PHILOSOPHICAL EXPLORATIONS

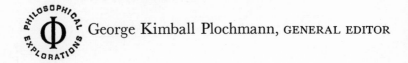

ROBERT STERNFELD

FREGE'S

LOGICAL THEORY

FOREWORD BY
George Kimball Plochmann

SOUTHERN ILLINOIS UNIVERSITY PRESS
Carbondale and Edwardsville

FOREWORD

IT WAS Abraham Mendelssohn who said: "Formerly I was known as the son of my father; now I am simply known as the father of my son." In much the same way, the historical function of Frege in America, except in the minds of a few initiates in the foundations of mathematics, was for a long time rather that of a middle term: first he was known as a correspondent of Russell, whom the latter had set right on an awkwardness in the theory of classes; and then it became known that he had had a small hand in helping the youthful Wittgenstein. Frege has always been mentioned with respect, mostly in papers, and in an impressive history of logic, but in the United States the literature of exposition and critique has until recently remained small, and it has only been in the last decade or so that the translations of Austin, Geach and Black and of Furth have brought his work to a wider dissemination.

But Frege's reputation in America is growing at last, more articles have been appearing, and just lately a book or two. He is by way of being fully accepted, and is now celebrated for his sharpness of vision, if not for any extra width of field. Thus Bochenski has said that Frege is the greatest logician since Aristotle, and that his precision was not again equalled until writers of the 1920's started publishing. Along with many other men, Peirce, Schröder, MacColl, and others, the work of Frege has led to the development of a new and growing body of knowledge, mathematical logic.

The peculiar position of Frege in a period of rapid transition, and the even more rapid transition in our own day, are both very good reasons for making him a subject of philosophic study. Commentary and critical interpretation are excellent types of contributions to philosophy at large, but their value is dependent upon whether the subject of the commentary is a worthwhile one, and upon whether the interpretation is able to outline the scope and detail of the text studied, placing it in a new context and thereby contributing to its classification. I have no hesitation in saying that on both counts Sternfeld's book is one to be included in the Philosophical Explorations Series.

The dilemma of permissible novelty is interesting. In Fregean terms, and paralleling his statement of the problem of the identity-sentence problem, we may put it thus: for an interpretation to be valuable, it must do more than merely duplicate the ideas of the thinker being interpreted. Yet if it is to be just, it cannot deviate significantly from the original formulation.

For me to expound Frege in this foreword would be an unnecessary duplication of Sternfeld's own exposition, and would only compound difficulties inherent in the dilemma just mentioned. Accordingly my remarks will be an attempt to justify Sternfeld's account of Frege by reviewing his own methodological approach. With Frege the available material is fairly well marked out—some "standard" books and papers, and relatively little else. Mr. Sternfeld has made a serious attempt to draw from all the material that has found its way into print, and has discarded the rest as not pertinent. But in the interpretation of the material admitted, a writer must take a certain risk, introducing some scheme of his own, for if he makes all the distinctions of his subject-philosopher, and only those, he perforce puts himself out of business. In consequence, the author of the present book keeps in mind some sets of terms which very likely would not have occurred to Frege. Thus Mr. Sternfeld speaks of Frege's *unit* of philosophic discourse as being the proposition rather than the term, and this strikes me as an importation. Moreover, one may discern in the treatment an emphasis distinct from that of Frege, who was clearly interested in mathematical logic as a developing scientific discipline, and who merely used the "philosophical underpinnings" for his own purposes. Sternfeld, on the other hand, has emphasized just those underpinnings, attempting to trace their effects throughout the scientific extensions of Frege's thought. In this same spirit Sternfeld criticizes Frege for having deserted his own principles in owning up to a "mistake" just where his logic is extended into a logistical structure. The psychological reasons for Frege's confession to a shortcoming in his work—in the "Nachwort" to the most nearly definitive statement of his views—concern Sternfeld not at all, and are to little purpose here. But now arises a nice question: we have Frege's explicit word that he owned up to a mistake. Can one understand and expound a man's philosophy properly and at the same time conclude that it is *sounder* than he himself thought it was? In his own contention, Sternfeld obviously diverges from the words of Frege, but he does this on grounds which he maintains are essentially Fregean.

A critic, then, must use a scheme not altogether explicitly discoverable in the text to which he is attending; nevertheless his *method*, to be fair, must bear close resemblance to the one he attempts to expound. Frege's method is very literal and so is Sternfeld's. Frege's purpose is to discern the least parts of each kind of proposition, keeping these parts and thereby the compounded propositions quite distinct in their definition. In many philosophers we find concepts merging into one another, so that for instance "proposition" and the concept "concept" become fused and inseparable; not so in Frege, and not so—this is important—in Sternfeld's account. For once *he* has established that Frege intends a distinction to hold, he does not blur this any more than the original text will permit him to, which is not at all. It is this that allows Professor Sternfeld to make one of the chief points of his book, which is that, taken seriously, the definitions and requirements laid down by Frege for framing propositions will keep the framer safely away from the clutches of self-contradiction. As has been shown over and over in modern logic, paradox is extremely easy to fall into; only the most precise of formulations have avoided it. Consequently it is encouraging to find that Frege's rigor and Sternfeld's acumen have combined to show that, closely observed, the class-of-classes difficulty which Russell insisted was inherent in Frege's way of grounding mathematical logic, need not arise.

In emphasizing the underpinnings of Frege's thought, Sternfeld offers a philosophical perspective of this mathematical logic, not in terms of its development as a science, but of the co-existence of contrasting philosophical bases for such a science. Perhaps this places its history in a new light and suggests threads of possible relations of logic cast into its new symbolic form with the traditional discipline of logic. But this digresses from Sternfeld's treatment. He takes much more trouble with the prior (and more necessary) details of Frege's own thoughts, exploring the scope and limits which the philosopher determines as the appropriate domain for logico-arithmetical science. Sternfeld does this in a context wherein he takes account of most of the criticism and interpretation to which Frege's work has been subjected, thus placing the work amid those contributions which today go by the label of "ordinary language analysis"; and he argues for the notion of ordinary language found in Frege himself, in contrast to the later efforts to amend Frege's appeal to common linguistic usage. This presentation, which is in such direct opposition to most of the current interpretations, is yet acknowledged by the author to have made use of those interpretations wherever possible. In his general result, one may say that Sternfeld has brought out a radical view, but he also tries to conserve the best of what his own predecessors in Frege scholarship have done. At the same time—and this should take care of the other horn of our old dilemma—he has managed also to preserve many of the admirable clarifications that Frege so painstakingly made to mathematical philosophy and logic.

George Kimball Plochmann

Southern Illinois University
January 22, 1966

PREFACE

PHILOSOPHY, whatever else it may be, at least is something that involves discourse. This study is a product of a discourse in which I have been engaged, and is moreover presented with the hope that it may engender further discourse on the important problems of contemporary logical theory. The long and intricate discourse which a person goes through in the formulation of his own conceptions is of little interest to others. But when this process entails indebtednesses to many other persons, due acknowledgement is certainly obligatory. And I wish to acknowledge gratefully my debt to the other commentators on Frege's work and to many writers on problems related to those Frege treated. I have been able to make reference here only to the works bearing directly on the problems growing out of Frege's approach to logical problems.

In addition, I have accumulated vast personal indebtednesses. I have sought criticism and help shamelessly and found friends and even strangers most willing and gracious. At the University of Illinois, Harry M. Tiebout, Leonard Linsky, and Nathaniel Lawrence (now of Williams College) have read various portions of this work and given criticism. At the University of Chicago, Manley H. Thompson, Herbert Lamm and Richard McKeon have worked through an early version of this study; Warner A. Wick has given valuable criticism which has led to the form in which the study is presented here. At the University of Kansas, E. S. Robinson and

Bruce Waters (now of the Texas Technological) have read earlier versions and been most helpful. Here at State University, Harold Zyskind has contributed helpful suggestions.

At one stage of this study I was in contact with Max Black, who generously criticized my work and sent me copies of translations of two of Frege's articles not available in English at that time—they have since been published in his and Geach's collection. In addition, an earlier version of this manuscript has been criticized by a friend who prefers to remain unidentified. His criticisms stem from the formalist school of mathematical logic, so when I quote his remarks I shall identify them as coming from my Formalist Friend. Last, but far from least, George Kimball Plochmann, the editor of this series, has given valuable criticism which has led to clarification of many points.

If, however, anyone should find any errors remaining, I must leave to him the problem of determining which of these scholars should be blamed. May I not disclaim all responsibility for error, since it is obvious that I have tried valiantly (and at considerable cost of time and effort to my obliging critics) to have the errors eliminated? Besides acknowledging these particular debts, I take this opportunity to acknowledge a long-standing, continuous, and more general debt to Richard McKeon. To those who have suffered from and been enlightened by his stimulating criticism, no explanation of this debt is needed. For those lacking this experience, no description of it would be adequate.

In addition, I wish to acknowledge my indebtedness to the University of Kansas for its support of my research by grants for secretarial aid and for partial support during the summers of 1954 and 1956—the latter grant being in the form of a Watkins Faculty Fellowship. I am also indebted to the Research Foundation of the State University of New York for similar aid in the later stages of preparation of the manuscript.

Now to the rationale of this discourse. I have attempted to present it in such a way as to interest both persons unacquainted with Frege's work or with little of the contemporary linguistic philosophies and those who know Frege's work intimately and for whom philosophy is essentially a study of language. For those not previously in contact with Frege's work, I have tried to present Frege's thought as a whole so that although they have had no such acquaintance, this will be no serious impediment to understanding Frege's thought. To this end, Chapter 2 has been composed as a summary of three key articles on which Frege's subsequent thought rests, and in view of which the arguments of Chapters 3–8 should be wholly intelligible. Further, there has been an effort throughout to keep in view the broad assumptions about the nature of the philosophical enterprise and the role of the linguistic philosophies in their historical contexts. I conceive this study as one way among many others by which a thinker whose major philosophical interests have been focused elsewhere might enlarge his understanding of some of the theoretic alternatives in contemporary logical theory.

For the readers especially interested in the technical problems of linguistic philosophy and who are already acquainted with Frege's most important papers, I believe I have been able to say something new and significant about Frege's work and about logical theory in Chapters 3–8, and am not repeating old opinions. I hope that the technically oriented linguistic philosophers of various persuasions will find in Frege's philosophy of language a challenging alternative to the prevailing approaches to contemporary problems. For Frege's thought is a technical, though quite unusual, philosophy in which the foundations of logic and mathematics are found in language. One extraordinary feature of Frege's thought is found in the grounding of his axiomatic system in a prior analysis of ordinary language— he thus combines *both* of the currently prominent approaches to language study!

Since Frege's philosophy is unique, it has followed (as has been shown me by the kinds of criticisms to which even this manuscript has been subjected) that several philosophers, each of whom appeals to diverging sets of principles, take exception to this analysis at various points. On the one hand, I have come to expect that the ordinary language analysts will claim Frege's conceptions of the sentence and its parts to be too rigid to apply to the variety of circumstances in which language is used. Or they will claim that Frege's notion of a concept is unclear and meaningless. On the other hand, those who believe that the solution to philosophical problems can be found only by first constructing an artificial language will hold that although Frege was the father of contemporary logistics, still he failed significantly because his system provided no means for avoiding the class-of-classes antinomy. But I shall demur to this: had he vigorously followed his own principles, he need never have admitted that the class-of-classes antinomy did damage to his system. I have taken note of these diverse criticisms, but I do not find that they present insuperable difficulties for Frege's philosophical thought. Moreover, taking account of Frege's ideas in the context of conflicting opinion has finally required an enlarged view of diverse relations among diverse conceptions of philosophy and logic. And, ultimately, this enlarged view is what this discourse is designed to develop—at least in outline form.

Robert Sternfeld

Stony Brook, New York
May 22, 1965

CONTENTS

CONTENTS

FREGE'S LOGICAL THEORY

PEIRCE'S LOGICAL THEORY

PART ONE

Frege's Matured Position

I

INTRODUCTION

I present this study of Frege's logic not merely to reassess the work of a prominent figure in the history of logical theory. Instead I do so because I believe Frege had something important and original to say about mathematical logic and that what he has said has been lost in the subsequent narrowing-down of the problems and of the accepted method for formulating mathematical logic today.

Frege's conception of language, and of logic as extending fruitfully into mathematics, places his work within that branch of contemporary thought which, for lack of better terminology, might be called "mathematical philosophy." For the practitioners of this mathematical philosophy, mathematical logic is something more than just one technical discipline among many, for it is not merely a science which is as autonomous and unphilosophical as number theory. Moreover, many of these practitioners seem to hold that it is a science of sciences, the architectonic science. For these men, since mathematics is the most general and abstract of all the sciences, the foundations of mathematics are the foundations of the whole system of the sciences.[1] Yet, I shall argue further that there are important—and quite different—conceptions of the proper bases for mathematical philosophies, of which we may distinguish for our purpose three in particular. To conclude, however, that there are important alternatives to the prevailing current conceptions of mathematical philosophy, I must first argue the values inherent in Frege's unique contribution.

Frege's contribution to mathematical philosophy has probably been neglected for many reasons: First of all, his ideography was typographically difficult and expensive to reproduce. Then again, some persons may have presumed that Russell culled the best from Frege, since Russell credited Frege with the prior discovery of the definition of cardinal number which he, Russell, had discovered independently. Thirdly, the prevailing formalist conception of a mathematical philosophy as based upon an empty formal schema has made Frege's alternative system seem old-fashioned, undeserving of attention. And finally, Frege's admission that his system contained a contradiction, the class-of-classes antinomy, combined with the prevailing formalists' predilections has undoubtedly reinforced the notion that Frege had little to offer beyond the ideas commonly attributed to him. These are some of the difficulties to be faced before one can conclude that there are live alternatives to the current mathematical philosophies. This means that I shall have to counter these objections by showing what is the significance of Frege's ideography as contrasted with the currently accepted symbolism, how Frege's definition of number differs from Russell's, that Frege was able to combine successfully logistical formalism and calculability with a content-bearing system of symbols, but, on the other hand, that he was wrong in admitting that the class-of-classes antinomy was properly derivable in his logistical system.

In chapters 6, 7, and 8 I hope to show that Frege's logic is consistent and that the charges of inconsistency arise from diverse conceptions of mathematical philosophy—conceptions which Frege himself mistakenly accepted when he admitted the presence of the antinomy. In addition, I shall argue that the conceptions of the role and import of the notion of consistency differ in these different mathematical philosophies. The argument of Part III rests upon the earlier elaboration of Frege's concepts in Part II. In Part II (Chapters 3, 4, and 5) I argue that Frege's philosophy can best be interpreted by examining three factors in his thought: content, power and unity. The content involves primarily Frege's ontology, the power is an account of Frege's notion of how logic extends into arithmetic, while the unity requires that we treat Frege's conception of the "combinatory structure" of the sentence and how this operates to unify his philosophy. But the argument of Part II rests upon the materials presented in Part I (Chapters 1 and 2). Chapter 2 is chiefly a restatement of the three basic papers containing Frege's matured thought. But even before I can do this, a prior difficulty has to be taken into account.

Besides the numerous criticisms and emendations of various points in Frege's writings (which the notes take care of at the appropriate points), there is a generally accepted notion that Frege did not use his technical term *"Bedeutung"* consistently. I must therefore show first of all, if I can, that he was consistent in this, and moreover that in order to make sense of what he is saying, one must assume that he was. Though the final proof that Frege's use of terms was consistent must rest upon a complete exposition of his thought, I hope to show in Chapter 1 that there is considerable direct internal evidence in Frege's own statements about the development of his thought that he used *"Bedeutung"* with great care and also that there is more than a little direct evidence that the charges of inconsistency have arisen from philosophic assumptions quite different from those underlying Frege's thought. Let us inquire therefore into the question of Frege's use of *"Bedeutung."*

There are two basic and opposed positions concerning Frege's use of the term *"Bedeutung"* (henceforth translated "reference" following Black's usage).[2] *a*] Various logicians (Max Black and William Marshall) have attributed some of the difficulties they have had in understanding Frege's philosophy to the fact that he used this term inconsistently.[3] They have held, for example, that his trouble with Russell's class-of-classes antinomy stems from the faulty use of this term, that sense can be made of his system only if one assumes he used this term inconsistently, and that other portions of his thought are incomprehensible because he was concerned too much with the "naming function" of language. They contend therefore that the use of *"Bedeutung"* and its cognate *"bedeuten"* with a proper noun, with a nominative expression (e.g., definite description), or with a sentence is technical and that the reference of such expressions is always an object as Frege held. But they balk at the notion that this same term is being used in its technical sense with predicate terms, because such terms are not properly names of objects and have only intensional conceptual content. *b*] On the other hand, several other interpreters (Michael Dummett and Rulon Wells)[4] have insisted that Frege does use the term "reference" in a technical sense with predicative terms parallel to its use with nominative expressions. These thinkers have found considerable evidence in Frege's work for justifying their notion that this term does function technically with predicative expressions. But their difficulties have centered around their attempts to *parallel* the use of this term for predicative terms with its use for nominative terms. For Frege, as we shall see, nominative expressions have two distinct elements of content, a sense, *Sinn*, and a reference, *Bedeutung*. And these thinkers in attempting to parallel the content of predicative expressions with those of nominative expressions have sought for a dual element of content for a predicative expression—its sense in addition to its reference. At this point, the first group of logicians can and do effectively criticize this second group of interpreters; for there is no statement in Frege's works which might lead anyone to suppose that a predicative expression expresses a *Sinn* separate from its reference, the concept or relation.[5] In fact, there has been a lively controversy between representatives of those two groups of interpreters—each of which can show that the other has difficulties in explaining various portions of Frege's writings. In summary then, the first criticizes the second for seeking a sense for predicative terms; the second criticizes the first for saying that Frege did not use the term "reference" with its technical significance for predicative terms. It is clear that for both of these interpretations, the problem begins with the function of the predicate term—subsequently widening out to include all the subsidiary problems connected with Frege's thought.

But let us turn now to Frege's own statements. He held that the three articles summarized in Chapter 2 of my exposition state his matured position. In his greatest work, his *Grundgesetze der Arithmetik* (henceforth *Grundgesetze*), Frege states: "From this it will be seen that the years have not passed in vain since the appearance of my *Begriffsschrift* and *Grundlagen*; they have brought my work to maturity."[6] At this very point he contrasts the more adequate treatment of his "Über Sinn und Bedeutung" and *Function und Begriff* with his *Begriffsschrift* and *Die Grundlagen der Arithmetik*. And since his "Über Begriff und Gegenstand" clearly was written in conjunction with, and makes reference to, the analysis of both his "Sinn und Bedeutung" and *Function und Begriff* and they in turn refer to it, it seems fair to hold that these three articles do state his mature position. This is not to reduce the importance of his earlier works and of his later basic *Grundgesetze* and other articles, and I shall of course refer to them where they illuminate the present exposition.

In detailing the internal evidence for consistency in the usage of "*Bedeutung*," I must take note of the historical development of Frege's thinking which leads up to his mature analysis. It is clear that Frege approaches logical problems from the point of view of a mathematician seeking a foundation for mathematics in logic.[7] He clearly seeks to show that arithmetic is analytic, in his sense of this term; that is, that arithmetic is derivable from non-empirical linguistic or logical principles. Conversely, he seeks to show that logic is progressive and fruitful as it expands into arithmetic. With this dual objective in mind, Frege, in common with many contemporary logicians, feels impelled to throw out the subject-predicate analysis of the sentence in favor of the function-argument analysis,[8] for this to him is more fruitful and makes possible the attainment of his goal.

It is obvious, I believe, that at this stage of his thinking Frege's technical vocabulary is not developed and that there is a glossing-over of what he later finds must be distinguished. For example, "pure thought" (*Reinen Denkens*") is not completely separated from "Concept" ("*Begriff*") in his earliest work and "*Gedanke*" does not enter as technically significant here. At this point, the total thought-element is the content ("*Inhalt*") of the symbols and is the meaning (*Bedeutung*) of the symbols. But even at this early stage of his thinking, Frege is committed to the principle that a logical analysis of language is essentially concerned with what can be discovered in the usage of ordinary language. He uses the metaphor of the microscope applied to ordinary language to reveal its structure.

At the next stage of his thinking (1884)[9] where he is exploring the foundations of arithmetic, Frege reveals the basic principles of his thought and specifies some of the basic terms on which it turns. Yet even here he has not clearly discovered the necessity for distinguishing the terms "sense" ("*Sinn*") and "reference" ("*Bedeutung*") as he so clearly states in his "Begriff und Gegenstand."[10] Even so, he does not use *Bedeutung* loosely at this stage. For this term is basic in his statement of the principle that the objective content of a word is found only when it is used in a sentence. Thus, he remarks, "Only in a proposition (*Satz*) have the words really a meaning (*Bedeutung*)."[11] Again, as the second in his list of three principles on which his *Grundlagen* is based, he cautions: "Never to ask for the meaning (*Bedeutung*) of a word in isolation, but only in the context of a proposition (*Satzzusammenhange*)."[12] For this reason, it seems right to hold that for Frege, the sentence is the philosophical principle of unity.[13] At this stage of his work, since he has not made the technical distinctions between "*Sinn*" and "*Bedeutung*," the only sense that we can associate properly with "*Bedeutung*" is that given us in the context of these three principles.

Frege feels that this second principle follows quite definitely from his first:[14] "If the second rule is not observed, one is almost forced to take as meanings (*Bedeutung*) of words mental pictures or acts of the individual mind, and so to offend against the first rule as well." The first rule reads, "Always to separate the psychological from the logical, the subjective from the objective." "*Bedeutung*" therefore apparently means for Frege the total objective content (as distinct from the subjective content) intended by the words being used. In this respect, then, the sentence is the source for determining objective content. And we must recognize also that at this stage the term "*Satz*" must imply more than the linguistic expression. (Austin's use of "proposition" to translate "*Satz*" seems to me quite fortunate. It emphasizes the objective content intended by Frege and shows that the term is not restricted to the mere symbols themselves.) It is in this way that Frege feels he is breaking away from the psychologistically-oriented philosophies of mathematics stemming from both "consciousness" and "associationist" doctrines of the nineteenth century (Wundt, Mill, etc.).

Frege's third principle gives further significance to the notion of objective content, or what is meant by "*Bedeutung*," by distinguishing two different kinds of content. It reads, "Never to lose sight of the distinction between concept and object." If the supposition made here is correct, it seems that "*Bedeutung*" is used to specify the *objective content* of words; objects or concepts. And Frege's later usage of "*Bedeutung*" reaffirms the truth of this supposition, even though a new element of objective content—not a reference (*Bedeutung*)—is added to complete the mature analysis. This new public element is of course the sense (*Sinn*) expressed by proper names. For even though Frege in his "Begriff und Gegenstand" notes that he had further refined the significance attached to the term "*Bedeutung*" in his "Sinn und Bedeutung," he still uses this term to apply to both objects and concepts: "We may say, in brief, taking 'subject' and 'predicate' in the linguistic sense: *A concept is the reference (Bedeutung) of a predicate.* An object is something that can never be the whole reference of a predicate, but can be the reference of a subject."[15] And again: "The concept (as I understand the word) is predicative," his footnote adding: "It is in fact the reference of a grammatical predicate."[16]

Three points must be noted in this final clarification of his technical terminology. *1]* What is new in this more mature expression of "Sinn und Bedeutung" is the separation of two elements of objective content associated with proper names, only one of which is a *Bedeutung.* This refinement is not inconsistent; it is merely a clarification which Frege found necessary as he became more aware of the logical problems he faced. *2]* Throughout all his thinking, he never uses the word *"Bedeutung"* as equivalent to *"Gegenstand"* ("object"); for "reference" has a larger region of application. In fact, expressions having references are proper names as subjects or as parts of grammatical predicates, sentences as a whole, and predicative expressions where the references are concepts, relations, or functions. Only the references of proper names and sentences are objects. Thus the two distinctions, object-concept and sense-reference are quite distinct.[17] *3]* What is of especial significance, Frege finds in this process of clarification (as other thinkers have also) that he has to reintroduce the subject-predicate distinction of the sentence in order to complete his logical inquiries. This subject-predicate distinction is not identical with the one he earlier rejected, and it is in fact rather more closely related to the later function-argument analysis introduced to replace the subject-predicate dichotomy. But it is in the development of the complexities of these correlated distinctions (function-object, subject-predicate, and sense-reference) that his mature philosophy receives its final expression, as I hope to show in the third, fourth, and fifth chapters of this book.

2

FREGE'S STATEMENT
OF HIS MATURE THOUGHT

The three principles cited from Frege's *Grundlagen* allow us to conclude that for him the sentence is the source of objective content and as such can be considered the principle of philosophic unity. The implications and significance of these three principles were explored at length in the three pivotal articles which stated his mature thought: "Begriff und Gegenstand," "Sinn und Bedeutung," *Function und Begriff*. Those three articles raise three basic sets of problems.

A] How are concepts and objects distinguished as different kinds of referential content (*Bedeutungen*) for different parts of sentences? And further, do these two kinds of *Bedeutungen* adequately account for the content of diverse sentential expressions—universal, particular, singular—which might be used to express the same thought (*Gedanke*)? Frege's "Begriff und Gegenstand" was written to answer these questions.

B] Are objects, as the *Bedeutungen* of nominative expressions, the only kind of objective content of such expressions, or is there an additional but different kind of objective content? And is this analysis of the objective content of nominative expressions adequate for *all kinds* of nominative expressions, including sentences themselves and clauses used in different contexts? "Sinn und Bedeutung" answers these questions.

c] Are concepts, as the referential content of predicative expressions, definable in terms of some more general kinds of *Bedeutungen* (called functions) on the basis of which arithmetic and other bodies of knowledge are seen to be an involved structure of specific relations between entities? In particular, what are the limits of generality of such kinds of *Bedeutungen,* and how are such kinds of content involved in the recasting of a given thought into different sentential forms or expressions? Frege's book, *Function und Begriff,* answers these questions.

It will be noted that these problems are formulated in terms of the notion of the *objective content* of language: i.e., the *Sinn* and the *Bedeutungen* of expressions. For Frege the question of the content of language is a fundamental one—and one which, as Chapter 3 will reveal, marks the distinctive feature of his approach to logical theory in contrast to other contemporary sentential philosophies. Nevertheless, the kinds of problems noted here in terms of the objective content of language could have been raised equally well in terms of the related problems of the fruitfulness or power of language and of the unity of a linguistic philosophy, as will be shown in Chapters 4 and 5 respectively.

A. *On concepts and objects as the only two kinds of referential content*

As Frege states,[1] Benno Kerry in a series of articles on intuition and its psychical elaboration referred to Frege's use of the term "concept" in the *Grundlagen.* Since Frege felt that Kerry had confused his logical notion with a psychological use of this term, and since his *Grundlagen* did not develop the meaning of this basic term, he wrote his "Begriff und Gegenstand." The special confusion Frege wished to eliminate arose from Kerry's insistence that objects can be concepts in different contexts. This is, of course, contrary to Frege's basic principle noted above—a principle he never changed throughout his life.

The basic distinction between object and concept is made first in terms of the references (*Bedeutungen*) of a subject and a predicate of a simple sentence. The reference of the subject, a proper name, is an object; whereas the reference of a predicate expression is a concept (*Begriff*).[2] A proper name functions in a sentence as a subject term or as a *part* of a predicate term, but it is never the whole predicate. In a simple sentence, the concept is attributed to whatever object is referred to by the subject. In some cases, this attribution is expressed by the simple connective copula "is," e.g., "John is falling" instead of "John falls." [3] This "is" does not mean "equals," and any statement such as "*a* equals *b*" is a correctly formed sentence when put in the logical form of "*a* is equivalent to *b*" wherein the phrase "is equivalent to *b*" (or "is not other than *b*") is a predicative phrase attributable to "*a*." "*b*" itself may be a proper name and by itself refer to an object, and this possibility, of course, can be shown by its functioning as a subject for some other sentence.[4] The differences between an equivalence and a correctly formed simple attributive sentence are clearly shown by Frege in his appeal to the facts: first, that the proper names in an identity sentence are reversible whereas the subject and predicate in a correctly formed statement are irreversible, and second, that the dropping of the "is" in an equivalence leaves the expression with no meaning, whereas the dropping of the copula in a correctly formed statement leaves the expression with the same adjectival attribution of a concept to an object.[5] Throughout his analysis Frege appeals to common-sense usage to make his distinctions. He even argues from the grammatical structure of the German language. He shows in particular, as one further indication of the importance of this distinction, that the definite article "the" is used with a noun to refer to a definite object, whereas nouns with indefinite articles refer to concepts.[6] Thus, at the first formulation, a sentence (considered with respect to its integral parts) is the attribution of a predicate to a subject, of a concept to an object, or—to view it from the other direction—it states that a given object falls under (*fällt unter*) a given concept.

Frege's defense of this distinction against Kerry's arguments makes it necessary for him to consider *a*] some special types of expressions which appear to confuse the issue, and *b*] some more complicated forms of sentences which also introduce different kinds of relations between parts of sentences and between the references of these parts.

A] Kerry introduces the expression "the concept *horse*" arguing that this refers to an object. Frege simply replies that this expression is indeed a proper name, which does indeed refer to an object, and therefore it is not a predicative expression referring to a concept as Kerry himself would have it. He further maintains that there is a commonly recognized use of the definite article to make a proper nominative expression which does refer to a single individual entity, an object. Thus he appeals to common usage as an aid to determine what the intended references of expressions may be. Such an appeal is consistent with his determination (mentioned above from *Begriffsschrift*) to use a microscope to examine ordinary language to determine its logical form. He recognizes, of course, that there are some uses of the definite article which are exceptions to this general principle, but he feels that the context of usage makes it easy to determine such special uses. In

The Turk besieged Vienna,

"the Turk" is a proper name of a people. But in

The horse is a four-legged animal,

we have a sentence of a different kind which Frege considers subsequently (see below).

Frege thus maintains his basic principle despite the fact that the expression "the concept . . ." appears to refer to a concept. He does indicate the special content of this expression, for its reference is an object falling under a special kind of concept (the reference of a special predicate-term) which cannot be attributed truly to other objects referred to by ordinary nominative expressions. Thus one can say

The concept *horse* is realized

and really mean

There is a horse,

but one cannot say

John is realized

because "is realized" refers to a special concept attributable only to these special kinds of object references. Or again, this special kind of expression may be used to turn a simple attributive sentence into a relational sentence.

John is a man

may be re-expressed as a relation between two objects; i.e.,

John falls under the concept *man*

where "falls under" by itself can be considered as a relational expression holding between two objects named respectively by the two proper name expressions "John" and "the concept *man*." One might of course consider the whole expression "falls under the concept *man*" as predicative and as referring to a concept. In this latter case, this concept contains, as a part, the object referred to by "the concept *man*." This is not unlike his argument that the identity sentence "*a* equals *b*" is properly a statement in which "equals *b*" or "is none other than *b*" is being attributed to the object referred to by the proper name "*a*", even though "*b*" itself is a proper name with an object as reference. But throughout, in using the expression "the concept . . .," Frege is quite careful to emphasize its special nature as derivative from a prior concept term.

B] The sentence

The horse is a four-legged animal,

introduces a new and more complicated form. For despite the apparent fact that "the horse" is a proper name-expression referring to an individual object (in accord with Frege's recognition that the definite article usually indicates such a proper name-expression), this general way of using the definite article does not apply here. Frege clearly recognizes that what is being said here is simply that

All horses are four-legged animals.

And this is a new kind of sentence—one in which there is no proper name-expression. Frege introduces a new term and a new idea for this. He states that this sentence is composed of two levels of concepts: those of first-level, and those of second-level. A second-level concept is being attributed to a first-level concept.

In contemporary terminology, the generally accepted notion most closely corresponding to Frege's notion of a second-level concept is that of a quantifier. Thus the sentence should read as follows:

For every *x*, if *x* is a horse, then *x* is a four-legged animal.

Here both "horse" and "four-legged animal" refer to first-level concepts.

Two kinds of subordination are indicated here. First, the concept *horse* is being subordinated to the concept *four-legged animal*. But we should note the difficulty in expressing what is meant. I do not mean that the object-reference of the expression "the concept *horse*" is subordinated to the object-reference of the expression "the concept *four-legged animal.*" Nor do I wish to refer to the symbols used to refer to the concepts. I wish merely to indicate that the concept referred to by the expression "four-legged animal" includes the concept referred to by the expression "horse". Thus, there are relations between intensional content referred to by such terms; that the extension of the term "four-legged animal" may include the extension of the term "horse" is of course another matter.

Second, and quite different, is the ordering between the first-level concept and the second-level concept. Frege never confuses the relation of subordination of one first-level concept to another with a first-level concept's falling within (*fallen in*) a second-level concept, though in his "Begriff und Gegenstand" he changes the terminology of the *Grundlagen* from that of first- and second-order to that of first- and second-level concepts.[7] This distinction holds between the reference of the phrase "for every *x*" and the references of the first-level predicative expressions "horse" and "four-legged animal."

Frege argues that the difference between second-level concepts (whether expressed by "all . . ." or "every . . .") and first-level concepts is clearly shown if one tries to negate a sentence such as

All horses are four-legged animals

by employing the symbol for negation "not" to modify the predicate term "are four-legged animals." This yields

All horses are not four-legged animals

which is, of course, not the strict contradictory of the universal affirmative statement. The proper negative requires a different position of the "not"—

Not all horses are four-legged animals—

showing a basic difference between this sentence and one such as

The concept *horse* is subordinate to the concept *four-legged animal*

which is properly negated by

The concept *horse* is not subordinate to the concept *four-legged animal.*

These examples illustrate the difference between the sentences in which a first-level concept is attributed to an object (or in which one object is related to another) and sentences in which a second-level concept is attributed to first-level concepts.

The reference of "there is . . ." is also a second-level concept. In the expression, "there is a square root of 4," "a square root of 4" does not refer to any single entity or object, say the number 2. It is a concept term referring to a first-level concept. And "there is" merely asserts the existence of at least one object of that kind. Thus, this latter expression refers to a second-level concept which is attributed to a first-level concept.

Frege further argues that the attribution of existence in a second-level concept to a first-level concept is analogous to the assertion of number; that is, that at least one object falls under the first-level concept in question. "In this respect existence is analogous to number. Affirmation of existence is in fact nothing but denial of the number, nought." [8] He then applies this to the ontological proof of God's existence. The basic error here, he says, stems from the application of a second-level concept to an object when the former should be applied to a first-level concept. Frege also puts this another way: "The ontological proof of God's existence suffers from the fallacy of treating existence as a first-level concept." [9] Such second-level concepts may be completed by any number of first-level concepts, but not by other second-level concepts, and certainly not by objects. Thus it makes no sense to say

There is Julius Caesar

(where "there" is not taken as an expression indicating a place) or

There is 2.

One cannot affirm a second-level concept of an object. Properly these sentences should read

There is a man called "Julius Caesar."

or

There is a number called "2."

where "a man . . ." and "a number . . ." are predicate expressions referring to first-level concepts. In more recent terminology, as we have already stated the second-level concept which Frege distinguishes so clearly here is the reference of quantifying phrases. But the peculiar use Frege makes of the references of such expressions as these to unite such content as number and existence marks his analysis as readily distinguishable from more recent logical work, which does not unite such content.

The distinction between the two levels of concepts is essentially the same as that made in his *Grundlagen;* but "Begriff und Gegenstand" places this distinction in the fuller context of a more general treatment of sentences, their various parts and kinds, whereas in the *Grundlagen,* his major concerns were to define number and to show the possibility of deriving arithmetic from logic. For the attributions of "4" to "moons of Jupiter," or of "existence" to "square root of 4," are statements attributing a second-level concept to a first-level concept. Number and existence are thus *properties* of a concept and as such are second-level concepts attributable to those of first level. This relation between a second-level and a first-level concept is similar in kind to the relation between a first-level concept and an object. Yet there are significant differences, for in a sentence composed of first- and second-level concept terms neither concept term can be considered as the subject of the sentence. Neither concept which is being referred to is an object, yet the sentence "can be regarded as expressing the fact that a concept falls under a higher one." [10] Thus what can be attributed to a first-level concept by a second-level concept is quite different from what can be attributed to an object by a first-level concept. Frege writes:

The relation of an object to a first-level concept that it falls under is different from the (admittedly similar) relation of a first-level to a second-level concept. (To do justice at once to the distinction and to the similarity, we might perhaps say: An object falls *under* a first-level concept; a concept falls *within* a second-level concept.) The distinction of concept and object thus still holds, with all its sharpness.[11]

The word "property," too, is ambiguous. A first-level concept, as attributable to an object, is a property of an object and a second-level concept, as attributable to a first-level concept, is a property of that in turn. Quite different from both the distinctions between the levels of concepts and the subordination of one first-level concept to another is the distinction between a *mark (Merkmal)* and a property. An object may be said to have a single property, albeit a complex one. Then each single distinct property which is a part of the complex property can be said to be a mark of the complex property. In

Two is a positive whole number less than ten

each concept (*positive number, whole number,* and *number less than ten*) can be taken as a mark or characteristic of the more restricted complex property embracing all three.

The substance of "Begriff und Gegenstand" is simply the basic distinctions between object and concept and between first and second-level concepts. Concepts are distinct from objects because concepts are incomplete by themselves, whereas objects are not. And this incompleteness is essential in some element in the content of a sentence. For if one tries to eliminate this incompleteness by rephrasing a sentence (whose subject and predicate refer respectively to an object and a concept) so that its parts refer to two objects, one finds that one has merely shifted the incomplete content to a relational term. Thus, in changing

Leo is a lion

to

Leo falls under the concept *lion,*

the relational term "falls under" is *still* incomplete. This sentence is similar in construction to

Venus is the morning star

where the "is" is an incomplete relational term with the content "is equivalent to." Conversely, one can express the sentence composed of concepts of two levels in terms of a sentence in which a concept is attributed to an object, thus;

There is one square root of 4

can be expressed as

The concept *square root of four* is realized

and in this form the expression "The concept *square root of four*" is a proper name (as shown by the definite article) referring to an individual object. This latter expression is therefore not a proper predicative or conceptual term; it has no incompleteness.

What Frege is maintaining here is simply this: that a given thought can be expressed in several different kinds of sentences; in sentences which are simple, involving merely a subject and predicate referring respectively to an object and a concept; in sentences in which two objects are related; or finally, in sentences in which a first-level concept falls within a second-level concept. Moreover, any of these sentences may contain complex expressions; but these must be used with great care and attention. Throughout, Frege repeatedly confesses his difficulties in trying to convey the meaning of "unsatisfied," "unsaturated," or "incomplete," ("abgeschlossen," "ungesättigt," or "unvollständig") yet he insists that these expressions are not to be taken literally. He admits that all he can do is to point to the need for an unsaturated portion of content as being necessary for all sentential usage in order to form complete thoughts. Any attempts to eliminate such portions only shift the burden of incompleteness of content to some other expression.

At this point, two avenues are open to us if we wish to follow up Frege's analysis. If we hope to determine more clearly what he means by "unsatisfied," "unsaturated," or "incomplete," he refers us to his *Function und Begriff* where he explains this in the context of explaining the meaning of the term "function" is in analysis. On the other hand, if we wish to follow up his assertion that a thought is a unit of content expressed by a sentence whether or not the sentence has one or another of a number of allowable linguistic forms, we must turn to his "Sinn und Bedeutung." The diversity of allowable linguistic forms is by no means unimportant, as we shall see later on (see Chapters 4 and 5). But now we summarize his "Sinn und Bedeutung" and *Function und Begriff* in turn to fill out this presentation of his mature analysis. (Frege's much later article, "Der Gedanke" [1919], develops the arguments of "Sinn und Bedeutung" about the proper status of a thought.)

B. *The objective content of all nominative expressions including sentences as nominative expressions*

Let us turn therefore to Frege's "Sinn und Bedeutung." In this famous article, Frege is concerned primarily with determining what is the content of the sentence as a whole. His analysis of this problem falls into three parts. First, he makes the basic distinction between the Sense and Reference (*Sinn* and *Bedeutung*) of proper names—a distinction which, as noted in Chapter 1, was not clear to him when he wrote the *Grundlagen*. Second, he shows the necessity for applying this distinction to sentences as wholes. And third, he demonstrates the adequacy of this distinction for all types of sentences and clauses.

I. PROPER NAMES AND DEFINITE DESCRIPTIONS

Frege comes to the distinction between Sense and Reference by way of an inquiry into the content of proper names—especially proper names as they function in identity-sentences. He is concerned both with the problem of separating the objective content of such words as they function in sentences from the associated subjective content, and with the problem of separating the kinds of objective content. The central point of this portion of Frege's "Sinn und Bedeutung" is the discovery of the *sense* as distinct from the reference on the one hand and from the private (subjective, psychological) content associated with a proper name on the other. For it is the sense of proper names which accounts for the difference between two or more proper names correctly used to refer to the same object. If there were no sense, then identity-sentences would either be mere tautologies with no cognitive content, since both names would refer to the same object with no difference, or else identity-sentences would be false, since the two names would *not* refer to the same object. Further, if the sense were not public and objective, there could be no objective science—every identity-sentence would have different private meaning for each person using the language. Communication and science would be impossible.

There are thus three levels of content associated with a proper name. (Levels of content among proper names are in no way connected with the notion of levels of concepts.) First, a proper name has a reference (*Bedeutung*)—its denoted object (*Gegenstand*). Second, a proper name expresses a public meaning or sense (*Sinn*). And third, there is associated with a name some private subjective representation (*Vorstellung*) or image (*Bild*) which must not be confused with the public sense.[12] Thus, if one considers the name "the lion" in "The lion roars," one must distinguish the object referred to from the public sense which everyone understands when using this sentence in the given context, and both of these from the private images or representations entertained owing to one's particular view of the lion. And by no stretch of the imagination can the sense be identified with the physical aspects of the word itself.[13]

Before turning to Frege's treatment of the content of sentences as a whole, three points about the applications of this conception of the content of the proper name must be clarified. *a*] In cases in which there is no reference for a given phrase which functions as a proper name (for example, "the lowest rational number") the phrase will be said to refer to the number zero. This device indicates that though the sense of the expression is clear, there is no proper reference for such a proper name. *b*] The reference-object of a given name may shift in certain uses so that the ordinary sense of a given name may become its reference-object. For example, the name "Richard III" is used in its direct and ordinary manner to refer to a particular King of England, but it is used also to refer to a play by Shakespeare—in which the public meaning or ordinary sense of the proper name in its original usage becomes the object being referred to (presuming here of course that Shakespeare's play reflects the public character of the King). In a case such as this, the ordinary sense is then said to have become the indirect reference-object. It is also true that an indirect sense of the term used this way is also introduced by this shift; that is, there is a publicly recognized meaning associated with the term "Richard III" when it is used to refer to Shakespeare's play. (This point will be significant when the problem of the sense and reference of a sentence and its clauses is discussed.) Further c], names may be used to refer to names, or to any linguistic expressions, as their intended objects; and in such cases, one should properly employ some marks, such as quotation marks around the expression in question, to indicate that the reference is the linguistic object and not the usual reference. The sense of such a proper name is simply the publicly accepted meaning attached to the usage of quotation marks.

Thus in all of these cases Frege maintains sense and reference as the dual elements of objective content for any proper name. He further takes note of the possible objections of idealists or sceptics that the objects named by proper names may not exist. And his answer reveals again the essentially linguistic basis of his analysis, for he holds that in so far as we use proper names, we intend to refer to such individual objects, and whether or not they are actually present does not invalidate the intentions of the language users as such. Frege's whole analysis is thus grounded on this notion of referring to individual objects. This explains in great measure Wells' feeling of strangeness in Frege's analyses and the difference between Frege's and Russell's approaches to logical theory—the latter reduces reference to individuals to the use of complex universals.[14]

II.   THE SENTENCE AS A WHOLE

The same dual elements of content are necessary for the sentence to function as a proper name. Frege proves this by showing first, that the thought of the sentence is not the reference but the sense; and second, that the thought or sense of the sentence cannot be the total content of the sentence; that is, it must also have a reference. The thought is the sense of the sentence, since two sentences which have an identical truth-value and whose subjects are two different proper names (with different senses) referring to the same object have different cognitive content. One may, in other words, know the truth-value of one of the sentences without knowing the truth-value of the other, e.g., "Tully was a great orator" and "The Scourge of Cataline was a great orator." That is his first point. Now to the second. The thought of the sentence cannot be the total objective content— there must be a reference of sentences, because the same thought can be understood merely as a literary construction or as a scientific and historical statement with a truth-value. This shows that the truth-value is the reference of sentences in their direct usage as proper names.

Thus the sense of a sentence is its proposition or thought (*Gedanke*), and the reference of a sentence is its truth-value. And Frege writes: "By the truth-value of a sentence I understand the circumstance that it is true or false. There are no further truth-values." [15] That is to say, all sentences have the True or the False as their references (*Bedeutungen*). These references are individual objects (*Gegenstände*). Frege further states that a judgment "advances from a thought to a truth-value," and again, that "in every judgment—no matter how trivial—the step from the level of thoughts to the level of the references (the objective) has already been taken." A judgment is not merely the apprehension of a proposition (that is, of the meaning of thought in combining a subject and a predicate), but also the assertion of its truth. But, on the other hand, "judgments are distinctions of parts within truth-values" [16] by means of the proposition (sense of the sentence). Frege distinguishes his use of "part" from the physical sense—that is, where a whole minus a part yields a determinate part as a remainder. This notion of "parts within truth-values" might be analogized, for explanatory purposes, to the notion of the way a name refers to an object by specifying only a fragmentary portion of a total object through a given sense; that is, "the Morning Star" does not express total content of the total object intended simply because the sense of the name is particular and limited by the context of its common usage. Frege argues further that the relation of a thought to the truth-value cannot be that of subject to predicate because such a sentence (e.g., "The thought that the world is round is true.") is redundant and is a misconstruction of the proper grounding of sentences. Further evidence that the truth-values are the references of sentences is found in the fact that substitution of different proper names (or definite descriptions) for the same objects mentioned in the sentence makes no change in the truth-value or reference of the sentence as a whole.

Thus, all true sentences have the same reference, the True, and all false sentences refer to the False. All distinctions are lost in the truth-value as object; but conversely without it, no statement has true scientific grounding. And, conversely, without the thought, distinctions between the content of sentences are impossible. It is therefore the commonly-accepted sense as the particular objective content, distinct from all subjective images, which is asserted as true in the judgment. And in the judgment, the proposition or common meaning is grounded objectively in the one object of all scientific discourse—the True. At this point, it is worth noting that commonsense in the form of ordinary meanings or sense in ordinary language usage has been appealed to in order to show *a*] that the references of the subject and predicate respectively are generally object and concept, *b*] that there is a public meaning distinct from private meanings on the one hand and from objects on the other, *c*] that objects named are presumed to exist and to be publicly recognizable and *d*] that "true" when used as a predicate is empty.[17]

III. COMPLEX SENTENCES AND THEIR CLAUSES: REFERENCES AND SENSES

Frege concludes his analysis of the sense and reference of proper names and of sentences functioning as proper names by showing that this distinction suffices for explaining the logical functions of all clauses, phrases, and expressions which function as parts of whole sentences. In particular, he states that he undertakes this analysis of compound sentences "to further test . . . the supposition that the truth-value of a sentence is its reference."[18] It is important to mention his insistence here that the investigation will proceed by a logical grouping. "Only a more thorough investigation can clarify this issue. In so doing, we shall not follow the grammatical categories strictly, but rather group together what is logically of the same kind." His insistence upon a logical taxonomy, as distinct from a grammatical one, indicates his need for an exhaustive treatment of this question in order to prove his point and is based upon the logical distinctions already clarified in his "Begriff und Gegenstand." Admittedly, he did restrict the argument of "Sinn und Bedeutung" to a discussion of proper names and their content, but he accomplishes his exhaustive treatment by a logical grouping in which concepts and relations enter as possible references of phrases and clauses. He thus states: "What I mean by an object can be more exactly discussed only in connection with concept and relation. I will reserve this for another article." [19] In this way he maintains his restriction of the subject matter of "Sinn und Bedeutung." "It is clear from the context that by 'sign' and 'name' I have here understood any designation representing a proper name, whose reference is thus a definite object (this word taken in the widest range), but no concept and no relation, which shall be discussed further in another article." [20] "Object" taken in its widest reference applies to any individually distinguishable entity, not just to physical objects or sense-data—but to senses and to thoughts as named.

In expanding the logical grouping Frege determines that a clause may have an indirect reference; that is, that it may refer to its thought as its object. He argues simply that in a sentence containing a clause in indirect discourse (e.g., "Copernicus believed the world was round") no other clause with merely the same truth-value as that referred to by "the world is round" can be substituted for that expression—for each would change the thought of the total sentence and some might change the truth-value of the total sentence. He concludes this first portion of his inquiry by noting that

> the subordinate clause (indirect discourse whose reference is not a truth-value, but a thought, a command, a request, a question, etc.) could be regarded as a noun indeed one could say: as a proper name of that thought, that command, etc., which it represented in the context of the sentence structure.[21]

Thus a thought, the sense of a sentence, can be an indirect reference, as can the sense of any proper name when used in certain contexts. As such it is an object, the reference of a proper name, as much as any object, physical entity, sense-datum object, or space-time event.

Frege then distinguishes no more than four simple usages of clauses in sentences. *a*] The first group names thoughts as objects referred to—as has been illustrated in the use of a sentence in indirect discourse above. *b*] The second group of clauses (subjective, relative adverbial—i.e., those involving temporal expressions, etc.) are those which, when taken alone, appear to be conceptual in nature (and may in some cases be so interpreted—see the third group below), but which are actually phrases qualifying other words, so that the total expression does in fact operate as a proper name to refer to an individual object. For example, in the sentence

He who discovered America was a great man,

the clause "who discovered America" does not by itself operate as a proper name, though the total subject does so operate. It is the fact that such phrases can be constructed without proper references that makes science and politics full of myth for Frege. c] The third group is closely connected with the second group and in effect involves the other interpretation of the second group —the interpretation which turns on the conceptual nature of the clause in question. It is at this point that the logical grouping according to the distinctions made in "Begriff und Gegenstand" became apparent. Thus the sentence just now framed could be shifted to read:

If anyone discovered America, he was a great man.

In this case the indeterminacy of the subject is brought out, and the first clause refers to a concept. This dual interpretation can be placed on other expressions found in the second group when the clause is taken as a conditional expression. But the third class extends beyond a mere shift in interpretation of the clauses found in the second class, for the interpretation which puts them in the second group is possible only when "the concept applies to one and only one single object." [22] If it applies to none or to more than a single object, the reference of such expressions taken as a proper name must be determined, even if only conventionally, as zero: its reference as a concept expression is of course the concept in question. The indeterminate character is recognizable not only in cases where there is only one object, but even more so in cases where "It is," as he says "by means of this very indeterminacy that the sense acquires the generality expected of a law." [23] This universal character appears in conditional clauses as joined to

concluding clauses, so that neither by itself is a complete judgment or proposition. This interpretation involving an indeterminacy is recognizable, according to Frege, in all forms of statements having subjective clauses, relative clauses, and temporal
indicators; since conditional clauses can be grammatically stated
in these forms. Thus a logical interpretation "must be read off
from the entire context" [24] in each grammatical usage of these
phrases. It is quite clear from Frege's argument that the reference
of the total sentence is the truth value, but that the clauses are
not complete expressions and have as such no independent object-references. The discussion of the reference of such expressions
must be made in the context of "Begriff und Gegenstand" where
Frege is concerned with the problem of concepts. *d*] The fourth
group may involve subjective and conditional clauses also grammatically speaking, but the important logical element in this
group is the fact that the dependent and main clauses each have
truth values as their references, and substitution for either is
possible without affecting the whole as long as the truth-value of
the total sentence remains the same. Thus, "If the sky is blue,
the ground is cold."

Frege summarizes by stating ɪ] that for those dependent
clauses whose sense is not a thought but only a part of one, the
reference is not a truth-value because either *a*] the reference is the
thought (the clause has an indirect reference) or *b*] some specific
object, or *c*] the clause is incomplete and refers to a concept
but does not express a thought; and ɪɪ] that for those clauses
whose sense is a complete thought, the reference is in fact a truth-
value. It may be noted here that the distinction between two
kinds of *Bedeutung* (concept and object) is basic, and that the
other logical difference in the usage of clauses arises simply from
the distinction in three different kinds of object-references: a
normal entity, a thought, and the truth-value. Further development of this analysis into more complex usages of phrases reveals
that there is no need to introduce additional kinds of references,
but merely that a given clause may be used with more than one
of the already discovered references intended. This enlarged
inquiry exhibits the flexibility of Frege's analysis of expressions
found in ordinary language, and the adequacy of his tools in
revealing the connections in complex sentences which defy analy-

sis by a simple conception that sentences with identical truth-values can be substituted freely for each other.

I shall note here three examples of his analysis of such sentences. In the first case, Frege uses a sentence each of whose clauses   a] expresses a thought and refers to the direct references of sentences—a truth-value, while   b] the sentence as a whole expresses a third thought and also has the direct reference—a truth-value. In the context of the sentence as a whole b] the clauses each have to be taken as having an indirect reference—that is, as also referring to the thought expressed when each clause is used as a sentence. This establishes the possibility of showing a connection between the thought expressed by the two clauses—that is, the contents of the sentences are treated as objects. His example,

> Napoleon, who recognized the danger to his right flank, himself led his guards against the enemy position

clearly indicates a causal connection between the first and second clauses. And no other clause with the same truth-value could be substituted for either of the two clauses in the sentence to yield the complete thought of the original sentence. Thus, this complex sentence involves a dual interpretation of these clauses, and in particular it involves a combination of groups one and four of the simple cases noted in the text. In the second case,

> Bebel mistakenly supposes that the return of Alsace-Lorraine would appease France's desire for revenge

Frege again combines a dual meaning for the clause in indirect discourse. It refers indirectly to its normal sense or thought as object. And secondly, it refers to the False—its normal direct reference-object. Again a combination of groups one and four of the simple cases. In the third case

> Because ice is less dense than water, it floats on water

each clause has its direct truth-value as reference on the one hand, and on the other, there is a third thought expressed—one involving the subordination of one first-level concept to another first-level concept by means of a universal quantifier or second-level concept. Thus,

> For any *x*, if *x* is less dense than water, it floats on water

is a third thought expressed and the reference-object is a truth-value. Here, therefore, each clause functions as referring both to a concept and to a truth-value, thus combining groups three and four of the simple cases.

This inquiry into complex cases is not exhaustive in the sense that all possible combinations of phrases and clauses are exhausted, but it *is* exhaustive in the sense that Frege believes he has shown that he can take account of any combination in terms of the four possible references of phrases and clauses:—truth-values as references, individual entities as references, thoughts as indirect references, and concepts as references of phrases. He thus feels he has sufficiently shown that his analysis is adequate to the variety of expressions used in complex sentences —and that such sentences cannot be read as being composed merely of clauses referring to truth-values alone: he has shown "essential reasons why a subordinate clause may not always be replaced by another of equal truth-value without harm to the truth of the whole sentence structure." [25]

Frege is thus quite aware of the complexities of ordinary language and the need for a detailed analysis of its content. He has devised, it seems to me, a remarkably successful method for treating these problems while at the same time he has laid the foundations for a formal symbolism grounded in objective content with objects as references. He can thus conclude that his analysis of the objective content (sense and reference) of proper names in general, and of sentences in particular, is adequate. His logical theory is thus grounded on a well-founded conception of a judgment which ties together the proposition or thought with the truth-value, thus yielding distinctiveness of content to each sentence while revealing the identity of references of all sentences in their truth-value (the True or the False). This is one side, and an important side, of Frege's conception that the sentence is the principle of unity in his philosophy. The other side of this conception is found in his *Function und Begriff*. It seems to me remarkable that he has accomplished this flexible analysis of sentential content while also grounding symbolic logic in objects as references. In order to see how he does this we turn now to his *Function und Begriff*.

C. *The referential content of nonproper name*
    expressions: generality and the limits of such
    referential content

The argument of *Function und Begriff* moves through
two stages: First, there is a statement of the meaning of the basic
terms "function," "argument," "value-range," and then follows
an expansion of the meanings of these basic terms throughout
the whole region of language usage.

1]   Frege's starting point in *Function und Begriff* is the
mathematical notion of function.[26] He then broadens this to lay
the foundations for the derivation of arithmetic from logic. In
defining a function Frege distinguishes two ways in which varia-
tions can take place in related expressions. First, as he has already
noted in his "Sinn und Bedeutung," there may be two different
names for the same object. And in mathematics, the difference
between symbols such as "2^2" and "2×2" must be found in
their senses and not in the object to which they refer. This
difference in sense arises out of a difference in the functional
relation between the numbers in these two names. In the one
case an exponential function is involved; in the other, a multi-
plicative function. In the second place, if we consider now only
one of these functions, we note a basic identity of operation
among differences of numbers in such cases as "3×3" and "$4 \times
4$." The same operation, that of the multiplication of a number
by itself, is involved in these two cases. This operation can be
symbolized generally as $A \times A$ where the "A" indicates merely
an open place which should be replaced by the same number
whenever filled in. Such a general expression symbolizes a function. A function is therefore the reference of an expression requiring completion by the filling in of an empty space with the
name of a definite object.

Frege's idea of a function has been criticized at some length
by contemporary thinkers. Part of the answer to these criticisms
can be found in Chapter 1, where the centrality of the controversy
surrounding the term *Bedeutung* as this is used with predicate
terms to refer to concepts was argued; further portions can be
found in Chapter 4 where the significance of this notion is more
fully developed. At this point, a simple comparison will perhaps

suffice. A functional expression for Frege is quite akin to the expressions going by the names "sentential function" and "relational expression" for more recent thinkers. Frege's notion of a function seems to me to combine meaningfully the sense of incompleteness of a verbal expression which requires existential grounding in some individual object on the one hand, and, on the other, the relational aspects of mathematical functions in which two values ("value" is not being used here in Frege's sense) are related to or mapped upon one another.[27] (I have taken the simplest example here—the one-one relation.) The first aspect is based, I believe, upon a simple common-sense recognition on Frege's part that it is the individual entities which exist—or are presumed to exist by our language usage—while the verbs refer to certain kinds of content which are within or are dependent upon the objects in question (assuming the complete sentence to be true). It should be noted here that this distinction does not lead to a substance-philosophy of the Aristotelian type, because for Frege the term "man" is a concept term just as is the term "white"—whereas Aristotle clearly distinguishes between general terms of these two types.[28]

Frege's insistence that the objective content of a word can be determined only as this word is used in a sentence might seem to imply that a proper name refers to an entity as incomplete as does a functional expression. But that this does not necessarily follow, and that for Frege an object is complete, means that existentially and linguistically there is a sense of completeness in the use of proper names even though the publicly recognized content of a proper name may depend upon its usage in a sentence. In contradistinction to the existential independence of the objects, Frege seeks isolated bits of content—content which cannot be further subdivided intensionally as the ultimate atomic references of functional expressions—references from which more complex functions and concepts can be built. He analogizes concepts and functions of the simple sort to chemical elements which can no longer be explained by their constituents. Thus, they have an intensional determinateness. What this content is for complex concepts depends in each case upon the definitions. For the most simple concepts or functions, Frege can only hint. But in spite of the intensional determinateness of functions, they still exhibit a basic existential incompleteness and require grounding in the extensional object-references of proper names. It should be noted here that Frege's approach to definition is not extensional. Even though extensional objects are existentially prior, intensional content (functions or concepts) is prior for cognitively precise science.

But let us return to the simple exposition of Frege's terms. An argument is merely the object which completes the function, the value of the function for an argument being "the result of completing the function with the argument." [29] A value is *always* an object. It should be noted, however, that even though the value of a function may be the same for all arguments, the function cannot be identified with this single value. Thus $2-x \cdot o$ is not identical with the number two, though it has the value of 2 for all arguments. The importance of this point is clear when the notion of value-range is introduced. For the value-range is that totality of argument-objects and value-objects tied together by the given function. In the function above, the value-range is representable in analytic geometry (assuming the arguments are represented by the ordinate and the values by the abscissa) by a straight line parallel to, and two units in the positive direction from, the ordinate line. Such a line stretches indefinitely from the abscissa line in both the positive and negative directions. This represents the value-range of the function, and shows intuitively the constancy of the value for any given argument.

The equality of value-ranges for two given functions is an indication that two such lines drawn on the same coordinate system will coincide. Such an equality also is merely the equality of the functions for all arguments, which leads Frege to state: "The possibility of regarding the equality holding generally between the values of functions as a (particular) equality, viz. an equality between ranges of values, is, I think, indemonstrable; it must be taken to be a fundamental law of logic." [30] In concluding this discussion, Frege introduces a special symbol for the notion of a value-range "'$\epsilon\phi(\epsilon)$'" and notes that though two functions in being equated do require the same symbol for the argument place in order to show that their equality depends upon being completed by the same argument, the value-ranges as total objects combining the arguments and values do not require the same symbol in order to be equated. Thus '$\epsilon f(\epsilon) = $'$\alpha g(\alpha)$ is an equation holding between different proper names (expressing diverse senses) of a single object. But one could equate two functions only if one indicated the identity of the argument for both functions. In contemporary symbolism "(x)[f(x) = g(x)]" shows this point.

2] Frege now extends the notion of function in two related directions: First, in terms of the operations; i.e., by adding functional expressions such as "is equal to," "is greater than," and "is less than" and second, in terms of the objects which can serve as values and arguments for functions. The expansion to include expressions such as "is equal to" requires the expansion of values of functions to include truth-values as objects, because these expressions when completed yield sentences, and we have seen in "Sinn und Bedeutung," the reference of the sentence is the True or the False. Two sentences whose values are both the True can therefore be equated regardless of their thought-content; for this is merely a more elaborate case, stated in terms of equality of value-ranges, of an identity sentence in which the senses are different but the references are the same. Thus, "snow is white equals (or is the same as) the earth has one natural moon," where "equals" means "refers to the same object, the truth-value, the True."

These expansions are the basis for showing how arithmetic is derivable from logic. For from the special functions (such as $x^2 = 1$ or, in English, "The square root of one") an indefinite number of sentences each dealing with different objects as arguments for the function (such as "1 is a square root of 1"; "2 is a square root of 1") can be generated. Only two of these refer to the True as its value; for the rest, the False is the value. Or again, the expression "horse" is completable by an indefinite number of proper names: "John is a horse," "Nellie is a horse," etc. Upon such completion, a sentence is formed and a truth-value is the value of such completion. This in turn allows Frege to define a concept as "a function whose value is always a truth-value.[31] And further, Frege carries over the notion of a value-range to these special functions or concepts calling them "the extensions of the concepts." He then shows that where the values of two functions (or extensions) are equivalent for all arguments, the value-ranges are equal. He adds "In logic this is called identity of the extension of the concepts. Hence we can designate as an extension the value-range of a function whose value for every argument is a truth-value." [32]

He further expands the notion of function to include those remaining portions of all statements and linguistic expressions which, upon the removal of a proper name, are incomplete. Thus, all objects whose names can be parts of a sentence can function as arguments and as values for various incomplete functional expressions. An object is therefore defined as "anything that is not a function, so that an expression for it does not contain an empty place." [33] The two truth-values are objects. The value-ranges and the extensions of concepts are objects. These expansions make necessary a definitive statement of the boundaries of each concept, so that for any object, it can be determined whether or not it falls under the concept. Further, since any function can be used as part of a concept (that is, as part of a function whose value is a truth-value), this means that for each function likewise such strict determination is necessary. What Frege is seeking here are strict determinations (in some cases, even by admittedly arbitrary decision) of the content of the various functions so that their usage is specified universally. He holds that piecemeal definition of terms for various kinds of objects as arguments misses the unity of meaning of such terms and also misses the possibility of establishing the foundations of arithmetic firmly in logic.[34]

Such determination may be arbitrary for many functions and concepts, but there is one function which cannot be treated arbitrarily. He introduces this function in order to complete his analysis of the expansion of functions and objects to the extent that all objects can be treated as arguments. For up to this point in the exposition of *Function und Begriff* truth-values have been treated as values only, not as arguments: thus "is white" has a truth-value—the True or the False when completed by "the snow" or "the crow" respectively. To complete his analysis, Frege introduces a function for which truth-values only can be arguments. This function is symbolized by the horizontal line "—ξ." Formerly, he called this the content line. Now, the value of this function is the True when the True is taken as argument, and false otherwise—when either the False or any other object is taken as object. Thus, whenever a true sentence follows the horizontal line, e.g., "—snow is white," the value of this completed function is the True; otherwise, its value is the False.[35] In addition, Frege introduces a vertical stroke to precede the horizontal line to indicate a completed judgment and not a mere supposition, thus: " ⊢." This separates the act of judgment from the subject, and indicates that "we are not just writing down a truth-value,... but also at the same time saying that it is the True." [36] Thus, the horizontal line is prefixed to a sentence and the total expression requires completion by the addition of the vertical stroke to turn a functional supposition into a complete act of assertion. "Of the two signs out of which the sign of assertion is composed the line of judgment alone contains the assertion." [37]

Frege now introduces several other symbols referring to functions whose arguments can be only truth-values—symbols such as those for negation and generality. In his "Die Verneinung," [38] Frege raises the problem of negative sentences in order to show that there are not negative thoughts as well as positive thoughts, negative assertions, judgments or truths, as well as affirmative assertions, judgments, or truths. He does this by reaffirming his distinction between the sense of a sentence, its thought, and the reference of a sentence, its truth-value. Here he gives three arguments: *a*] A question has a sense, but presumably, its reference or truth-value is undetermined. *b*] There is a common meaning distinct from the private meanings of such questions as those questions raised before a jury. *c*] There are hypothetical sentences in which the truth or falsity of the antecedent and consequence may not be determined though each has a sense. Ultimately Frege argues that the word for negation, "not," is essentially a functional term completable only by a thought as a unit of meaning. Thus, "the negation of..." is completable only by a thought, that is, the direct sense of a sentence in its normal use. This later statement of his position is quite compatible with his introduction of the special symbol for negation in his *Function und Begriff*, a short vertical line drawn below and attached at the top to the horizontal content line to indicate the negation of the thought expressed by the sentence: "⊤ξ." Since the horizontal line was designed as a functional expression which could take truth-values as arguments, clearly the symbol for negation refers to a function which applies either to the thought of the sentence whose reference is a truth-value or to the sense of any expression which might be incorrectly used as an argument term in this functional expression. Thus "⊤ snow is black" or "⊤ horse" indicates the falsity of the argument in completing the function referred to by the horizontal line.

As for generality, Frege introduces a symbol—a depressed curve to fit the middle of the horizontal line—in order to provide the symbolic place for the universal quantifier which is then placed in this concave section, thus: "—ɑ—" to stand for "for every a" as does the current symbol "(a)." On the surface of course, the difference in symbolism seems immaterial, and since our symbolism is typographically simpler, it has replaced Frege's symbolism. Actually, of course, this technique of combining the horizontal line-function with the quantification function implies a totally different conception of symbolic logic, as I shall argue in Chapter 4 below. From the symbols for generality and negation all the expressions for universal, existential, affirmative, and negative sentences can be expressed. Thus, the universal affirmative is simply "—ɑ—"; the universal negative is "—ɑ⊤"; the particular affirmative is "⊤ɑ⊤"; and the particular negative is "⊤ɑ—." From this beginning his whole ideography is constructed to depict the total content of single sentences.

He also introduces the very important notion of a *relation* as a function with two empty places completable by two arguments and whose value is a truth-value. This notion is basic to the definition of number. In particular, the definition of number ultimately depends upon the concept of equinumerousness which in turn is definable in terms of the one-one relation.[39] Moreover, Frege defines the relation of equals as that holding between two object-names when the references of the object-names are the same object and the reference of the identity sentence is the True.[40] He defines the function of material implication as simply a relation in which each argument is a truth-value, and in which the total expression refers to the False only if the first argument refers to the True while the second refers to the False. Symbolically for Frege, $a \rightarrow b$ is $\vdash\genfrac{}{}{0pt}{}{\xi}{\zeta}$. Frege then introduces the distinction between first and second-level functions and the corresponding first and second-level concepts. This latter distinction was noted in his "Begriff und Gegenstand" and ties in directly with the symbolism for generality and negation indicated above. A second-level function can be completed only by a first-level function; for only a first-level function can be completed by an object. Frege concludes his *Function und Begriff* by indicating both the complexities possible with two levels of functions and two or more possible argument places in a relation, and the uses of such complexities in mathematics. He finally summarizes the history of the expansion of the idea of a function and surmises that it is unlikely that further expansion into levels higher than the second will prove fruitful.

This ends our presentation of the content of Frege's *Function und Begriff* and of the three basic articles stating Frege's matured thought. In the final portions of Frege's *Function und Begriff*, one recognizes multiple connections of the ideas he expresses there with the ideas expressed in the other two articles. In Frege's ideography, we may see that he has reached a basis upon which to ground his logical system. This, it seems to me, is another aspect of the conception that for Frege the sentence is the philosophic principle of unity as will be argued in Chapter 5. In this chapter, I have not attempted to develop very fully the significance of Frege's thought. I have merely indicated some points of difference between Frege's ideas and those of other, more recent thinkers. In subsequent chapters, I shall develop an interpretation of this material in an attempt to show the significance of Frege's philosophic foundations of arithmetic as this comes into conflict with other diverse conceptions of language, of logic, and of mathematics in our more recent philosophies.

PART TWO

The Content, Power, and Unity
of Frege's Philosophy

3

LINGUISTIC AND LOGICAL CONTENT
IN FREGE'S THOUGHT

My last chapter was a summary of the subject-matter of Frege's three basic articles. We can now develop the significance of his thought as he viewed the major problems of logico-mathematical theory. Throughout all of his works, Frege was concerned with two problems: the content of logic and arithmetic, and the power of logic as it expands into arithmetic (or conversely, the analytic nature of arithmetic as it can be shown to derive from logic). These two problems will be discussed in this and the following chapter respectively. But there is also a third major problem to be faced in regard to Frege's philosophic system: that of the unity of his thought. How is his notion of content united to his notion of the power of logic?[1] As might be surmised from Chapter 1, this turns on the notion of the sentence as the basis for determining the objective content of words. And since the sentence has become a principle for many subsequent philosophies as well as Frege's, it seems especially worth while to show just how the sentence functions to unify Frege's thought. This problem will be treated in Chapter 5.

Turning now to the problem of this chapter—that of

linguistic and logical content—I shall argue that for Frege, linguistic content arises from, but is not wholly restricted to, the use of proper names. We turn to his "Sinn und Bedeutung," his study of proper names. His "Begriff und Gegenstand" distinguishes the kinds of references (*Bedeutungen*), as we have noted, and his *Function und Begriff*, the *Grundlagen*, and the *Grundgesetze* complete the account of content by revealing its basis for logic and arithmetic. Chronologically, Frege's thought started with his interest in clarifying mathematical symbolism; that is, in determining the content of concept writing. It developed further and more specifically toward the derivation of arithmetic from logic. This led to the discovery of concepts of such a sort that they could be used to define individual entities—numbers. Thus, though his logical problems began with concepts, they ultimately led back to objects as the source of content. Since this chapter is concerned primarily with Frege's final logical discovery, it reverses the direction of his intellectual growth.

The fact that objects play such a prominent place in Frege's logical system is indicated by the attention given to his ontology by many recent commentators.[2] Thus it seems appropriate to begin with a statement of his ontology. Second, the particular significance of the content of logic itself requires elaboration. And finally, the general significance of objects for his total system will be reviewed.

A. *Frege's ontology*

Rulon Wells and others have given different lists of entities which presumably constitute Frege's ontology, and they have also given various reasons for their lists. This is perhaps a suitable way to examine Frege's ontology. With one exception, the list given below is simply an extraction of objects, which Frege indicated as appropriate references of proper names in the context of the articles discussed in Chapter 2 above. The first five can be found in his "Sinn und Bedeutung;" the sixth, in his "Begriff und Gegenstand;" the seventh, in his *Function und Begriff*. The eighth, number, does not come from these three articles. We must turn to his *Grundlagen* and his *Grundgesetze* for the expansion of his logic into arithmetic to find the detailed account of this object. It is important to note, however, that his analysis of logic ultimately depends upon the identification of this arithmetical element, number.

The list is as follows:

1] any physical or psychological object to which one may care to refer.

2] the two truth-values, The True and the False.

3] the sense of any proper name.

4] any name or linguistic object or symbol or groups of symbols to which one may wish to refer.

5] a thought, the sense of a sentence.

6] a concept or function when referred to by the nominative expression "the concept *x*" or "the function *y*."

7] an extension of a concept or more generally, a value range of a function.

8] a number (which is an extension of a second-level concept).

Let us comment on each of these in turn.

1] Despite the questions raised by idealists and skeptics about the existence of physical objects as named, it is clear that language is used to refer to such objects. For ordinary commonsense usage there is no problem in using proper names to refer to the physical or even phenomenal (sense-data) objects around us; and if the scientists prefer more accuracy in such usage, they can attain it by their techniques of inquiry in their respective fields. Exactly the same is true for psychological entities, ideas (*Vorstellungen*), considered not as mere private content of proper names when used but as facts in the history of a given individual. Though each person's ideas are private, we may refer to and discuss another's ideas as a doctor may discuss a man's pain even though he does not feel it. Whether or not the pain is there or is merely feigned is a problem which the doctor may determine by inquiry. Frege argues that even though many of our private ideas (including our ideas of self) may not be a part of the content of any objective object, selves as the bearers of private ideas should be objective objects even for skeptics and rash solipsistic idealists—and they should be objects to which reference can be made by proper names expressing senses or public meanings.

2] For Frege, any sentence has at least one object-reference:

its truth-value, the True or the False. This, for Frege, is the fundamental grounding for all sentences. Some sentences may also have other object-references as parts of their content. Thus, the subject of a simple sentence always has an object-reference, and relational sentences may have two or more object-references. Other sentences may have no apparent object-references—for example, those which express the thought that a first-level concept falls within a second-level concept. But even in such sentences, I shall argue that there are concealed object-references in the very structure of the second-level concepts (see section 3 below). All the *objects* (1, 3–8), in the present list may enter as parts of the referential content of any complete sentence whose total reference is always a truth-value. Yet for Frege the expressions, "the True" or "the False" are not themselves appropriate proper names. For only sentences properly refer to the True or the False, and these expressions, "The True" and "The False" have neither thoughts as senses nor ordinary senses which could distinguish them from other proper names. The importance of this point will appear in Chapters 5 and 6 below.

3]   As indicated in Chapter 2, one can name the sense of a proper name as an object and thereby focus attention upon the public meaning associated with that name. These names as so used with indirect references also have an indirect sense, the public meaning associated with the usage of a name to refer to its direct sense.[3] Two points must be made, however, the first of them being that the normal or direct sense of a proper name is an object only when it is the indirect reference of a name. As such, it no longer functions as either the direct or indirect sense expressed by the proper name. To argue that the sense as used is a concept[4] or an object[5] is to reduce the distinction between sense-reference of proper names to that of the referential distinctions of object-concept. Such reductions open up fantastic possibilities for discovering differences in objects—requiring subscripts: objects$_1$ vs. objects$_2$,[6] or for explaining how senses are concepts. There is no ground in Frege for such reductions, nor for the premise that "all is either an object or a function."[7] If this were the case, then the discovery of the sense-reference distinction *after* the writing of the *Grundlagen* could never have been such an important logical discovery as he felt it was. My second point is that, as we noted in Chapter 1, some thinkers[8] have attempted to parallel the objective content of concept terms with the dual objective content of proper names, so that concept terms are assumed to express a sense independent of its reference, the concept. It is true that there are places where Frege does write of the incompleteness of the sense of the concept term as the reason for holding that the term or sign is incomplete.[9] However, at no point in Frege's writings does he specify that there is a sense expressed by a concept term different from the referential content of the concept term, the concept itself. There are instead clear statements that concept expressions in fact have no sense or thought in addition to the reference-concept.[10]

That this is the case seems clear also if we recall that the sense expressed by a proper name is a part of the content of the object-reference of that proper name. If a similar part-whole relation between the sense expressed by a concept-term and its reference (the concept) obtains, difficulties ensue. For simple concepts are indivisible units of intensional content and there are no publicly recognizable "parts" which could be expressed by the concept term. For complex concepts, each part is a *mark* of the total concept or property of which it is a part. In no sense can such a part be a sense expressed by the concept term. Rather, a concept is such a definitively bounded unit of content (as contrasted with the object which is an inexhaustible content source) that it is meaningless to hold that a concept-term expresses only a part of the content of the reference-concept. To hold otherwise is to treat the concept as an object and miss the importance of this distinction for Frege.

In conclusion, though it is true that Frege does state that the sense of a predicative term is incomplete, this is not done in a context in which he is distinguishing the sense of a predicative term from its reference; and his statement is merely another way of saying that the content of a predicative term is incomplete. Normally he identifies this content as the reference of the predicative term. Caton's attempt[11] to interpret the sense expressed by a predicative term as its incompleteness and to set up various degrees of incompleteness seems to me to build a meaningless structure which has no direct relevance to the problems Frege is treating. If this were the case, then why is not completeness the sense expressed by proper names? Rather, is it not possible that the redundant use of such terms as "complete-ness-incompleteness," "satisfiedness-unsatisfiedness," "saturated-ness-unsaturatedness" is Frege's way of trying to convey by hints the differences in referential content of proper names and predi-cative terms.

4] A name or any other linguistic expression—e.g., a whole sentence—can become an object referred to by another proper name. As we saw above, such a reference is indicated by quota-tion marks. It should be noted that such usage restricts the refer-ence-object to a grammatical or a physical content. The difference between these last two corresponds roughly to the difference be-tween the sign as a grammatical entity or as a mere physical vehicle. Thus, one can say "The word 'red' has three letters" or "The word 'red' in the line above is black." In the first case, the entity is merely the grammatical entity recognized as such—a single identifiable element in the structure of a language. The whole language—its proper name, conjunctions, prepositions, etc., its structure and usage even—can be referred to by a name, The English language. We should note here that for Frege such an entity is not a class of sense-data or physical instances of such occasions of use. Since Frege's analysis is focused on the content of ordinary language usage, and since he makes no reductive physicalistic assumptions about ultimate sense-data, he determines that "In speaking of the same sign, the coincidence of the refer-ence is transferred to the sign."

The importance of quotation marks to indicate that the reference of an expression is the linguistic element rather than the normal object cannot be overemphasized. For Frege, the formalists confused the objects of arithmetic (numbers) with the signs (the numerals) used to refer to them. Alonzo Church has called particular attention to this point in Frege's "Über Sinn und Bedeutung." [12] This important logical distinction does not involve the type-token distinction. Since Frege assumed no physicalistic sense-data as the beginning for his analysis, this dis-tinction is not of importance for his constructions. Certainly in ordinary usages the context determines readily whether the ob-ject referred to by a proper name in quotation marks is the grammatical or physical entity. The sense of the proper name as well as its reference is thus clearly indicated.

5]   As we noted above, when one uses a clause in indirect discourse, the clause is not being used to refer to a truth-value as in its ordinary usage; for the total sentence might not be true if any other clause with the same truth-value were substituted for it. Rather, its reference is its normal thought or sense; and such an expression can be replaced only by an expression having the same thought. Thus, the thought is an object referred to by a clause in indirect discourse. And Frege points out carefully that this proper name (i.e., the clause) does not have a thought as its sense; rather, its sense is basically the same as the sense of any ordinary proper name. Thus Frege writes: "In this case, then, the subordinate clause has for its reference a thought, not a truth-value; as sense, not a thought but the sense of the words 'the thought that . . . ,' which is only a part of the thought of the entire complex sentence." [13] Frege's clear statements on this point are important because of later interpretations of his thought and the subsequent developments in logical theory. Alonzo Church,[14] for example, treats Frege's distinction between sense and reference as leading to two infinite extensional hierarchies—one for ordinary names and one for sentences. Church recognizes that he has gone beyond Frege in his development of Frege's distinction, but he believes that he is working within the spirit of Frege's conception of the problem. At least it seems clear that, for Frege, when the reference of a clause is its thought, the sense associated with the clause is *not* a thought but a mere sense, as it would be for any other proper name. There are no dual extensional hierarchies of sense and reference in Frege's theory. Furthermore, Frege's development of formal symbolic logic is built upon the analysis of the functional or intensional side of his analysis—not upon the extensional sense-reference side, as will be shown in Chapter 4 below.

Rudolf Carnap thinks of Frege's sense-reference distinction as being one possible solution to "the antinomy of the name relation." [15] But in developing arguments for his notion of the intension-extension distinction as a more adequate solution, Carnap himself criticizes the sense-reference distinction as it applies to sentences because he believes that a complex sentence using several attitudinal or modal phrases may create an infinite hierarchy of indirect thoughts and references. Now Carnap's fear of an infinite hierarchy is ungrounded for these reasons. First, any hierarchy exists only as needed and only as actually expressed by referring to the senses of proper names or the senses of clauses in indirect discourse. We have already noted, the hierarchy of clauses used in indirect discourse merges with, or is identical in kind with, the hierarchy created by referring to the sense expressed by any proper name. Next, this single hierarchy loses its content at the second level, for once we consider the sense of a proper name used indirectly—that is, the way in which a sense is held publicly as a reference-object—a further regress adds nothing new. All that is meant by this is that a proper name, referring to the *indirect* sense of another proper name used indirectly to refer to its *normal* sense, would have little individualized content of its own as compared with that of another proper name being used in the same way. It is unlikely that any language usage, other than the excessively subtle probings of a logician, would ever occasion the use of a proper name of this kind. Finally, though the use of a single modal or attitudinal expression does involve the direct sense of the indirect clause as its reference, the introduction of the second attitudinal or modal phrase as applying to the total first expression merely makes that total first modal or attitudinal expression refer to its direct sense. It does not affect or generate another "indirect-indirect" reference (i.e., the indirect sense of the clause used to refer to its direct sense). Rather, the reference of the original clause in the "inner" modal or attitudinal expression remains exactly the same—its direct sense. For this reason, the case which Carnap envisions involves no hierarchy at all.

Frege's method seems to me a rather simple and direct device for making a series of distinctions in complex sentences. Suffice it to say that one does not create objects in Frege's view, except in the sense that man, in talking and writing, adds something to the sum-total of what is already in the world. Nor is there any way, it seems to me, of cutting down the number of objects of this kind being created every day. The only limit to such action would seem to be the fruitfulness of it. Would not every philosopher subscribe to this?

We pointed out above that the sort of objects 1], 2], 3], 4], 5] all appear in the exposition of Frege's "Sinn und Bedeutung." In order to deal with objects 6], 7], and 8], we must turn to his "Begriff und Gegenstand," *Function und Begriff, Grundlagen,* and *Grundgesetze.* Our primary interest in developing this portion of his thought will merely be to explain the objects referred to by the special proper names introduced in these works. The problem here is just that of applying the proper–name analysis of "Sinn und Bedeutung" to the diverse kinds of linguistic content introduced by these other works. The objects introduced are those referred to by [6] "the concept x" or "the function y," [7] "the extension of the concept x" or "the value-range of the function y," [8] "seven," "10," etc.

As we noted in Chapter 2, a concept is first a reference of a predicate attributed to a subject which in turn is a proper name, whose reference is an object. In some sense, then (assuming in this example that the sentence is true), the content of a concept derives from the object. But further, if the sentence is known to be true, the concept must derive from that aspect of the object expressed by the sense of the proper name that refers to it. Thus one can know the truth of "Leo is yellow" because yellow is a part of the vaguely outlined, yet public, content associated with the name "Leo" when it refers to a given lion. The concept, on the contrary, has clear boundaries, and therefore more precise knowledge is conveyed by specifying the particular concepts attributable to a given object. One can hold, therefore, that the content of a concept derives from an object as a specified portion of the sense of a given proper name. (This does not mean that sentences with empirical content are analytically true, for Frege.)

At this point no new kind of object other than the five we have described has been introduced. One might *derive* another object, on the other hand, from such a process as the following without *creating* a new kind of object. One might say for example, in pointing to Leo "That yellow is dull"—thus specifying the color as a specific object. Such an object is also of kind [1]. Similarly one can coin proper names from predicative terms, if one knows that only one object falls under the concept in question; thus, "Two is a positive square root of four" is true, and since there is only one object which falls under the concept referred to by that predicate, one may coin the proper name "the positive square root of four" to refer to the same object referred to by the proper name "two." This latter example employs objects of kind [8] which so far have not been discussed in detail.

Now, if one wishes to mention the content of a concept, one cannot express this by putting the terms in quotation marks; "yellow" refers to the grammatical or physical object. Frege, therefore, has introduced the expressions "the concept x" or "the function y" to refer to the content of the concept or function. Further, "the concept *yellow*" or "the function *positive square root of*" does not refer to any specific spot of color or any specific number but to the content of the concept or function itself. Frege used such expressions to turn a simple sentence, in which a concept is being attributed to an object, into a relational sentence. Thus: "Leo is yellow" becomes "Leo falls under the concept *yellow*." The expression "the concept *yellow*" is not attributive; its reference is therefore an object. What has taken place here is this: The conceptual content has simply been referred to as an object and is not being treated attributively. And, similarly, this is the case for all functions referred to by such linguistic expressions.[16]

The objects of kind [7], the extension of the concept x and the value-range of function y, also derive from the use of the predicative expressions "x" and "y." The relation of this kind of object to the objects of kind [6], the concept x and the function y, requires clarification. In his early work, Frege himself was somewhat unclear on this point. In his *Grundlagen* in defining "the Number which belongs to the concept f" as "the extension of the concept 'equinumerous to the concept f,'" he gave two reasons for using the expression "the extension of the concept . . . ." One, the expression "the extension of the concept" rather than "the concept" was needed to insure recognition that an object was the reference, and the other that the extension of two concepts might be identical, whereas the content of the concepts might not.[17] His first reason is apparently not needed, since he insisted in "Begriff und Gegenstand" and even a few pages before in the *Grundlagen*[18] that the expression "the concept f" did refer to an object. Yet this reason is necessary; for in the statement of the definition of number given above, the expressions "the concept f" and "the concept 'equinumerous to the concept f'" must both be taken to refer to the concepts actually being used attributively and not to refer to the objects to which such nominative expressions with the definite article "the" usually refer. Otherwise the definition makes no sense at all. The criticism of Benno Kerry was the occasion for Frege's writing his "Bergriff und Gegenstand," partially in order to clarify this point. His second reason is important because the extension of two concepts: equilateral triangle and equiangular triangle, are the same though the content of the concepts is not the same.

What emerges here is that the references of the predicative expressions as used, actually have two distinct kinds of content. To begin with, there is the special content of each concept: e.g., yellow as distinct from red or blue or short or square root of one. Then, there is the general applicability of every concept—that is, the fact that it can be attributed to many different objects or be denied of many different objects. Now the expressions, "the concept x," or "the function y," clearly refer to the special content of the concept or function in question, while the expressions "the extension of the concept x," or "the value-range of the function y," refer to an object that is created to take account of the general applicability of the particular concept or function in question. From the general applicability of the concept or function, that is, from the circumstance that expressions for them can be completed by many different proper names referring to many different object arguments to yield completed expressions whose references are value-objects, two related developments flow: The extension of a concept is first of all defined, that is, an object of type [7] can be specified. And second, the notion of a second-level function or concept is introduced.

For Frege, a concept is the reference of a predicative term as noted above, but it is also defined by him as a function whose value is a truth-value; that is "is white" when completed by "This sheet of paper" as subject term becomes the total sentence: "This sheet of paper is white" which has as its value, a truth-value, the True. Other functional expressions, such as "x^2" when completed with a given numeral referring to an object, a number, yield another number as its value. Now, for such mathematical functions as the squaring function, the value-range of the function is an object. It is the totality of argument-objects used to complete the function combined with the corresponding value-objects referred to by the completed function. It is thus a complex object, and for a mathematical function of this sort, if the argument-objects are real numbers, the corresponding value-arguments are real numbers (for non-numeral objects as arguments, the value-arguments may be defined as zero) and the value-range may be represented on a Cartesian co–ordinated plane as a parabola. Non-mathematical functional expressions, e.g. "the capital city of..." refer to a function such that when nations are the argument-objects, cities are the value-objects (and for all other argument-objects, the value-objects are zero). The value-range is then a complex object in which all the argument-objects are combined with the corresponding value-objects.

Now since a concept is a function whose value for every argument is a truth-value, Frege in his *Function und Begriff* defines the extension of a concept as simply the value-range of a function whose value for every argument is a truth-value. Frege works out this simple definition after his original supposition in his *Grundlagen* that the notion of an extension was clear enough for everyone and prior to his later problems in the "Nachwort" of his *Grundgesetze* and in his notes to Jourdain's article.[19] This definition clearly specifies, as in case for other functions, that the extension is a complex whole entity with ordered parts combining argument-objects with value-objects, in this case truth-values. This complex object contains two distinct parts: all those argument-objects, which when used to complete the concept yield the value-object, the True, combined with the True as value, and all those argument-objects which when used to complete the concept yield the value-object, the False, combined with the False, as value. Since any concept must yield a value for all possible objects as arguments, a sentence such as "This cow equals $3 - 2$" must refer to the False as its value. And the extension of the concept *"is the same as $3 - 2$"* thus combines the totality of objects in the universe ordered into two distinct parts.

The distinction between objects [6] the concept x and the function y and objects [7] the extension of the concept x and the value-range of the function y thus seems clear. The one is used to refer to the special content of the concept or function while the other refers to the complex object, in which all objects are appropriately grouped. If this distinction is collapsed, Frege's analyses lose their peculiar significance and seem to lead to nonsense. Thus, each properly delimited concept must contain as part of its content the complete possibility of its applicability. One might suppose that this general applicability part of the content of a concept would carry over into the simpler expression "The concept *yellow*" in "Leo falls under the concept *yellow*," but this is not the case. For this simpler expression is used to refer to the special content of the concept without reference to the general attributive character of the original concept. In fact, the general attributive character has been taken over by the relational expression "falls under."

But this complexity of content found in predicate concepts has occasioned some difficulties of understanding for some of Frege's interpreters. Thus Peter Geach writes: "Frege holds not merely that the abstract expression ("the concept *man*") does not stand for a concept, but also that it does stand for an object; he is inclined to think that 'the extension of the concept *man*' or 'the class of all men' stands for the same object." [20] It seems to me Geach collapses an important distinction in Frege's system and furthermore arbitrarily identifies these technical expressions with the expression "the class of all men." Geach further discusses Frege's special use of "the concept *x*" in such sentences as "The concept *square root of 4*, is realized" to mean "There is at least one square root of 4." Yet he holds that such sentences are not false but meaningless. Geach also dislikes the expression "the concept *x*" because it is "stylistically clumsy and philosophically dangerous." He holds also that Frege "is led to give false analyses" [21] because he uses this expression (along with some others that seem to be equally barbarous for Mr. Geach). Max Black also criticizes this expression "the concept *x*" as senseless, misleading, and adding to the mystification in Frege's philosophy.[22]

Frege may not have been elegant here. Whatever this is I must leave to others. Certainly any expression used carelessly is "philosophically dangerous," as Frege so well knew. I do agree with Mr. Geach that it is just in this very maze of terminology that the class-of-classes antinomy arises, but I believe it arises not because Frege makes these important distinctions, but because he did not clearly and carefully use these distinctions to solve the antinomy when Russell wrote him about it. But I must leave this for Chapter 7. It is pertinent here to note however that during most of his life, Frege criticizes vigorously the various notions of "classes of objects." The only time he fails to criticize this notion is in his "Nachwort" to the *Grundgesetze* when he mistakenly allows his notion of the extension of a concept to be identified with Russell's notion of a class. What he argues against is any arbitrarily invented or constructed group or heap; he is maintaining that any grouping has to be united in a definitive way by a definitive unit of intensional content through which argument-objects and value-objects are appropriately united. The expression "the concept x" does not do this job, because it refers only to the particular content of the concept. Only the expression "the extension of a concept x" performs the function of referring to a complex object containing other objects as properly grouped parts. Geach seems to me to miss a vital distinction and to slur over Frege's rejection of ordinary class-objects in spite of the fact that he also notes that Frege rejected the notion of a "class of all objects" as merely an invented group entity.

We turn now to objects of kind [8]. The special nature of numbers as objects in Frege's system is overlooked simply because of the widespread acceptance of Russell's definition of number which is, on the surface, so similar to Frege's notion of number. But actually, the place of numbers as objects in Frege's system is quite different from the place they have in Russell's logico-mathematics. I leave most of this for Chapter 7 below, so I shall merely indicate here the major elements entering into Frege's analysis.

In discussing the distinction between the expressions, "the concept x" and "the extension of the concept x" above, I noted that the latter was specifically concerned with the general applicability of the concept in question. I also indicated that the notion of a second-level concept or function entered. For the second-level concept is, as we have noted, one which is expressed by what we today call quantifiers: "for every $x \ldots$," "there is an x, such that $\ldots$." For Frege the term "quantifier" would have been quite apt, for he treated the quantifiers or second-level concepts as quantitative devices for specifying the general applicability of the concept in question. Now, it is not the case that the specification is always exact. We say "There is a square root of four" when we mean that "There is at least one square root of four" and we know more specifically that there are two and only two square roots of four. And similarly we may say "All men die" without any notion of how many men this statement may or will apply to. Thus, the quantitative factor involved in the general applicability of concepts—as expressed in second-level concepts—is generally in a none-, one-, or many-form. For example, as noted above, the usual existential sentence asserts that at least one object has the property in question; that is, the first-level concept is realized in at least one object. The universal affirmative sentence asserts that no object (the quantity here is zero) has the first property and not the second property. Thus, "All men are mortal" simply asserts that there are no objects which are men and not mortal. Frege's way of doing this is sometimes not clearly seen in view of the prevailing "class-of-classes" analysis which superseded his approach. Quine's treatment of the binding of variables by quantifiers as involving the existence of objects is similar to Frege's notion[23] but for Frege the existence statement is bound up with the notion of number itself.

At this point, Frege's problem shapes up roughly as follows: he has constructed a philosophy based on the notion that the content of language derives from objects which are the references of proper names. It is clear that language may even be used to refer to itself in cases in which one uses names to name names or other words. But even these object-references are subject-matter for non-logical disciplines; that is, a word may become an object of study for philological, grammatical, anthropological, or psychological purposes—or even for physical ones (the size, shape, color of written words or the intensity of sound). The question being raised here on the other hand is simply this: Is the subject-matter of logic merely a series or network of functions; or does logic also have some definite objects which define its proper subject-matter—its range or scope?[24] This problem actually touches on the power of logic, which depends, of course, on the possibility of identifying the subject-matter of arithmetic within the structure of language itself (see Chapter 4 below). This question leads directly to the problem of the kind of objects referred to by the names for numbers [8] as a part of Frege's total ontology. Frege is asking simply whether it is possible to define these objects totally within the confines of linguistic subject-matter alone. If this can be done, the particular subject-matter of logic will have been discovered.

Since the second-level concept does contain numerical content specifying the scope of the first-level concept, Frege, in the *Grundlagen*, defines as follows: "the Number belonging to the concept *f* is the extension of the concept 'equinumerous (*gleichzahlig*) to the concept *f*'." [25] This definition was achieved after having specified in a noncircular and nonintuitive manner the notion of "equinumerous to the concept *f*." He accomplished this by using the notion of the one-one relation—the notion of relation (or relation-concept as he called it at that stage of his work) ultimately being defined in terms of the notion of function. My concern here is not that of explaining the special functions or function-signs introduced to formalize the definition,[26] but merely to note that the definition is of the concept *number* attributable to individual entities N, M, . . . , i.e., of objects which fall under the concept. "N is a number" means "There is a concept such that N is the number which belongs to it." Since the number belonging to a concept was defined in terms of the concept *equinumerous*, Frege does thus construct a definition of a concept of individual objects, of cardinal numbers, thus extracting in determinate form the content of the second-level concept.

B.   *The content of logic*

Frege's discovery that he could define cardinal numbers within the context of general language usage as he conceived it, that is, in terms of objects and concepts as the references of all possible linguistic expressions, rested on the unique role of the second-level concepts. These second-level concepts are of course the logical concepts: the concepts referred to by the logical particles: "all," "some," "no," etc., out of which general sentences are constructed. Logic therefore had cardinal numbers as its subject-matter, since these were properties affirmable (or deniable) of all concepts. However, numbers play a dual role. On the one hand, as noted above, they are the substantial content of logical or second-level concepts. On the other, they are individual entities which can be named by proper names and function as the reference of a subject of a sentence as can any other object; e.g., "Two is a positive whole number." In this latter role, a number is an object to which other concepts are properly attributable. It should be noted, therefore, that though the attribution of a number to a first-level concept: "There are *two* square roots of nine," constitutes a logical or second-level concept, a number by itself is not such a second-level concept. Numbers, therefore, are clearly not concepts, but objects—individual specifiable entities.

There is no inconsistency in having an object function as part of a concept, no matter whether of first or second-level; thus, in "Venus is the same as the evening star," "the evening star" is the proper name of a reference-object and at the same time is a part of the predicate "is the same as . . ." which refers to a concept. Similarly, "two" is a proper name of a reference-object and at the same time is a part of the second-level concept "there are two" which is attributed to the first-level concept in the sentence: "there are two square roots of nine." This analogy of the role of a number as a part of a second-level concept with the role of an object as a part of a first-level concept is not intended to suggest the reduction of the second-level concept to a first-level concept. The character of these two levels of concept is quite distinct; for a second-level concept can be completed only by a first-level concept. In neither case can the attribution of an object to another object take place except when one object is an element in the content of an attributive concept.

Several further points must now be made. First, the attribution of number to a given concept is the same in content as a statement expressing the existence or nonexistence of objects falling under the concept in question. To say of any object that it exists is to make the mistake of attributing a second-level concept directly to an object; this is the trouble with such ontological statements as "God exists" or even "Julius Caesar exists." What one can say properly is "There is one object which we call God," or again, "There is one man called Julius Caesar," or "There is one even prime number." Thus, the general problem of existence is simply replaced by arithemetical attribution, plus Frege's philosophic superstructure. And this portion of metaphysics is replaced by arithmetic.

Second, Frege does write of third-level functions in *Function und Begriff* and in the *Grundgesetze*.[27] In the former work, he symbolizes a total judgment or assertion involving differentials with two levels of functions. In the latter work, the incompleteness of a definite concept f is shown by the use of a Latin letter "f" in the expression "$f(\xi)$." This stands for a definite concept of first-level. It becomes a determinate sentence referring to a truthvalue either by the introduction of a proper name yielding "$f(\mathfrak{a})$" or by the use of a second-level concept to complete it yielding "$\underline{\;\;}\mathfrak{a}\text{---}f(\mathfrak{a})$." Similarly, Frege states: "A concept of second level is thus $\neg_{\mathfrak{a}}- \phi(\mathfrak{a})$," where the Greek letter "ϕ" (and "ξ" above) indicates the empty place requiring some first-level functional expression to complete the total expression. This letter merely indicates (*andeutet*) and does not refer to (*bedeutet*) anything.[28] As we stated above, Frege does speculate on the possibility of introducing a third-level function and does introduce symbolic means for this. He doubted the usefulness of such further levels of functions—despite the linguistic possibilities for expression. He nowhere actually says anything about a third-level concept, though he is aware of the symbolic possibility, such as $-_{\mathfrak{f}}-$ $\mathfrak{f}(\mathfrak{a})$, where the German letter "$\mathfrak{f}$" indicates that the first-level function is bound. Frege does use such higher level concepts to define the concepts *following in a series,* by means of which mathematical induction is reduced to the general laws of logic.[29] Yet "for every $\mathfrak{f}$, $\mathfrak{f}(\mathfrak{a})$" or "There is no property which is not attributable of a" can be transposed to reveal the same numerical content of the second-level concept; e.g. "Zero is the extension of the concept 'equinumerous to the concept *property not attributable of a*'." This reduction is compatible with the tendency in Frege's logic to reduce higher levels to lower ones. Once more it is noteworthy that Frege does not indicate any content for second-level concepts other than numbers. Even the attribution of number to numerical concepts; e.g.

There are aleph zero positive whole numbers,

or

There are two square roots of four,

is still within this notion of a second-level concept. This is obvious because the numerical concepts are merely first-level concepts on the same level with concepts expressed by such words as "yellow" or "red" when attributed to objects in simple sentences; e.g.

Two is a positive whole number.

Even Cantor's infinite numbers of infinite numbers are mere objects on the same level as other numbers.[30] And such constructions as are made to define such entities do not use concepts of higher than the second-level. They may require quite involved first-level concepts, of course. In this way Frege is able to connect these higher level analyses with his essentially non-hierarchical logical analysis grounded in ordinary language.

Third, for sentences in which a first-level concept is stated as falling within a second-level concept, the first-level concept is not to be taken as the subject of the sentence. As noted above, properly speaking these sentences have no subjects, because the function-object distinction is primary in this kind of sentence. Nevertheless, it is clear that for Frege a thought expressed this way can also be expressed in many other ways. It is particularly important that the number being attributed to the first-level concepts can be treated as the subject of the sentence by a shift, thus:

> There is at least one square root of four,

becomes

> the number one is the same as or less than the extension of the concept "equinumerous to the concept, *square root of four.*"

Frege shows another way of making a number the subject of a sentence so as to express the thought of a sentence attributing a second-level concept of a first-level concept. Thus, the existential sentence above could be re-expressed as,

> The number four has the property that there is something of which it is the square.[31]

This sentence does not focus on the numerical content of the second-level concept; rather, it focuses on the numerical content of the first-level numerical concept. But the special numerical content of the second-level concept can be elicited in sentences which have no first-level numerical concept.

> All mammals are hot-blooded (or, for all *x*, if *x* is a mammal, *x* is hot-blooded)

becomes

> The number, zero, is the extension of the concept, "equinumerous to the concept, *mammal-not hot-blooded.*"

This shift does not change the sense-thought or the reference truth-value of the original sentence although the form of the original sentence has been changed. Here, the numerical content of the second-level concept becomes the subject of the sentence, and this is what I meant when I stated earlier that even sentences composed of two levels of concepts have at least a concealed reference to a second object; that is, a number (the first object being of course the truth-value reference of the sentence as a whole).

Fourth, Frege answers the question he raised about the content of logic. Numbers are the proper objects grounding this discipline and giving it its particular range or scope. Logic is therefore as extensive as the science of arithmetic. Frege later qualifies this.[32] This point shows clearly that Frege's uniting of logic with arithmetic must take place through the notion of content—which arises from objects, the references of proper names.

Finally, most contemporary logicians have accepted this reflexive definition of the notion of number in one form or another. Thus, Russell's class-of-classes definition has been widely accepted. Yet the importance of the method Frege uses is generally missed. For him, the definition does not simply involve a higher level of abstraction. Certainly a higher-level concept is needed, but the basic point is *the return in the higher level (second-level) to a fundamental object, which is properly the reference of a proper name.*

Further differences in the treatment of the whole question of the relation of logic to mathematics follow: For Frege this question must be treated as one of showing that the content of arithmetic is definable in the context of logic. Again, this problem is not one involving mere references to signs or classes of signs as the content of higher-level mathematical abstractions.[33] There is here no need for a Russellian theory of types or metalinguistic devices for separating levels of languages. Thus all the formalistic devices are unnecessary, because the problem of content is primary and is not confused with the symbols used. Frege would certainly view such devices as techniques of a revived formalism —the formalism which he argued against so vigorously throughout his lifetime. But these questions take us into the general problem of the power and limitations of Frege's logic (see Chapter 4).

C. *The general significance of objects*

In conclusion, then it seems important to review what Frege does mean by an object. He gives three accounts. In his "Sinn und Bedeutung," an object is the reference of any proper name; in his "Begriff und Gegenstand," an object is the reference of the subject of a simple sentence; and in his *Function und Begriff*, an object is that which is referred to by a complete or satisfied expression. In sum, then, an object is defined as a reference of a kind of linguistic expression, a proper name, which can function either as the subject of a sentence, as an argument expression to complete an incomplete functional expression, or as the value of the completed expression.

Throughout all these characterizations, one point is clear. First, a particular linguistic expression is being used with the intention of indicating unambiguously a single individual entity complete in itself. This notion of singularity or individuality is fundamental for Frege. Implicit in it is the notion of existence. In section *B* above, it was noted that the *general* problem of existence was bound up with the use of the logical or second-level concepts. But this general solution rests ultimately upon the existence of unique entities nameable by proper names or equivalent definite descriptions.

Perhaps Frege grounds his logical and philosophical system upon objects, as the appropriate existential grounds, because he had been led to search for such unique entities in his approach to arithmetic and mathematics generally. There is indeed a special kind of precision associated with unique existence proofs in mathematics. This does not mean however that Frege is constructing a Platonic heaven.[34] It merely means that Frege recognized a basic difference between certain elements of language which had unique references, individual entities, and others which did not have such individual entities as references. For these latter expressions Frege avoided the designation of "common name" in order to emphasize the notion that a proper name did indeed refer to a single entity. These latter expressions were of course his concept terms.

Since Russell's work on definite descriptions, it has been customary to treat such expressions (proper names) as having meaning (a complex set of properties) but no reference. Thus, if "author of Waverly" is signified by "f," then one states that there is only one by the following expression "$(\exists x)[(f(x)) \bullet (y)(f(y) \rightarrow (x = y))]$." In Russell's system, there remain certain basic epistemological problems in the use of the logical particles "all," "there is," etc. In addition, Russell holds that there are particulars—but these are based on an entirely different principle (an epistemological one) from that of the simple naming function to which Frege makes appeal. Quine has carried Russell's work on definite descriptions even further: he reduces meaning to a non-ontological linguistic network as a basis upon which thinkers may ontologize different elements, thus making his pragmatic choices based upon particular interests.

Now for Frege these attempts to rid language of its implicit ontological content are self-evidently futile, for they reduce ordinary commonsense language to an artificial structure. The outcome of such reductions is a specification of a variety of logical and mathematical entities; that is, linguistic constructs. Thus in apparently ridding the world of its natural entities, they create artificial ones. But to Frege, no natural object is created by human manipulation. If it could be, all science would be mere make-believe, subject to imagination and whim. Science is a process of discovery, not invention.[35] Objects are present as references for our proper names as we see fit to name certain ones for our particular purposes. It is obvious that some objects that we name may not really be as we think they are, and that our intentions in so naming them will miscarry. Nevertheless, the naming process itself indicates our belief that we can and do deal with specific objects. If we make a mistake, a physical or psychological inquiry may reveal the causes of error. The logician's task is to determine through analysis what are the references implied in determinate linguistic usage. He is concerned merely with the linguistic side of language usage. In particular, he must specify the diverse kinds of objects and concepts introduced by the diverse kinds of expressions introduced by language usage.

This is clearly Frege's conception of what he has accomplished in the three basic articles discussed in Chapter 2 above. And the summary of objects discussed in section A above is merely a restatement of the individual entities (not concepts as used) implicit in Frege's breakdown of the content of language.

Since language is apparently a natural function of man, Frege makes no point of the distinction between natural and artificial entities. Rather, what does become clear in the context of his analysis of linguistic usage is that from the philosophic standpoint there are essentially three different kinds of objects in Frege's sententially oriented system.

First, there are the philosophic objects, the two truth-values. These are the references of special linguistic expressions, sentences. Only through sentences can objective content of all other linguistic expressions be determined.

Second, there are numbers, which are special objects. They are the substantial content of the logical or second-level concepts. These objects serve to extend logic into arithmetic (or derive arithmetic from logic); since they are definable within the structure of sentences themselves. As the peculiar subject-matter grounding logic, these objects occupy a special place in Frege's ontology. And further, whether or not there exist any other objects (skeptics and idealists might bring objections against any additional objects), no one who uses language can question the objects of the first or second kind.

Third, there are all the other objects listed in section A above: that is, the references of proper names of all the other kinds: physical objects, ideas as named, senses (*Sinnen*) as objects named, linguistic expressions as objects named (by words in quotation marks), thoughts (*Gedanken*) as objects named, concepts and functions (when preceded by expressions like "the concept" or "the function") as objects named. These objects are, to begin with, the normal references of proper names used in ordinary language and in the sciences. But added to these are the various kinds of objects which result from Frege's own distinctive breakdown of linguistic content. Thus, reference to the sense of a proper name, to the sense of a sentence (a thought), to a linguistic entity (all linguistic expressions: names, phrases, and sentences as named), or, finally, to concepts or functions (by nominative expressions) adds to the kinds of objects found in Frege's system. All of these kinds play essentially the same role in his system as do the objects referred to in ordinary language and in the sciences. They add no new dimension to his logic, nor do they have a special role setting them apart from the ordinary references of ordinary proper names. Thus, all these kinds of objects constitute merely a third group alongside the philosophic entities, the truth-values, and the logical entities, numbers. These latter two thus have the special philosophic and logical functions not found in entities of this third class.

As for the value-range of a function, this is merely a complex object composed of a set of objects functioning as arguments and another set functioning as values. And since any function must be defined so that it has an object-value for any object as argument, the value-range of a function groups all possible objects of classes two and three above. Thus the function "x^2" would have the value zero for all argument-objects except numbers, and the function "the capital city of..." would have the value zero for all argument-objects except countries or states. And since the extension of a concept is the value-range of a function whose value is a truth-value, clearly this complex object is composed of objects of class one united with objects of classes two or three above. Thus, in the case of these complex entities, no new class of object, distinct from the three noted above, is introduced. These three classes of objects and the properties of these objects constitute the total content of Frege's philosophic system. In the next chapter we turn to the power of Frege's logic as it expands into mathematics.

4

THE POWER OF FREGE'S LOGIC

Power, as a property of a logical system, refers to the expansibility of the principles of logic to include mathematical principles, or conversely, the reducibility of the latter to the former. The power of Frege's logic requires another view of the material covered in Chapter 3 together with some additions from his *Grundlagen* and his *Grundgesetze*. The philosophical portion of these two works is found in summary fashion in his *Function und Begriff,* and the content of these three, when developed in accord with the underlying principles stated in "Sinn und Bedeutung" and "Begriff und Gegenstand," give a unique conception of the power of logic. This parallels and indeed interlocks with the question of content. Overemphasis upon the content tends toward a reduction of his logic to a peculiar ontology; conversely, over-emphasis upon the fruitfulness of his system appears to reduce it to a network of concepts and functions. The problem of the power of his logic is essentially a two-fold one: First, the power of Frege's logic must be viewed internally in terms of the unique set of principles he uses to make it an expansive and fruitful discipline. Second, the power of Frege's logic should be viewed in terms of his conception of the role of logic as a discipline alongside other disciplines in a system of sciences. In this latter view, Frege's treatment of logical problems can be illuminated somewhat by contrasting his conception of logic with those of certain other writers.

CONTENT, POWER, AND UNITY

A. Sources of power in Frege's concept-writing

Frege was forced into the problems of logic in his search for an adequate conceptual basis for arithmetic—a conceptual basis which would satisfy his notions of what constituted a properly precise scientific statement. Precision for him depended upon the unambiguous use of each sign in a system in which every reference (object or concept) involved was adequately represented by an appropriate sign. The problem of the power of logic then arose for Frege in his treatment of symbols and their content.

I. THE SYMBOLS

Frege's first important work, the *Begriffsschrift,* was designed solely for the purpose of constructing a way of symbolizing concepts which would reveal the general logical structure in symbolic usage—even in the usage of ordinary language. In this respect, Frege's objective appears to be identical with the objectives of many of his own contemporaries and of later thinkers. Nevertheless, even in this early work, he conceived of this problem as involving symbolic content (*Inhalt*) in the very ideography which he constructed to reveal the structure of linguistic usage in its barest form. The ideography was designed to lay bare in a simple geometric picture the actual structure of language and "thought" (non-psychological) as expressed by language.[1] Jourdain, for example, notes that it was conceived as a device for determining the empirical as distinct from the logical basis of arithmetic.[2] It was not devised merely for simplicity or facility of symbolic transformations, but to reveal the connections and the source of the content of given concepts. Frege distinguished clearly his use of concept-writing from that of Peano; for Frege intended to combine clarity of content (*lingua characterica*) with calculative power (*calculus ratiocinator*). In Frege's opinion, Peano's symbolism failed because it used signs having more than one kind of content. For example, Peano used no sign of assertion, hence his primary relational symbols in a sentence not only had to refer to their special content, but also had to function as an assertive function-sign.[3] This same point is made in Frege's criticism of Schröder's lack of an assertion sign. Such a lack indicates a basically incorrect orientation; i.e., that a logic of classes is prior to a logic of judgments or truth-values. Such an orientation is not properly based upon content-bearing sign usage and leads to the kind of formalism Frege criticized so forcefully (see below—section B 2). Thus in spite of the refinements in his analysis of the content of symbols in his later work—refinements which, as he noted, did in fact change the significance of his ideography—the ideography apparently still serves the purpose in his mature and basic work, his *Grundgesetze*, of revealing in as clear a form as possible all relevant and distinct elements which enter into the structure of linguistic usage. Such pictorial revelation eliminates appeals to intuitive self-evidence, and apparently achieves the goal of presenting, in a completely unambiguous form, symbols whose references are absolutely determinate. This is the method he used in laying the foundations for arithmetic in the logical analysis of judgments and their contents.

II. THE CONTENT OF THE SYMBOLS AS THE SOURCE OF POWER

Frege was a part of the modern movement in logical theory which rejected most of the Aristotelian logic in favor of a more powerful and flexible symbolic approach to logic. Early in his career, Frege achieved this stand by rejecting the older subject-predicate analyses of sentences for a new function-object approach to logic, yet in his "Begriff und Gegenstand," he found it necessary to formulate a new analysis of the simple sentence (that composed of a subject and predicate). What was being accomplished, in effect, was a fusion of the older notion of a predicate as attributing some property to an object with the mathematical notion of a function as being filled in with or being completed by appropriate objects. Certainly this changed the older notion of the role of predicates in sentences by providing the enlarged context for treating adjectival expressions. This led (as noted in Chapter 2 above) to the definition of concepts as functions with one argument whose value is a truth-value, to the definition of relations as functions with two or more arguments whose value is a truth-value, and to the notion of second-level concepts (analogous to second-level functions) from which ultimately the definition of number was attained. This, then, combines the two roles: that of being a property of an object and therefore a concept attributable to it (the object), and that of being an operational function applicable to an object (the argument) in terms of which it (the object) is placed in relation to another object (the value). Thus it gives immense scope to Frege's logic. But in performing these roles, the simple concepts are in fact the rock-bottom unde-composable intensional units (they can not be explained in terms of their parts).[4] Further, this dual role makes necessary clear delimitations of all functions (concepts and relations) so that proper determination of the objects to which they apply can be made and sentences (equations, etc.) in which they are used can be determined to refer to the True or the False. In simple sentences, Frege is concerned merely with that characteristic of first-level concepts which allow them to be attributed to the object named by the subject of the sentence. The functional nature of the concept derives, of course, from the fact that the subject of the sentence may be changed to yield an indefinite number of similar sentences.

The introduction of the second-level concept brings out the fact that one may summarize in such a concept the total num-ber of such objects as may properly fall under a given first-level concept. And this second-level concept in turn may apply indefi-nitely to any number of such first-level concepts. In this way, con-cepts are functional because of their general applicability. The only limit to an expansion of concepts is of course the ingenuity of the language-user in noting the properties of objects and de-termining their range of truth-applicability. The fact that num-bers form the substantive part of second-level concepts gives Frege the basis for the expansion of logic into arithmetic. This for Frege proves to be the most fruitful of the consequences of his system: the analyticity of arithmetic and the progressive nature of logic. But this involves the discovery that the notion of identity (or equality), a primary arithmetic function and logical relation, (A) reveals the source of fruitfulness of the dual content of proper names and (B) underlies the definition of number.

A]   As stated in Chapter 2 above, Frege defines the identity-relation as the reference of a special sign which holds between two proper names when their references are a single object and the reference of the whole sentence is the True.[5] It is in this same context of his "Sinn und Bedeutung" that he discovers the need for the notion of a public sense (*Sinn*) as well as a reference for proper names in order to account for the truth and cognitive significance of an identity-sentence. The point here is that this dual content of proper names is the source in language of the potentialities for indefinite expansion and fruitful development of significances of proper names and of predicate terms by means of which concepts are attributed to objects, the references of proper names. (This is all the more the case in dealing with sentences and the net-work of interrelations possible in an expanding sentential structure.)

B]   When, in addition, Frege achieves the definition of number and of individual numbers as identifiable entities by the use of this relation, identity, the power of his analysis is increased and at the same time the analyticity of arithmetic is shown. Frege achieves this by means of the two levels of concepts. Yet the important point is the return at the second-level to the discovery of an individual entity, whose content can be identified purely linguistically. This was achieved in a rough manner in his *Grundlagen* through the special concept "equinumerous to the concept *f*." The content of this concept derives both from the singleness of the particular content referred to by "the concept *f*," and from the singleness and individuality of all objects falling under the concept. In this case of course, no attention is directed to the diverse content of the objects in question; i.e., no proper name for each object is involved. Only the individuality of the objects is involved. It is this singleness which allows them to be placed in one-one relation. In this way numbers are identified as objects. The concept "equinumerous with the concept *f*" thus ties together the singularity of the concept *f* with the multiplicity of the objects falling under the concept and allows the extraction of a new proper name of a new object (e.g., a numeral). Thus, these two distinctions, sense-reference and object-concept, underlie the power of the statement for Frege for they allow the development of logic into arithmetic. We noted above (Chapter 3, section A, object 8) that this analysis depends upon reaching a single object definable purely linguistically. In this analysis, concepts are references of predicative expressions which have no associated senses, so it is not surprising that Frege's first studies in this direction missed this basic distinction which is so essential to his whole analysis. Only in dealing with expressions for objects, i.e., with proper names, is the necessity for the distinction between sense and reference apparent. But once this distinction is made, the significance of the shift from the predicate expression for a concept to the nominative expression whose reference is an object becomes most clear. When the definite article "the" is used before the concept (under which only one object falls to yield the value, True), the content of the concept is split into its reference, which is the object, and its sense, which is the particular public meaning expressed by that proper name. Thus, the concept expression is very similar to the proper name of the object; the content of the concept is very similar to the sense, and the object falling under the concept is the reference of the proper name. For example, "*an* even prime number" and "*the* even prime number" function in this way.

But there is a difference between these two types of expressions and their respective contents: there is a basic shift from a function-object analysis, in which a constant element makes possible a multiplicity of argument-value relations, to a sense-reference analysis of the content of the proper name, in which the focus is upon the object and the public meaning associated with the proper name of the object. In the first analysis, the delimited concept retains its attributive nature; whereas the sense expressed by the proper name is merely the partial content of the object. Thus, the special case in which there is only one object falling under a concept yielding the True as value is indeed the focus of Frege's logico-mathematical system; for in this case the content of the delimited concept is an adequate definition of the object and becomes the public sense. And the use of the definite article (and the special symbol "$/\xi$") to turn a conceptual phrase into a nominative expression for an individual entity in effect completes the process of extracting the particular argument-object for which the concept is True from all other argument-values (those for which the concept is False) as well as from the True itself as value-object. Thus, the proper name for the simple object is derived from the complex proper name for the argument-value complex object—the extension of the concept f. And the fruitfulness and precision of Frege's system is just this result brought about by the shift in the content of the expressions from function-object to sense-reference. (One can prove "The even prime number is the same as the positive square root of four," thus establishing the identity of references for these two proper names despite the differences of the concepts from which these names derive.) Thus, the symbol ("=") for such a complex relational content which ties together expressions and the content of such expressions is the center of great fruitfulness for Frege's system. For it is by means of this relation that arithmetic has been shown to deal with objects (numbers) wholly linguistically definable, though such objects are not mere marks or classes of mere marks on white paper. And, of course, the only limit to the development of an arithmetical system is the limit of man's ability to discover properties and construct relations between the properties of the arithmetical objects, numbers.

Frege's *Grundgesetze* is organized on just these principles. First, he restates the principles of his concept-writing in accord with his mature determination of the proper content of different kinds of symbols.[6] He specifies the proper kinds of symbolic constructions, the kinds of content for the different kinds of constructions, the basic laws of arithmetic upon which the whole logical and arithmetical system is built, and the basic rules of inference by means of which the system is developed. Second, he formulates proofs of the basic theorems.[7] And third, he investigates the conceptual difficulties surrounding the notion of irrational numbers.[8] He begins this last inquiry by specifying the principles governing appropriate definitions: completeness (not piecemeal definitions) and simplicity (direct, non-impredicative). He first reviews the contributions of Cantor, Heine and Thomae (in which he develops fully the deficiencies of formal arithmetic as compared with contentful arithmetic), those of Dedekind, Hankel, and Stolz (in which the problem of formulating properly restricted and determinate constructs based ultimately on the basic laws he originally formulated at the beginning of the *Grundgesetze*), and that of Weierstrass (in which fundamental ambiguities in concepts occurred). Frege then states the problem of defining real numbers without basing the definition on the signs themselves (which would be a return to the errors of formal arithmetic) or on notions of extension, line or plane (which would involve the grounding of these numbers on a yet unclear notion outside arithmetic and logic).[9] Frege thus insists upon distinguishing between an extension and a number-measure, though extensions, times, masses, etc. are all quantitative, as is that which is measured. Frege's problem then becomes one of maintaining logical formality, defining real numbers without geometric references, and at the same time with adequate logical content; that is, without reference to mere signs. The problem reduces finally to specifying the reference of the word "quantity." The problem then turns upon the construction of a concept whose extension (or class) is a quantitative region.[10] And a definition of such a concept is ultimately based upon the notion of a relation. So Frege concludes that real numbers are definable purely arithmetically or logically as relations of demonstrated existing quantities (cardinal numbers).

In the statement of the basic laws, Frege emphasizes that these are not mere conventions, nor mere beliefs, but statements whose references are the True.[11] Similarly, he argues that the rules of inference are justified because the negation of the conclusion (that is, to hold that the conclusion refers to the False) would entail a negation of a premise whose reference is the True. Thus, the basic elements of a truth-table analysis are present in Frege's work, and *modus ponens* is the primary rule of inference for the total body of logico-arithmetic. What Frege maintains is that though the signs are constructs, the whole system is grounded in determinate objects and functions.[12] Throughout the *Grundgesetze*, the emphasis is not upon separating out and analyzing various regions for proof constructions and determining the limitations of such different modes of proof. Rather the object is just that of the expansion of logic into arithmetic as far as the determination of definitive concepts and objects allow. All the laws of arithmetic and the rules of proof are laid down at once, as these are expressions and transformations ultimately based on the True.

B. *The proper province of logic*

In viewing the extent and limits of logic as a discipline for Frege, one chief point emerges; that is, the fact that geometry plays a distinctive role in the system of the sciences Frege envisaged. Around this central fact, three primary points are of concern: first, Frege's controversy with Hilbert and Korselt about the fundamental notions of geometry, second, Frege's way of raising and solving problems concerning the organization of the sciences, and third, Frege's special notion of logic within his system of the sciences as contrasted with other pertinent conceptions in the history of logic. I treat these three points in turn:

I. CONTROVERSY BETWEEN FREGE AND HILBERT-KORSELT

In order to pin down this analysis of the power of logic and the limitations of such power for Frege, I shall summarize his criticism of Hilbert's *Foundations of Geometry* and the ensuing controversy with Korselt.[13] But before making the summary itself, it seems desirable to explain my reasons for elaborating Frege's thought in this direction. Some may feel that this controversy is merely an expression of the more general differences in the conceptions of the foundations of mathematics—differences which have been attached to the contrasting labels "logicists" and "formalists." I postpone to Chapter 8 a discussion of the general differences in the treatments of the foundations of mathematics, though it is true that Frege attacks the formalists' conception of empty symbolism. At this point, however, my primary purpose is that of determining the principles to which Frege makes appeal as he criticizes the work of the formalists and attempts to take account of their work within the structure of his conception of mathematics. I have chosen to elaborate Frege's arguments against Hilbert and the ensuing controversy with Korselt rather than his arguments against Thomae, Heine, and other mathematicians who worked within the formalist tradition for these reasons:

A] Hilbert is without doubt the greatest mathematician within this tradition and possibly within the whole of mathematics during the first half of the twentieth century, so Frege's arguments against Hilbert should lead to a clearer notion both of Frege's thought and of how Frege could take account of the vital discoveries Hilbert made in geometry.

B] Frege's arguments against the formalist tradition as it came to grips with arithmetical problems turned primarily upon the simple but basic distinction between a sign and the reference of a sign. In this restricted field, we have already developed Frege's position fairly fully, so that the application of his analyses to arithmetical problems would not shed much new light upon his thought in this region of mathematics. Furthermore, in Chapter 7 below, I shall consider once again Frege's notion of number in contrast with Russell's notion as a part of the argument proving that Frege need not have admitted the class-of-classes antinomy into his system. In this argument, the difference between Frege's notion of number and Russell's notion that number is a constructed extensional counterpart of predicative or intensional terms will give us a similar (though not identical) notion to that of the formalist arithmeticians; for they solved arithmetic problems by using the notions of constructed classes. On the contrary, it seems especially appropriate to take account of Frege's treatment of geometric problems in order to determine what for him would be the limits of the power of logico-arithmetic. And the fullest expression of Frege's notions about geometry is given in this controversy.

c]   Frege's criticism of Thomae and the other formalist arithmeticians has been translated and is already fairly well known, but there are only a few references to Frege's original article against Hilbert's book, and there is little account of Frege's arguments against Hilbert's conception of geometry. This is most probably owing to the vast scope and consequent success of Hilbert's contributions to geometry—these alone making Frege's criticisms *seem* old-fashioned, meaninglessly limited, carping, and irrelevant in the light of the new discoveries. More interesting is the fact that Frege's later reply to Korselt opens up in a new and fresh way an old and fundamental philosophic problem: the organization of the sciences. Frege carefully distinguished Hilbert's original statements from the additions of Korselt—additions which he felt derived in great measure from Thomae and Heine. So I shall first deal with his arguments against Hilbert's position as found in his original article, and then summarize Korselt's reply and finally Frege's final statement.

Frege criticizes Hilbert for confusing the functions of definitions and axioms, and for making axioms bear the burden of defining the terms they involve. This leads to a possibility that no single identifiable reference can be determined for a given term, as the given term may (and generally does) function in several different axioms. The point clearly follows from Frege's insistence that every term have a specified reference in order that it be used in a sentential context. For Frege a definition is properly a method for introducing a short term for an involved and longer one referring to a complex content. Therefore, the definitional statement itself has no true cognitive content. But equalities which function as definitions and axioms for Hilbert are not simply sterile substitutions of convenient terms for inconvenient ones. Rather, the content of particular terms in such axiom-definitions can be determined only in conjunction with the significance of the terms as they function in other coordinate axiom–definitions. Frege argues that the law of identity (or equality) itself is a simple axiom, and other identities can be considered as examples of this law. Such confusion of axioms and definitions leads to logical jugglery, according to Frege. "Für die Strenge der mathematischen Untersuchung ist es durchaus wesentlich, den Unterschied zwischen Definitionen und allen andern Sätzen nicht zu verwischen." [14]

As for Hilbert's central problem of the consistency of the axioms, Frege holds simply: "Die Axiome widersprechen einander nicht, da sie wahr sind; das bedarf keines Beweises. Die Definitionen dürfen einander nicht widersprechen. Für das Definieren müssen solche Grundsätze aufgestellt werden, dass kein Widerspruch auftreten kann." [15] Hilbert's problem really derives from the multiplicity of significances given to terms in combinations of axiom–definitions. Similarly the central problem of the independence of the axioms arises because of the involvement of the basic terms in various of the basic axiom–definitions. For Frege, the axiom–definitions cannot be independent simply because they are so involved one with the other in the very meanings of the terms used in them. Frege ultimately feels these questions are answerable simply in terms of the properties being attributed to the objects in question: "Wenn diese einander widersprächen, so gäbe es keinen Gegenstand, an dem diese beiden Eigenschaften gefunden werden könnten..." [16] And similarly, "Wenn man einen Gegenstand aufweisen kann, der die erste Eigenschaft hat, nicht aber die zweite, so ist das zweite Merkmal unabhängig vom ersten." [17] He further states that this way of treating these two problems is approximately the same as Hilbert's way of showing consistency and independence.

But what derives from Hilbert's approach to mathematics as revealed by this confusion of axiom and definition is his double way of defining and explaining the reference of a term. Ultimately this double way turns on Hilbert's confusion of first and second-level concepts. And Frege shows this by examples drawn from Hilbert's work—examples involving the concepts "between" and "congruence" which Frege parallels to the use of the proper name "God." [18] This parallel is introduced in order to carry forward his argument that Hilbert's terms have no determinate references. He shows this to be the case by arguing that it is impossible to determine from Hilbert's axiom-definitions whether or not his conception of point is applicable to Frege's pocket watch. This clearly indicates what is necessary according to Frege in order to formulate an adequate definition: one must be able to determine whether it applies to any object. Thus, he is carrying out his stated criterion for consistency and independence of axioms in seeking for objects by means of which we can determine the adequacy of the content of our technical terminology. This is clearly consistent with his approach to logical and mathematical problems as growing out of common-sense language and as based upon definitive content derived from individual objects as the references of proper names. The impossibility of showing whether or not a pocket watch is a point proves for Frege the emptiness of the term "point" and its dependence upon the whole system of axioms involving all the other terms. And even if one considers this whole system, one is still unable to determine whether or not the term "point," or any other term or group of terms, applies to Frege's pocket watch. This leads, as we saw, Frege to use Hilbert's language to construct the ontological proof of God's existence.

At this point Frege's basic distinctions between object and concept, and first-level and second-level concept, enter. The determination of these distinctions is logically prior to the establishment of mathematical definitions and axioms. He therefore proceeds to state the distinctions which have been summarized already in this paper in Chapter 2 in the discussion of his "Begriff und Gegenstand." He then shows that since each individual point is an object, "is a point" is a first-level concept which must be describable by properties or marks of first-level, and that on the contrary Hilbert has attempted to descibe them in terms of second-level concepts, properties, and marks. In the process, of course, all the other terms such as "straight line" and "even" enter into his definitions. Frege now raises the question whether Hilbert's definitions have any meaning for Euclidean points, which are defined by first-level concepts and are applicable to objects directly. This indicates the basic problem in Hilbertian geometry. In one sense, it attempts to generalize Euclidean geometry, but it does so at the expense of not being any geometry at all, or of being a nest of geometries whose significance can be kept straight only by distinguishing "geometry-A" from "geometry-B" and "parallel axiom-A" from "parallel axiom-B" etc.[19]

In reply, Korselt[20] argues that Frege's demand for a *Bedeutung* for a sign is unnecessary, that the meaning of a sign depends upon its context of usage. Korselt further holds that an axiom is a rule for determining the use of a sign and that, in modern mathematics, signs merely indicate (*andeuten*) and have no content or meaning. Meaning arises only in the applications of signs to different areas of experience. In this way greater generality of applicability is possible and economy in proofs is achieved (one proof applies to many diverse subject-matters whose structure is the same). Such formal theories are object-oriented (*gegenständlich,* not *objectiven*) and in this way reveal the consistency of the axioms of the system. Further, such a formal system embraces the older mathematical constructions as mere parts of a larger system. Such a formal theory is based upon a general formal theory whose interpretation constitutes formal logic, without which no derivation or proof is possible. Whether or not a given formal theory applies to Frege's pocket watch is clearly a matter of meanings derived from experience and in no way involves a criticism of the formal theory itself. For Korselt, old-style definitions (e.g., of Euclidean point) are useless and arbitrary. The demand for a determinate reference for a formal theory is unsuitable and incorrect, and the use of existential sentences as axioms are nothing more than certain assumptions for a formal development. Hence, Frege's use of the ontological proof of God to refute Hilbert's type of axioms is groundless. Korselt gives credit to Bolzano (as an opponent of Kantian intuitionistic mathematics) for the ideas he expresses in defence of Hilbert, and traces the modern conception of mathematics back to Leibniz.

Korselt's criticism of Frege's original criticism of Hilbert forced Frege to state even more sharply his criticisms of the Korselt-Hilbert conception of the foundations of mathematics. Frege notes that Korselt not only confuses the notion of an axiom, as a basic assertion, with that of a definition, which is concerned merely with the determination of meanings, but he also adds to this mixture the notions of rules determining use, of sentences indicating (*andeuten*) but not designating anything, and of such sentences as binding experienced objects together in some structure.[21] Frege argues that if the interpretation of a schema must be used to determine consistency, how can one tell whether a contradiction is due to the particular interpretation chosen or to the formal structure being interpreted. Frege expresses once again the necessity for a prior determination of the fundamental logical notions upon which proofs are based; that is, he distinguishes the philosophy of science from the science itself which is based upon it. He thus distinguishes such prior determinations of basic terms from the merely derivative definitions of terms in a formal system, and argues that one cannot seek beginning points for a formal system in derivative definitions since these in turn are based upon primitive terms of a system assumed to have some references.[22] If one seeks greater generality of content in the reformulation of the bases of a science, one may extend the range of references of the terms as one chooses, but this does not mean that one should attempt to construct a meaningless (referenceless) formal system. Such empty formal systems are completely ambiguous and cannot themselves be used as proofs at all. "Was nur mittels vieldeutiger Zeichen bewiesen werden kann, das kann nicht bewiesen werden." [23]

One of Frege's clearest arguments[24] occurs in his examination of the devices for achieving generality of content in the formal systems of Hilbert (and as defended by Korselt). Generality of content arises in these systems by the use of symbols which merely indicate (*andeutet*) an empty place and by the use of strings of hypothetical clauses—all of which ultimately depend for their content on a correlated assumed conditional sentence. In such a hypothetical system, no clause by itself is a proper sentence having a truth-value as reference. Each clause merely contains a predicative expression joined to other such predicative expressions—the whole string requiring completion. Such expressions have references: the first-level concepts, relations, or second-level concepts, but the total system has no sense, because such predicative expressions have no sense. The whole sign-system therefore constitutes an unsatisfied predicative expression requiring completion even to determine whether it is true or false. Some proper name (or properly comprehensive second-level concept) is needed before the question of the adequacy of the analysis can be raised. Further, the question of the independence of axioms becomes, in this system, a question of the ordering of concepts of first-level or of relations. In none of this is one actually concerned with the signs themselves—but only with the predicative content of the signs. Signs function for Hilbert in two ways, according to Frege: they indicate (*andeutet*), thus allowing generality and as such have no reference, and furthermore, they appear to carry the conceptual content found in signs in Euclidean geometry. This dual function appears to Frege to be the substance of Korselt's claim that modern mathematics is quite different from older mathematics.

In his concluding argument. Frege raises the question of the independence of proper axioms.[25] By "proper axiom" he means the thought (*Gedanke*) of a proper sentence. By "proper sentence," he means a complete sentence and not one of the Hilbertian dangling incomplete hypothetical expressions. He thus raises in his own system the problem which derives from Hilbert's formalism. Here he is primarily concerned with the significance of such a problem in the context of his more adequate (in his opinion) approach to logic. In effect, the question of dependency is essentially as he first formulated it: whether or not a given thought (the sense of a given sentence) is derivable from a group of thoughts. Yet he restates this question, and shows that the dependency of a given thought on a group of thoughts (axioms) implies the truth of the axioms. This indicates that "nur wahre Gedanken Prämissen von Schlüssen sein können." [26]

Yet even here he feels something else is needed in order to complete the argument about the independence of axioms. He does not feel he can show exactly what is contained in the notion of independence itself, yet he opens up the problem by supposing that there are two parallel portions of a given language in which the dependence or independence of a statement depends upon the relations established in each portion, and between the por-

tions so constituted. This formalistic construction appears to be
Frege's conception of the Hilbertian technique of the modeling
of an uninterpreted series of symbols in another meaningful
language, whereby Hilbert investigates the independency of the
axioms in terms of the relations the interpreted symbols have to
one another. Frege is saying merely that any conclusions drawn
from such a "paralleling technique" derive as much from the assumptions of modeling and the original nature of the uninterpreted symbols as it does from the meaningful language itself—
in fact the meaningful language adds nothing to the process
without this "paralleling technique." But what Frege draws from
this formalistic construction is that any object and any concept
is as good as any other object or concept for logic and can be
exchanged for any other. For him, this is meaningless formalistic
nonsense and is not logic at all. Logic has its own content as does
any other science. Moreover, "Keine Wissenschaft ist ganz formal." [27] One science may be formal relatively to another; e.g.,
gravitational mechanics to chemistry. And logic may be formal
in relation to mathematics. Nevertheless, it is concerned with
such concepts as negation, identity, ordering of concepts, etc.
And these are quite different from the content of a study about
lines and points.

　　Substitution of diverse expressions in the conclusions of
one portion of such a paralleled language does not affect the truth
of the premises, but substitution of a geometric statement for an
axiom of logic (e.g., identity) may lead to complete non-corre-
spondence of the two paralleled portions of the language. This
indicates the importance of the content of logical laws themselves. What Frege is indicating here is another sense of independence: that holding between the axioms of different sciences
with diverse subject-matters. This sense of independence is itself
independent of the notion of independence as found in the relation of a given statement to other statements within the same field
of subject-matter. He recognizes that he has not stated this basic
principle of science exactly, yet it has led him to determine more
clearly what a logical conclusion is and what belongs properly
to logic. And further, he recognizes that one must prove some
sentences, such as those stating that "the concept, point, or the
relation between points and straight lines do not belong to logic"
in order to maintain the independence of logic and geometry.

Perhaps, he surmises, these are axiomatic, but certainly, they are not geometrical and cannot be used in geometry. "Aber wir befinden uns hier auf einen Neulande." [28] And Frege declines to pursue the problem of the organization of the sciences any further. He feels he had clearly indicated the necessity for distinguishing subject-matters despite his inability to bring the argument to an exact and completely satisfactory state.

Korselt replies to this argument of Frege's. He restates at greater length Bolzano's position, basing his analysis on the notion of the *Vorstellung* of a sign, which of course is for Frege only a private content. Throughout his argument, he clearly rejects Frege's limitations on the content of logic as contrasted with the content of geometry. And in concluding, he clearly indicates he has never understood what Frege meant by a second-level concept as distinct from a first-level concept, and by an object as distinct from a concept.[29] And, of course, in Korselt's arguments we find the use of an empty schema of the formalistic conceptions of mathematics. Such use has depended, so Frege argued, on symbols meaning nothing and yet everything. Such meanings must, according to Frege, lead to still greater problems. Further, for Frege, the linguistic bases of generality ("all," "some") by which logical content does enter into the analysis of geometrical problems are here used without recognizing their proper content. Though of course Frege has not said the last word on the significance of the quantifiers for logic, he did treat logical subject-matters as more than a network of concepts and/or of black marks on white paper, whose use is arbitrarily determined by semantical rules.

II. FREGE'S SYSTEM OF THE SCIENCES

Now this *Neulande*—this unexplored country—involves the problems of the organization of the sciences—a problem not entirely new to him. For, much earlier in his *Rechnungsmethoden*,[30] Frege distinguishes arithmetic from geometry because the elements of geometry are intuitive and those of arithmetic are not. In his *Grundlagen*,[31] he agrees with Kant that geometry is synthetic since its subject-matter goes beyond what can be defined within the structure of logic itself. In the following year,[32] Frege holds that the axioms of geometry are concerned with space. And he holds later[33] that "the truths of geometry, in particular the axioms, are not facts of experience, at least if by that is meant that they are founded on sense perception."

Now since Frege uses the distinctions between the a] a posteriori-a priori and b] the synthetic-analytic to classify the various sciences, there is in fact a rudimentary basis for considering the organization of the sciences in Frege's system. A science is a posteriori for Frege if the *source* of its principles are obtained by induction from experience. It is a priori if the principles are not based upon such an inductive procedure from experience. What does not come by induction from experience may come from the content of language-usage or from ordered relations independent of experience, etc. He leaves the latter possibility rather vague, but it is clear that Frege is not using the Kantian psychologistically-oriented notion of the a priori. The distinction between the analytic or synthetic properties of a science is a question not of source or content, but of the dependence or independence (or justification) of the laws governing a given subject-matter, as organized in a given science. This again is not Kantian or even Leibnizian, but neither is it Carnapian. The notion of the analytic is not defined in terms of the containment of the content of the predicate in the content of the subject. Nor does analyticity depend upon what can be defined or derived in an L-true logical system. Frege holds, rather, that a science is analytic if it depends solely "on general logical laws and definitions ... which themselves neither need nor admit of proof." [34] Any dependence on other laws than those found within logic itself clearly marks a science as synthetic.

Frege would not understand any question such as "Is logic analytic?" or "Are there analytic propositions?" because the question of analyticity is defined by sole dependence upon logical laws. Now, the problem Frege raises and solves to his satisfaction in the *Grundlagen* (which was dealt with in Chapter 3 above) is whether logic is merely concerned with a network of functions or whether it has an identifiable subject-matter of its own—that is, whether it has objects, the references of proper names, which are inherently bound up in language usage itself (as language is the medium for all statements involving all other subject-matters). Frege concludes that arithmetic is analytic, not that logic is analytic. Logic consists of general laws which neither need nor admit of proof. What is shown is that arithmetic objects, numbers, are definable within logic, as the substantive part of the purely logical concepts. Frege thus distinguishes the sciences by the differences in the subject-matters or types of objects each investigates. These objects and the scientific structure about them determine in turn the sources of the subject-matter of the science and the structural relation of one science to another. Only logic and arithmetic are analytic and a priori. Logic is distinguished from arithmetic in Frege's later work because arithmetic uses concepts (plus and minus, e.g.) which are not properly germane to logic. Nevertheless, arithmetic is analytic because its content or subject-matter is definable within logic. The physical sciences (including psychology and social sciences) are synthetic a posteriori. Their principles are arrived at by induction and they employ laws other than logical ones.

Finally, there remains geometry, which according to Frege, is a synthetic a priori science. It is synthetic simply because its subject-matter is not derivable from logico-arithmetic alone. In the *Grundgesetze,* (as we noted) Frege determines that real numbers could be defined as relational quantities, but that they also had to be distinguished from the measurable quantities of space, time, mass, etc. Geometry treats of space or spatial relations and order. These are not derivable from logical laws and definitions. In this sense, it cannot be analytic. But at the same time, the particular principles of geometry are not justified by an appeal to experience. True enough, we would have no science, not even logic and arithmetic, without experience. But this does not mean that the source of the principles of logic, arithmetic, and geometry is induction from experience. The question remains: how the special principles of geometry arise a priori, so that the science of geometry can be considered to be synthetic a priori in Frege's sense. Frege evidently holds that the science of geometry has as its own subject-matter such entities as points, lines, etc. with specifiable properties and determinable relations holding between them. Such entities are never the objects of experience. In this sense then, the objects of geometry are defined entities—abstracted or considered apart from the gross objects of our sensations. The principles of geometry—definitions, axioms, and postulates—are thus independent of experience and are justifiable purely on the basis of the relations between the abstracted and defined entities. The principles are not then gained inductively and the truths are not empirical.

Now, Hilbert's extension of geometry has for Frege apparently diverted attention away from the entities of geometry focussing it instead upon the relations and order of undefined objects. In this case, naturally, the relations between the entities of Euclidean geometry can be shown to be quite similar to relations between unspecified entities or classes.[35] (And since Frege did accept set theory as a derivative discipline, it is appropriate to consider the possible significance of this for him.) Thus, insofar as the formalists choose certain relations as beginning points for constructing their generalized system, some content remains within the generalized symbolic or linguistic forms which can be used to order other interpretive material to which the forms may be considered to apply. As such, these forms have distinguishable conceptual or relational content and are not merely empty formal schemata as claimed. Further, there is no restriction upon the application of the content (conceptual or relational) of such symbols to themselves in their relations to each other: spatially, i.e., how they occur in a string, or definitionally, i.e., how they can be ordered arbitrarily.[36] But the significance of such "orderings" is entirely dependent upon the conceptual content of the devices one employs. For Frege, the truth of such conclusions as one may draw from such procedures is entirely dependent upon how one is able to pin down such formalistic procedures to logical, arithmetical or geometrical entities.

What should be noticed of course is that linguistic expressions are not the objects or entities of such a system and can only incidentally be used to pin down such a system. By "incidentally" I mean only insofar as they are considered to be standing for bona fide arithmetical or geometrical entities. As physical marks, clearly, they cannot serve the purpose of proving the consistency or validity of the system itself. Thus, a treatment of classes and their members as interpretations of formal schemata of the same kind as a spatial interpretation (lines and points) merely indicates that geometry deals with certain relations which are extendable beyond the spatial entities abstracted from experience—or that there are other kinds of relations which are essentially spatial in this broad, abstracted sense. Such relations may derive from experience, but their ultimate justification, if geometry is to be a priori, must be found in some non-experiential objects. One cannot show the validity of geometry by applying a given system to physical nature itself. It is the case that symbols for such Fregean logical concepts as "for every *x*" or "there is" can be ordered in some linguistic system and that one can establish certain relations between such spatially related entities or such defined entities. But even this does not, in Frege's view, justify the reduction of logic and arithmetic to geometry in some all-embracing foundation of mathematics. The reason for this is that the content of logical concepts are numbers, and these very concepts are used in the formulation of any axiomatic system itself. Logic and arithmetic, together thus constitute a prior science with its special subject-matter, and as such, the fact that the symbols they use can also be subject to geometric techniques does not justify the reduction of these prior sciences to merely interpretive instances of a more general symbolic system. Any treatment of the symbols as physical entities or symbolic entities (classes of such physical entities) is a matter entirely separate from the primary content of logic and arithmetic.

III. LOGICO-MATHEMATICS AND LOGIC

The Power of Logic One of the most persistent claims for contemporary logic is that in breaking away from the limitations of traditional Aristotelean logic, it has become a powerful science, progressively developing in its own right. Contrary to such thinkers as Kant and Poincare, who held that mathematical statements, including arithmetic, must be synthetic because the mathematical sciences are progressive and developing, Ayer and others have argued that analyticity does not necessarily imply sterility nor that growth or progress in a science imply the existence of synthetic statements.[37] Frege in arguing for the analyticity of arithmetic clearly agrees with the contemporary movement in logic.

It is generally recognized therefore that the power of logic is conceived as directly related to the derivability of mathematics from logic. Quine writes: "In Whitehead and Russell's *Principia Mathematica* we have good evidence that all mathematics is translatable into logic." [38] He elaborates this:

Mathematics, in the sense here intended, may be understood as embracing everything which is traditionally classed as pure mathematics. In *Principia,* Whitehead and Russell present the constructions of the essential notions of set theory, arithmetic, algebra, and analysis from the notions of logic. Geometry is thereby provided for as well, if we think of geometrical notions as identified with algebraic ones through the correlations of analytical geometry. The theory of abstract algebras is derivable from the logic of relations which is developed in *Principia.*

It must be admitted that the logic which generates all this is a more powerful engine than the one provided by Aristotle.[39]

Now, Frege found no difficulty in accepting most of the recognized portions of the mathematics of his day. He accepted Cantor's work on transfinite numbers. He considered Dedekind's work interesting but hesitated about accepting it because he thought it based on unclear notions, improperly worked out. He found the treatment of classes posterior to the basic notions upon which he based his system: object and concept; but he was willing to admit them into the mathematical arena. This would mean that set theory and its related disciplines would be derivative and could not be taken as the foundations of mathematics. What would be needed in each case for Frege was a clear determination of the objects and concepts constituting the subject-matter of the various branches of mathematics. If these could be defined solely in terms of logical laws, the latter would be analytic extensions of logic. Where (as in geometry) additional elements entered involving concepts of order (not contained in the logical concepts) a new kind of discipline, a synthetic one, has its origin. Thus, in contrast to Quine, for whom it is important to separate the conceptual structures of the various parts of logic in order to distinguish the differences both in the inferential possibilities and in the ontological commitments of logico-mathematics, Frege argues that where conceptual elements, which are not the references of logical expressions, enter into a mathematical system, there must be new entities as the subject-matter of such a system. For such concepts imply the existence of objects of which they are the properties; that is, that there are objects which fall under the concepts. Otherwise, the system is an empty, meaningless, and possibly contradictory structure.

It should be noted here that the problem is not that of the application of logic; as, for Aristotle and all other logicians, logic is an instrument for organizing the content of other sciences. The problem here is simply that of the limits of the expansiveness of logic itself. And the diversity of answers even within contemporary logic (where the power of logic is a desirable attribute) is clearly a matter of philosophical assumptions about the role of symbols: the presence or absence of content of symbols, the variety of kinds of content of symbols, etc. What also is implicitly involved are such philosophical problems as that centering around the search for a unity of science on the one hand as contrasted with the search for appropriate means for differentiating and organizing the sciences on the other.

Axiomatics The push toward the unification of knowledge through the axiomatization and development of logic as a discipline expanding into mathematics is clearly a part of the geometrizing of knowledge which began in modern times with Descartes, Spinoza, and Hobbes, though of course there were anticipations of it in Plato. Leibniz is the person generally credited with first having anticipated the possibilities for mathematical logic. And Frege clearly conceived of his work as an extension of the Leibniz-Boole conceptions of logic and mathematics.[40] Other recent logicians and philosophers of mathematics also have felt they were following this same tradition. Leibniz's conception of a universal characteristic and of a calculus clearly seem to anticipate the objective of Frege and other more recent thinkers. Yet Frege and the others have moved in contrary directions in their development of this tradition. For Frege, the centrality of the notion of identity and the founding of his analysis upon individual entities with properties seem close to Leibniz's entities, though it is obvious, of course, that Frege's entities are grasped through common language usage, whereas Leibniz's entities are the monads, at best highly speculative entities. For many other logicians, the central notion is the elaboration of a formal system of symbols somewhat reminiscent of Leibniz's realm of pure mathematical possibility (governed by the law of contradiction), yet again, recent thinkers emphasize the purely constructive and arbitrary character of these symbolic constructs, whereas for Leibniz, the relations and the corresponding relata (ideas) were by no means merely symbolic constructs. Further, Frege's debt to the Leibniz-Boole tradition is quite different from that of Russell, Zermelo, and other logicians. Whereas these other logicians sought to treat the formal aspects of logic (the structure of a sentence or inferential schema) by means of mathematical techniques, Frege sought for and found the union of logic and arithmetic in the existence of numbers, the content of the second-level concepts or quantifiers.

Other contemporary logicians continued the process of geometrizing knowledge far beyond the earlier steps taken by Descartes, Spinoza, Leibniz, and others of the seventeenth and eighteenth centuries. For not only did these later men employ the geometrical structure of axiomatization, but they also reduced the content of knowledge to empty elements which could be treated purely in terms of formal notions of order, relation, and arrangements.[41] On the other hand, Frege, though equally interested in the axiomatizing of logic and arithmetic and in the applications of such an axiomatic system to all knowledge, emphasized differences in different branches of knowledge—differences based on differences in subject-matters. Many mathematical logicians honor Frege as the discoverer of *the* logistic method, despite Frege's assertions that he was merely following Euclid's approach to axiomatics in geometry and despite his criticism of Hilbert's logistic.[42] He did in fact formulate a logistic in his *Grundgesetze,* but this formal system was not empty. It was grounded on axioms referring to the True and was developed by inference rules also insuring that the conclusion referred to the True.

Thus, for Frege there are different kinds of logistical systems with different axioms because there are different kinds of content of such systems. Though Quine recognizes that Frege's treatment of an extension of a concept is quite different both from Zermelo's use of the abstraction principle and from Whitehead and Russell's use of the extensional counterparts of propositional functions as the bases for a logistical system, and though he does recognize that these extensions are "rock-bottom" objects for Frege's logistic,[43] he does not treat the differences in philosophical principles underlying these logistical systems and the implications for the role of logic in a system of sciences.

Logic and Symbols   As we noted above, there is much in common between Frege's total philosophic-scientific system and that of more recent logicians; e.g., the construction of a logico-mathematical symbolism which sets a scientific standard and is applicable to all subject-matters. The common elements have made it easy to interpret Frege's work as a lisping anticipation of the more contemporary approach. Thus Frege's work is criticized for not having gotten much beyond the elementary portions of the problem, for being strange, for being old-fashioned and Platonic,[44] etc.

Now, Frege himself accused many of his contemporaries of formalism.[45] In particular, he attacked formalism in arithmetic and geometry, and an extension of his criticisms can be made to all logic itself. For him, black marks, or classes of black marks, on white paper could in no way be taken as an adequate conception of a number. And since numbers constituted the substantive content of logic (see Chapter 3 above), similar use of empty symbols as a beginning point for the analysis of logic would certainly smack of the same kind of formalism in logic against which he waged war in his day in arithmetic and geometry. Further, the attempt to define such basic content-terms as "true," "provable," "satisfies," "belonging to," etc., by use of uninterpreted symbols and their relations is a reversal of his approach in which language must have content before it can be properly used. For Frege, this reversal confuses the primary problem of logical theory with the extension of logic into mathematics to the detriment of both.[46] Hence, throughout much of his work Frege emphasizes the priority of the logical task over the mathematical task; logic is a prerequisite for determining the allowable modes of proof and the assumptions to be made about objects when one employs constructions in mathematical proofs. Such logical determinations are not definitional in character. They deal with the ultimate simples which, by their nature, are essentially indefinable—but in terms of which other notions may be definable. He therefore repeats that he can only hint at the logical principles—not prove them or define them.[47] This is so just because they are *principles* or the beginning points for all proof.

Frege's analysis needs no subsidiary devices for distinguishing between linguistically created entities at various levels; e.g., type theory, metalanguages, etc.; because he determines at the very beginning a basis for distinguishing the content of symbols, especially arithmetic symbols. This does not mean that all linguistic constructions are invalid, but it does mean that the content of all legitimate constructions must be clearly specified and properly delimited. Only in this way can possible contradictions in such freely created linguistic entities be avoided. Frege sees clearly the assumptions about logic and language which the formalists make—i.e., that there could be a constructional method in which content problems merely concerned the interpretations of symbolic constructions exhibiting relations between symbols. Such formalistic symbolic structures destroy both the distinction between sense and reference and that between object and concept, so that such expressions as "the concept x," "the sense," or "the thought" all have extensional and intensional content. Numbers as special kinds of objects no longer have significance, becoming merely the extensional content of certain expressions of a given higher type. From Frege's point of view, the confusion of the intensional and extensional content of expressions and the assumed constructed nature of numbers would appear to destroy any distinction between the number signs as constructed and the numbers themselves. This raises all the problems of type distinctions, or levels of language, distinctions which never arose in Frege's system.

Thus, though Frege does distinguish between object and concept, first- and second-level concepts, and the levels of content of proper names, these are not type distinctions holding between linguistic entities made for the purpose of avoiding a merging of levels of language which might lead to contradictions.[48] Objectivity therefore rests on distinguishing the references of proper names from the references of predicative expressions, since objective content arises from the objects referred to. Where this is not done, formalism, psychologism, physicalism, and subjectivity follow. These philosophical errors have given rise to the belief that objects of arithmetic, numbers, are created by language users. This is subjective psychologism and nonsense for Frege. Physicalism is merely another aspect of the psychologism and formalism of recent logical theory. In summary then, Frege does not criticize the use of linguistic elements in formulating his own logical and mathematical system (e.g., his definition of the identity relation involves the proper names and their references as well as the sentence and its reference), yet each such function (concept or relation) so defined must contain determinate content.

Historically, in the logico-mathematics to which Frege conceived of his work as primarily contributing, he has had the least influence. This is in spite of the fact that in publishing the *Grundgesetze*, he did achieve the recognition that he had felt himself lacking heretofore. He engaged in lengthy controversies with many of the major figures of his day, as Jourdain has noted.[49] That he was unable to persuade them of his conceptions of logic and its relations to the various branches of mathematics is evidence, it seems to me, not so much of the obvious "truth" of the logic of his philosophical opponents, but of the attractions associated with the mathematical expansiveness of the formalistic way of approaching problems of logico-arithmetic. Frege's greatest influence has been upon those thinkers who have agreed with him that the problems of logic arise in the analysis of ordinary language, albeit those who have agreed with him in principle have not been interested in laying a precise foundation for logico-arithmetic. And they also have disagreed with his analysis of the content of language and logic. Perhaps Frege's greatest contributions to philosophy lie in the very peculiarities of his way of stating and solving problems. He has stated many of the arguments by which the continuing criticism and evaluation of logics in general and of philosophies of mathematics may be carried on and developed.

5

THE SENTENCE AS THE PRINCIPLE
OF PHILOSOPHIC UNITY

Frege held that the objective content of a word could be distinguished from the subjective elements of content associated with its usage only as that word functioned in the context of a complete sentence (see Chapter 1). Since the objective elements of content are the sense expressed and the object referred to by a proper name, and the concept, relation, or function referred to by a predicative expression, these of course constitute the complete catalogue intended by the expression "objective content." To make the sentence the basis for determining the objective content of all expressions is to hold the sentence to be the principle of philosophic unity. This statement involves two closely related points: *a*] We must determine how the sentence functions as a unit of content for Frege; that is, how its unity is constituted. And this will reveal how the objective content of expressions enters into and is intricately bound up with the structure of the sentence itself. *b*] We must also determine what is meant by saying that the sentence is the philosophic principle of unity; that is, how the sentence functions as the ultimate unit of assertion in which Frege's philosophy reaches a reflexive terminal point. The phrase "reflexive terminal point" must be understood as applying only to the problem of the sentence considered as the source of philosophic unity. The significance of this phrase will become clear as the argument of this chapter develops. Here again, as in Chapters 3 and 4, the same material which was presented in Chapter 2 is the subject-matter for the discussion. In this case, the analysis centers around Frege's "Begriff und Gegenstand" wherein he was particularly concerned with the proper parts of the sentence. But in order to complete the analysis by considering the diverse functions of a sentence, we must of course turn to both his "Sinn und Bedeutung" and his *Function und Begriff*.

A. *The sentence as a unit of content*

This problem falls into two parts, corresponding to the two kinds of sentences Frege distinguished: 1] the simple sentence composed of a subject and predicate and 2] what we call today the general sentence or what Frege called a sentence composed of a first- and second-level concept.

I. THE SIMPLE SENTENCE

This sentence clearly gets its unity from the attributive and incomplete nature of the concept, on the one hand, and from the public sense associated with the proper name of the object on the other. For it is from the public sense (expressed by the name), which is a partial but objective part of the content of the object named, that the concept can be seen to be truly or falsely attributed to the object named. Thus, though the truth-value of a sentence is unchanged when a different proper name referring to the same object is substituted for the original proper name, the sense of the sentence (the thought) changes, as does the sense of the subject term, when a new proper name replaces the original. Such a substitution may create a cognitive gap; that is, though the truth-value of the second sentence is the same as the first and the truth-value of the original sentence is known, the truth-value of the second sentence may not be known.[1] Thus, until the two names have been recognized as referring to the same object, doubt may remain as to whether the concept is properly attributable to the object named by the second proper name. Once the identity of the object referred to by the two names is recognized, (as, for example, when the relevant identity-sentence is seen to be true), the concept-word is then accepted as properly attributable to either proper name. Thus, the sense of the proper name forms the cognitive connective link between the object and the concept, and gives the cognitive basis for grasping the identity of the truth-value of the two sentences. For instance, if we know that the morning star appears in the heavens just before dawn and also that the morning star is the same as the evening star, we could properly say, with Frege, that we know that the evening star appears in the heavens just before dawn. In addition, the content of a predicative word in referring to a function or concept is incomplete or unsatisfied. This incompleteness is existential and is removed in a simple sentence by the attribution of the concept to an object. This incompleteness cannot be due to the special content of the concept or function, which had to be clearly limited and determined in order that the objects to which it is attributable negatively or positively could be strictly determined. From this side then, the unity of the simple sentence involves the notion of the existence or non-existence of an object with the given property—which is being attributed as a concept to that object.

Five points are noteworthy here: First, the unity of the sentence derives from a natural source of ordinary language usage. It is not a matter of artificial construction based on some semantical, syntactical, or axiomatic rule, as it would be for Carnap or Tarski. Nor does this natural relation involve a notion of objects mutually interlinked in a chain as for Wittgenstein in the *Tractatus*. Further, for Frege there is no strained epistemological analysis involving problems of how one builds up knowledge by description from atomistic sense-data with which we are acquainted, as for Russell. He simply analyzes the structure of ordinary language as it is used every day.

Second, there is no danger of referential opacity in the use of a proper name. This danger, so Quine has argued, may occur when a name or phrase is used in indirect discourse or modal sentences. In the example given above, one might hesitate to say "The evening star appears in the heavens just before dawn," but this hesitancy is not owing to any opacity. Rather it is owing to the fact that the connecting link between the object referred to by the subject and the concept referred to by the predicate is not obviously present in the sentence. The knowledge of the truth of this sentence is dependent upon the scientific sophistication of the persons using the sentence, when, on the face of it, the sentence itself appears false. This indicates the important point for Frege, that in using language, one can merge the content of proper names by establishing identities. This is possible (and referential opacity is avoided at the same time) by distinguishing clearly the publicly recognized sense of a proper name from the object referred to and from the proper name itself.

Third, the concept is seen to be one of the elements of content separated from the sense of the subject-name. This sense may be rather vaguely understood; whereas the concept is a properly delimited and sharply defined content. Thus one may say "Leo roars" or "Leo is yellow" or . . . and each of these statements can be true because the sense associated with the name "Leo" contains the content of all of these concepts. The concept has the further advantage of being completable by proper names of a number of other individual objects—and thus allows the expansion of a system of interconnected objects and concepts extending to the second-level, as we noted in Chapter 4. This function of object, sense, and concept therefore serves to solve the problem of the unity of the simple sentence as well as to solve the problems of its content and power. (We note in passing that the unifying function of the sense of a proper name does not imply that every sentence is analytic. For Frege "analytic" is defined in terms of derivability from the laws of logic alone. For objects which are known by experience (a posteriori) no proposition can be analytic. The notion that analyticity is a matter of the unifying principle of sentences is foreign to Frege and stems from diverse philosophical principles; e.g., those of Leibniz and Kant.)

Fourth, the objective content of the proper name is separated from the subjective content associated with its use by any person, simply because the delimited concept can be publicly cognized as attributable to the object in question only by persons who understand the properly accepted sense of the proper name being used. In the example given above, primitive men who had not yet established the identity between the evening and morning stars could not cognize the truth of the sentence. And only when the public sense of the term "the morning star" has been enlarged by public recognition (scientific or more popular) of this identity to include the sense associated with "the evening star" can the truth of the sentence be recognized. Thus, Frege's notion of a sense embodies all those elements of agreement of meaning which underlie all human communication, both popular and scientific. Finally, Frege does recognize the rather obvious and natural assumptions made by users of ordinary language; that is, that objects or entities exist and that properties exist in such objects. This natural assumption is reflected in the very structure of the simple sentence itself. In conclusion, then, it is clear that the unity of the simple sentence derives from the existential unity of the object and the existential and/or predicative dependence of the property upon the object, as well as from the particular way in which that object is grasped by persons using the proper name referring to the object.

II. THE GENERAL SENTENCE

Let us now turn to the question of the unity of a sentence of the second type—one composed of a first-level and a second-level concept. In this type of sentence, clearly the unity does not depend upon the sense of a proper name which functions as the subject of the sentence, for there is no such name. The unity in this case derives from the peculiar affinity of these two different levels of concepts. This affinity arises, as has been noted above, from the general applicability of the first-level concept, for this is the feature which becomes specified in the content of the second-level concept. But if we ask what is meant by "general applicability," we find that what is really *meant* here carries with it existential content. We are in fact concerned in sentences of this kind with specifying the existence or non-existence of objects which fall under the first-level concept in question. Such specification takes place without the use of proper names to refer to the diverse objects in question. And as has already been shown in Chapter 3, this specification involves objects of an entirely different kind—numbers. The unity of these sentences derives, then, from the unity of the specific content of the given first-level concept and from the linguistic possibility (found in numbers) of referring definitively (but without specific reference to the individual entities themselves) to the total possibilities for attributing the concept in question. Thus, the second-level concept is the reference of an expression which attributes this property to the first-level concept or property.

A number by itself could not be a second-level concept and could not by itself be united with a first-level concept or be a simple property of the concept. In addition, the special content of the concept "equinumerous to the concept *f*" is bound up with the numerical content to form an attributive expression. Thus, the unity of the sentence derives both from the unity of the content of the first-level concept and from the unity of the substantive content of the second-level concept as this is determined to be the extension of the concept "equinumerous to the concept *f*." For example, the sentence, "There are two square roots of nine" could be transformed into "Two is the same as the extension of the concept, equinumerous to the concept, square root of nine." There is thus a concealed notion of the identity-relation embedded in the use of general sentences. And the unity of the sentences depends upon both the existence of a multiplicity of objects falling under the first-level concept and upon the unity of objective existential entities, numbers, whose content can be attributed as a property of the first-level concept.

Again we may summarize the discussion of the unity of the general sentence in five points, some of which the reader will quickly note as being similar to the account of the unity of the simple sentence: First, the unity of these sentences derives from a natural source of ordinary language usage and in particular from the special portion of language with which logic is concerned—the second-level concepts with their numerical content. It is worth noting that these functions are not determined by semantical, syntactical, or axiomatic rules. Nor is Frege concerned with the epistemological niceties involved in the use of the term "all" as this might involve a commitment to a total examination of everything that has been or might exist. Second, in the general sentence, the second-level concept is drawn from the first-level concept because of the vaguely contained notion of its general applicability. Thus, though the content of the concept itself is delimited intensionally, its extensional applicability still requires delimitation by further refinement at the second level. Third, the objective content of the first- and second-level concepts is found in their being clearly delimited and defined as they mutually complete each other in a general sentence. Fourth, existence in the general sentence implies a two-fold reference: to the objects falling under the first-level concept and to the number which is the content of the second-level or logical concept. (Here it is worth noting that Frege would agree with Strawson[2] that the use of a nominative referential expression implies the existence of the object referred to. Frege would insist, however, that a simple sentence using such a proper name could be re-expressed in a general sentence—each having exactly the same thought. For example, the thought of "Two is a square root of four" can be re-expressed by saying "There is a number named '2' which is a square root of four." The parts of the sentences given here are different; the source of unity of these two sentences is different. But the thought [*Gedanke*] is identical for Frege.)

Finally, since for Frege the second-level concepts involve numbers as objects, a general sentence cannot be equated with a sum or product of individual simple sentences. If this were attempted, the unity of the general sentence as it expresses a particular thought would be broken up into a sum or product of many individual thoughts. What is lacking here of course is the singleness and unity of the original thought as this was expressed by the second-level concept. This does not mean that one cannot tie together a number of individual sentences to make a compound sentence. But then each sentence must be treated as referring to an individual truth-value which in turn can be related to other truth-values in a complex net of relations. And in order to deal with such a problem as this, the larger question of how the sentence functions as the principle of philosophic unity enters (see B below). Even here, though, Frege would not equate a general sentence with a series of simple sentences. The reason is not that the word "all" might involve the sum or product of an infinite series of simple sentences, but that such a reduction leaves out the numerical content which gives unity to a general sentence. The unity of a sentence ultimately turns on the notion of a complete and identifiable thought and finally on the ultimate references of all sentences, their truth-values as objects. This latter point indicates once again the importance in Frege's philosophy of grounding the unity of sentences in particular individual objects of all three classes: Truth-values, numbers, and ordinary objects.

B. *The sentence as the principle of philosophic unity*

Now to the problem of how the sentence functions as the philosophic principle of unity for Frege. The two aspects of unity indicated above, in the simple sentence and the quantified sentence, derive respectively from the difference in the treatment of the problem from the standpoint of "Sinn und Bedeutung" on the one hand and from the standpoint of *Function und Begriff* on the other. The first turns on the distinction between the sense and reference of a proper name, the second on the distinction between the functional content and its unsatisfied nature taken in conjunction with the multiplicity of objects which complete a concept. Similarly, we must look in both of these directions in order to consider fully the dual aspects of the sentence as a whole as it is a philosophic principle of unity. According to "Sinn und Bedeutung," the sentence gets its special content from the particular thought *(Gedanke)* it expresses as the sense *(Sinn)* of the sentence and its scientific grounding from its object-reference *(Bedeutung-Gegenstand)*, its truth-value. From this direction sentences are independent units expressing public objective content—partial though it may be—about a total object, its truth-value reference. According to *Function und Begriff,* where the function-object distinction replaces the sense-reference distinction as basic to the analysis, the whole sentence, in referring to an object-reference, is used as an argument-name in completing a special function term, the horizontal line "—ξ." The horizontal line refers to a function which has as its value, the True, when it has the True as argument, and the False, when it is completed by any other object. Since the values of this function are truth-values, this function appears to be a concept.

At this point, Frege's philosophic system reaches what I have called "a reflexive terminal point" when considered from the aspect of its unity. Seven remarks need to be made here. First, this function operates in a converse manner to the role played by the definite article in turning a conceptual expression into a nominative one (a definite description). Thus, "an even prime number" yields the nominative expression "the even prime number" which refers to the number two. In this case, he specifically designs a function which facilitates the separation of sentences referring to the True from all other linguistic expressions and which is itself incomplete or functional in character.

Second, sentences are treated in "Sinn und Bedeutung" as independent units referring to truth-values. Even general sentences (those composed of first- and second-level concepts) are treated there only for the purpose of specifying the references of the clauses of such sentences. Nevertheless, the placing of sentences after the horizontal line makes the total expression incomplete, much as "is the same as the morning star" and "there are two . . ." are incomplete. This becomes all the more obvious when the horizontal line is combined with other symbols to symbolize the conditional, the negative, the existential, and the universal sentences. In these latter symbolizations, Frege insists that the force of the horizontal line holds throughout.[3]

Third, in the treatment of the general sentences (existential and universal), the second-level concept is symbolized by the combination of the horizontal line with the concave line and the negation sign. The second-level concept whose content is essentially numerical thus plays a significant role when symbolized in this process of "functionalization" of the sentence; that is, in the process of reaching this reflexive terminal point. That this symbolization of these concepts enters into this process of functionalizing the sentence in the formalization of a total judgment seems quite compatible with the role of numbers as the subject-matter of logic and the source of the power of logic as it extends into arithmetic. This symbolism is thus significant in the total context of an expanding symbolic network.

Fourth, the horizontal line followed by a sentence does refer to a function, for this expression and its reference is incomplete. It must be completed by another symbol, the vertical line to form the complex and now familiar signpost " $\vdash$." Since the total horizontal-line-sentential expression is incomplete and conceptual in character, the vertical line which completes it probably should be taken as a proper name expression referring to an object (but note qualifications below). But the total expression is an act of judgment or assertion. And Frege specifically points out that this total expression cannot be taken as either the name of an object or of a concept. The act cannot function as an argument or value for other functions, nor is it something which requires completion or can become part of a functional expression itself. That is, it cannot be further "functionalized" by some special function such as the horizontal line itself. "The assertion sign (Urtheilsstrich) cannot be used to construct a functional expression; for it does not serve in conjunction with other signs to designate an object. ' $\vdash 2 + 3 = 5$ does not designate; it asserts something." [4]

Fifth, insofar as the horizontal line function has a truth-value as value and is completable by any proper name, it conforms to the definition of a concept. But in requiring completion by another symbol, the vertical line, the horizontal one might be taken as referring to a relation holding between two objects. Yet the total expression has no value in the ordinary sense as does any ordinary function (i.e. a relation) when it is completed. It is merely an act of assertion, the final act of linguistic usage.

Sixth, and of historical interest, Frege's interpretation of the total act of judgment changed from his *Begriffsschrift* to the view found in his matured expression. In the early work, he wrote:

> Here we can indeed, if we wish, distinguish subject and predicate, but the subject contains the whole content, and the sole aim of the predicate is to make it a judgment. Such a language, which has one and the same predicate—namely, "is a fact"—for all judgments, is the *Begriffsschrift,* and the sign (that is, the vertical line) is its common predicate for all judgments.[5]

After he had arrived at his matured expression, he wrote:

> The old fundamental signs, which reappear outwardly unchanged and whose algorithm has also hardly changed, have nevertheless been supplied with other explanation. The former "content-stroke" (*Inhaltsstrich*) reappears as a horizontal (*Wagerechter*). These are consequences of an energetic development of my logical views. Formerly, I distinguished two elements in that which takes the external form of an assertoric sentence: a] the acknowledgement of truth; b] the content which is acknowledged to be true. The content I called the "possible content of a judgment." This has now split up into what I call "thought" and "truth value"; a consequence of the distinction between the sense and reference of a sign. In this case the sense of the sentence is the thought and its reference is the truth-value. Besides this, there is the acknowledgment that the truth-value is the True. (I distinguish two truth-values: the True and the False.)[6]

Frege also writes: "My *Begriffsschrift* no longer corresponds to my

present view, and thus should only be used with caution to eluci-
date what I said here [*Function und Begriff* and 'Begriff und
Gegenstand']." [7] It seems not unlikely that one of the basic
changes is in the reversal of the roles played by the subject and
predicate in the act of judgment; that is, that the predicate contains the total conceptual content being affirmed of the True
as subject. This analysis fits most closely to his statement of the
subject-predicate relation in his "Begriff und Gegenstand" and
his treatment of truth-values as reference-objects and not as concepts in his "Sinn und Bedeutung." Of more general logical and
historical interest is the obvious fact that though many other
logicians have adopted the signpost as a proper logical symbol,
none has given it the particular significance found in Frege's
writings.[8]

Seventh and last, the total judgment as the philosophic
principle of unity can be seen by viewing the sentence with its
dual elements of content, its sense and its reference, in the context of its being asserted. The linguistic expression, the sentence,
functions in two ways in two different contexts. As the proper
name expressing a thought and referring to its truth-value, the
sentence is seen as an independent unit of meaning. But as the
name of a concept, the multiple possibilities for connecting such
a concept with other concepts in a vast network is revealed.

It should be noted that an object is not being identified
with a concept here; rather, a sentence functions in two ways in
different contexts. The references of the sentence in these two
contexts differ. Clearly, for the sentence as a proper name, the
reference is the truth-value, and all sentences are identical in
this respect. The reference of the sentence in the horizontal line
context, i.e. as the name of a concept, is just the given concept.
But in this case the concept as a concept is being asserted of the
True as subject. Thus, the dual status of the sentence makes
necessary a dual status of the True as an object referred to by all
sentences and as an object which falls under all such sentential
concepts.[9] As the object named by any sentence, the True cannot
be symbolized as a part of the sentence; for it is that to which the
sentence refers. But as the object which falls under the concept
named by the sentence, it must be symbolized as the single objective ground for all sentential concepts. Otherwise this peculiar
function in which truth-values are arguments is never properly
completed.

The vertical line as symbolizing the True is a special proper name symbol. It expresses no sense. In thus expressing no content, this symbol depicts the impossibility of the act of assertion itself being further postulated (as a part of another enlarged concept) by another function (or horizontal line). This also shows that the unity of the assertion, in which a sentence as the name of a truth-value is attached to the vertical line by means of the postulating function (the horizontal line), does not derive from the sense of the special proper name, but from the peculiar postulating function which mediates between the truth-value and the vertical line. Further, the special character of a total assertion, e.g., "Truth is such (or, It is true) that there is a positive square root of four" is indicated by noting that though the clause is grammatically in indirect discourse, logically its reference is not merely its thought as in the case of "Copernicus believes that . . . ." Logical indirect reference involves the attachment of the thought to someone who had that thought—whereas the assertion involves no such attachment.[10] In fact, it is the very nature of the assertion that it be strictly objective and final.

But in addition, the reference of the clause cannot be the mere truth-value, for then the assertion is merely that "Truth is such that it is true." This means that the horizontal line cannot function as an identity expression; for the identity relation holds between two properly constituted proper names which refer to the same object. But the vertical line is not a properly constituted proper name; it has no sense. And further, any sentence expresses merely a part of the totality of the object to which it refers, or of which it is attributed as a concept. To interpret the horizontal line as an identity expression is therefore impossible. This shows then, that the reference of the total functional expression is the postulated truth-value of a given thought; and this is in effect, a special concept of the True when the functional expression is completed with the vertical line.

Thus, the dual role of the sentence requires a dual role for the object, the True, and for the thought, the sense of the sentence. In "Sinn und Bedeutung," the thought is treated as the content expressed by the combination of the subject and predicate of the simple sentence; whereas, in *Function und Begriff*, the distinctions of subject and predicate have given way to the function-object analysis. And the total functional expression has no sense or thought. The advantages of this dual treatment are obvious.

On the one hand it allows Frege to base his analysis of logical problems on the everyday common-sense language, with the public senses and thoughts expressed by such usage; on the other hand, since all concepts are clearly defined and bounded, he can achieve the precision needed for careful logical and mathematical analysis. The possibilities for achieving such precision within the context of everyday language is based directly on the dual function of the thought. Such precision without antinomies or the artificial devices of type theories or metalanguages is indeed an accomplishment.

Therefore, the partial grasp (the thought) of the True becomes a bounded property or attribute (concept) of the True. The one is an expression of the independence of content, the other, a method for developing a multiplicity of relations between concepts and the objects falling under them—a particularly valuable feature where the expansion of logic and mathematics is concerned. And in this functional context, it appears that the function referred to by the horizontal line serves the same role that the sense of the proper name—the subject of an ordinary sentence—serves in a sentence. It is the device for connecting the delimited concept to the object named by the vertical line in the absence of any sense for this expression. In view of the limited content of the concept (reference of the sentence in this functional structure), it cannot be equated with the True which contains the totality of content of all sentential concepts. And conversely, in view of the fact that the vertical line has no associated sense by which it is delimited, the horizontal line which replaces the sense as the unifying factor in the functional context has universal applicability, so that all sentential concepts can be attached to the True through this device, which has no special content. Further, the modifications (negation, generality, and implication) have each in various combinations only partial applicability to sentential concepts, depending upon the special logical meanings attached to each special sign. These are, in effect, delimitations of the universal sense symbolized by the horizontal line alone.

In summary then, the thought is the basis of the difference between sentences which have different content though referring to the same object, the True; whereas, the horizontal or content line merges this thought content with the postulated truth-value to form a definite concept attributable to the subject which completes it, the True. It is not surprising then that Frege in his later life re-emphasized the objective public character of thoughts—and their independence of being apprehended. He clearly prepared in "Sinn und Bedeutung" for their status as different from objects on the one hand and the private images of a person on the other. Since thoughts are the public or common objective independent units of content expressed by sentences, they suffer little transposition as they become "functionalized" into concept form where their clarity and precision is seen in the context of their relations to other thoughts. It should be noted that in this discussion of the sentence as the name of an object and of a concept in different context, of the vertical line as a special name of the True, and of the horizontal line as a "sense-like" functional expression, the terms "object," "concept," "sense," "proper name," "concept term," etc. have all been transmuted in this enlarged context. However, such transmutations derive directly from the original usages as found in the three articles discussed in Chapter 2 above.

Thus, Frege's philosophy, considered from the three points of view, of content, of power, and of unity, is based upon the sentence. With the sentence as the philosophic principle of unity, Frege maintains contact with definite objects and attains power through the network of concepts and relations. And the basis for constructing this contentful, powerful, and united philosophical-logico-mathematical system is the logical and mathematical object, number. With this logical basis and with Frege's determination that truth-values are the philosophic objects, Frege has been able to show that the sentence is the principle of unity for philosophy as it unites the subject and predicate and in effect functions as the name of an object and of a concept in a realm of commonly accepted senses and strictly delimitable concepts on the basis of which the True is referred to and known conceptually.

PART THREE

Consistency in Frege

6

PROBLEM OF INCONSISTENCY

In Chapter 1, I stated that two primary criticisms have been directed against Frege's philosophical system. Some have held that his treatment of predicates as referring to functions, concepts, or relations was unsatisfactory, and others that his original logico-mathematical system was weakened, if not destroyed, by the class-of-classes antinomy. In Chapters 1–5, I have argued that Frege's philosophical system makes sense only if predicates refer to concepts (functions and relations), atomistic units of intensional content (or complexes of them). Such references of predicative terms are necessary if we are to understand the content, the power, and the unity of the sentence as it functions in Frege's philosophic system. These notions are presented in contrast with diverse treatments of these same problems by other logicians. Thus, the general philosophic context in which Frege develops his ideas and in which his ideas in turn are interpreted has been kept in view in an attempt to clarify the diversity of bases to which appeal is made as different logicians struggle with roughly the same problems. It seems not inappropriate, therefore, to conclude that Frege's position, the criticisms to which it is subjected, and the diverse bases from which they stem mutually clarify each other. In the light of the criticisms and the possible counter-criticisms available to Frege, his treatment of the reference of a predicative expression seems no less satisfactory than the numerous alternatives proposed since his day. Regarding the second criticism that Frege's system did contain an ineradicable antinomy, it seems especially appropriate to raise the general question of consistency in Frege's system.

A. *The general problem*

At this point, there remain two important problems surrounding the whole question of consistency in Frege's thought: 1] What method can we use to argue that Frege's total system does not contain a contradiction? This in turn is a double-barrelled question. First, it involves the question of Frege's *total* system. By this I mean, how can we be assured that, even if it can be shown that Frege's system does not contain the class-of-classes antinomy, it does not contain any *other* kind of logical inconsistency? Second, it involves the question of what *method* is the proper one to be used to solve any question of inconsistency in Frege's system. These two problems are closely related because Frege's philosophic system must contain the *method* for showing both the *exhaustiveness* of any proof of consistency in his system and the non-existence of any contradiction in his system. 2] Once it has been shown that there is no inconsistency in Frege's system, there still remains the larger problem of the meaning of the term "consistency" as used in Frege's system in contrast to its usage in other logical and mathematical systems. It seems to me even the question of the existence of an inconsistency in a philosophical system cannot be completely detached from the meaning and function of the notion of inconsistency in the system in question.

This statement should not be taken to imply any "dialectical" assumptions about the nature of knowledge, such as the supposition that the presence of contradiction is the necessary step which leads to a higher level of truth. Nor should it be taken as a denial that sometimes from given premises in an axiomatic system, contradictory conclusions may be drawn. Such conclusions would of course invalidate the alleged body of knowledge thus constituted, and would necessitate a revision of the premises before the body of knowledge in question would be scientifically acceptable. So I omit here all dialectical constructions of philosophy and knowledge; what remains are those philosophies which are concerned with the sciences as literal bodies of knowledge—the statement of which must be consistent in order to be true and intelligible. Above this minimum condition of intelligibility and truth, the importance, meaning, and function of the notion of consistency varies significantly in mathematical philosophies; and the question of the existence of an inconsistency in any given system may well imply something quite different from unintelligibility and falsity. In other words, in a philosophic system (as distinct from an axiomatically organized body of statements), one thinker often finds inconsistencies in another's work. There are two unique factors about this situation. First, the contemporary linguistic philosophies were formulated to combine logic and mathematics in precise scientific structures, yet these philosophic differences still emerge. Second, Frege himself diverged temporarily from his original principles when, in a moment of confusion, he accepted the imputation that his system contained an antinomy.

Historically, the contemporary problem of inconsistency in linguistically oriented systems was pushed most vigorously by Russell.[1] He made a strenuous effort to collect all inconsistencies in language usage because he thought such puzzles were useful devices for revealing the logical principles which he was seeking to discover. He further held that they all had a common fault—universal self-reference—and he introduced the theory of types to prevent such inconsistencies. Later, F. P. Ramsey[2] distinguished the linguistic (or semantical) from the logical (or mathematical) inconsistencies, analyzing meanings to remove the former and retaining a simplified version of theory of types to prevent the latter.[3] Later, Tarski[4] sought a definition of the concept of truth in order to avoid the liar paradox which he believed was inherent in ordinary language. He outlined a formal discipline of semantics to be constructed at the highest level of an open hierarchy of artificially constructed formal languages as the appropriate way for defining such basic "syntactical" concepts of logic and mathematics as truth, consequence, etc. This sketchy review allows us to make three points: First, since Russell attempted to make his collection of puzzles comprehensive, I assume his collection is exhaustive in the sense that all kinds of puzzles are represented. For Russell, for whom they are all of the same kind, classification of puzzles is no problem. Second, Ramsey has introduced this problem of classification, and it is one which will aid in our argument that Frege's total system is consistent. Finally, since for Frege, inconsistency as such is no special problem, nor does some particular inconsistency raise any problem requiring special treatment (as for Tarski), the principle of classification by means of which we can argue for the total consistency of Frege's system must come from philosophically prior principles.

Because Frege held that content is basic to logic and mathematics, and that content derives from objects referred to by proper names or nominative expressions (see Chapter 3), it is fitting to use this principle as Frege's basis for classifying possible inconsistencies. In Chapter 3 we distinguished three different kinds of objects: ordinary objects of reference (physical objects, sense-data as objects, senses, thoughts, words and linguistic expressions as references of names); philosophic objects, that is, truth values as the references of sentences; and logical and arithmetic objects, that is, numbers. Corresponding to these kinds we may distinguish three *possible* sorts of inconsistencies in Frege's total system, as follows: paralogisms in linguistic usage as applied to ordinary objects, the paradox of the liar as concerning the references of sentences, and the class-of-classes antinomy as concerning the references of expressions closely akin to those used to define number. Three new points must be made here. First, although "paralogism" has obvious affinities with Kant's use of the term to refer to projections into linguistic usage of content which is not originally present, Frege clearly is not employing Kantian principles. Frege's philosophy is grounded in linguistic principles whereas Kant's is based on principles derived from the faculties of the mind. Frege accused Kant, as we have already noted, of having psychologized the problems of philosophy. Second, the term "ordinary object" in the broadest sense refers to entities denoted by *accepted* proper names. One example to be examined below is a paralogism involving an arithmetic object, a number, as this is referred to by different proper names. In this case, number is an ordinary object because the paralogism turns on the ordinary name used to refer to it—not on the special logical devices used to define it. Third, since the class-of-classes antinomy arises in the reflexive construction of a class-of-classes—and it is in such a reflexive construction that number is defined (as a class-of-classes or a second-level concept, a property of a concept)—this notion of inconsistency arises in the treatment of logical and arithmetic objects, numbers. Because the class-of-classes antinomy involves a complex of elements—some of them found in simpler form in the other two kinds of inconsistency, I examine it in the subsequent chapter.

B. *The paralogisms of ordinary language*

In this first class of inconsistencies would fall those which turn on using the linguistic characteristics of words for generating a contradiction. And this can evidently be done with words which function as proper names as well as with those which function as predicative expressions. Thus, "the least integer not nameable in fewer than nineteen syllables" is a proper name of an apparently identifiable object; whereas Grelling's heterological contradiction turns on the meaning associated with an attributive predicative term.

In either case, I call these paralogisms.

1] "The least integer" contradiction is generated in an obvious way. In the reference to nineteen syllables, one is clearly referring to the normal naming process for numbers as a particular sort of object—whatever system one may choose makes no difference. But then, one later takes the "nineteen syllables" also to apply to any definite descriptive phrase which can be used to identify an object of any sort, such as a string of words. In this last usage, apparently the "nineteen syllables" can be used to refer to the total descriptive phrase itself ("the least integer not nameable in fewer than nineteen syllables") which is made up of only eighteen syllables; and thus a contradiction follows. This contradiction is clearly the result of importing arbitrary linguistic content as part of the sense expressed by the name of a mathematical object. Clearly, one may generate endless contradictions of this sort. The device open to Frege for handling such situations is simple. Since the concept "least integer ..." is contradictory, no object can fall under it.[5] Hence one can say, in the logical formulation, "There are no least integers ..." or, "The number zero, is the extension of the concept 'equal to

...' "; that is, the proper name constructed from this concept is said to refer to the object-number, zero. As noted above, Frege uses this device for such mathematical proper names as "the least rational number" where the expression has a sense (obviously derived from the concept) but no reference. What is needed to make such a phrase non-contradictory is some simple interpolated phrase such as "The least integer not nameable *by accepted mathematical terminology* in fewer than thirty-three syllables".

2] The "heterological" contradiction has received adequate attention recently,[6] so an expansion of Frege's criticism of this is not necessary. Simply stated, the contradiction is generated by noting that some words appear to be subject to having their content attributed to themselves; for example,

"Short" is short.

Others appear not to be reflexive in this way;

"Long" is not long.

The first type of term is called "autological," that is self-applying. The second is called "heterological," that is, non-self applying. At this point the question arises, "Is 'heterological' heterological?" And one may note that if the answer is affirmative, then it should not be taken as applying to itself. And conversely, if one says it does not apply to itself, then one says it does. A variety of suggestions have been offered as solutions to this paradox. Frege's method is quite effective.

First, for Frege, when one puts a word in quotation marks, the reference of that word is either the physical sign vehicle itself, to which one can attribute a physical concept: red, long, loud, soft, etc., or else the reference of the word is the grammatical unit to which one may attribute grammatical concepts: noun, verb, etc. In neither of these cases can one become concerned with the *content*. But if one wishes to ask about the content of a word (that is, the sense or reference of a proper name, or the reference of a predicative expression, as these may be used in a given sentence), then he must put his question in a different form: "Is the reference of the word 'heterological' heterological?" or "Is the concept *heterological* heterological?" Even at this point, it is clear that the rephrasing destroys any possible paralogism because the *reference* of the predicate "heterological" cannot properly be used in a sentence to apply to itself, for its reference is a concept applying to an object that falls under it, and its application to the subject term, "the concept *heterological*," is not an application to itself. From Chapter 3 we recall that "the concept *x*" refers to the linguistic expression, the concept *x,* which in turn refers to an object, as in the sentence "The concept *x* is realized." But still hidden even in this corrected form is another double use of the predicate term 'heterological' as both a predicate concept term and as only a part of a predicate expression—that part which is a name referring to an object. The question should therefore be changed still further to read "Does the concept *heterological* apply or not apply to the concept *heterological*?" But a development of this point will be made below in considering the class-of-classes antinomy. It is clear that what happens in constructing such paralogisms is that an expression is being used to refer to a linguistic object, to an object which contains the content of a concept (e.g., the reference of an expression such as "The concept *f*") and to a concept—all quite contrary to Frege's admonitions about the slipperiness of language in such circumstances.

C. *The paradox of the liar*

The Paradox of the Liar has a long history, the very value of which has also been the subject of some discussion. Reduced to its simplest linguistic elements, the paradox rests on a single statement "This sentence is false." From this sentence, it appears that if it is true, it is false; and if false, it is true. The diverse solutions offered for this problem reflect clearly diverse philosophical principles. Thus, as Koyré has shown, the classical solution is based upon showing that the object referred to by the subject of the given sentence, "this sentence," is not a proper sentence and therefore cannot properly receive the attribution of either the predicate "true" or the predicate "false." [7] Or again, C. S. Peirce, who holds that "no proposition can mean nothing but the assertion of its own falsity," [8] has dissociated the problem of the Liar Paradox from that of a purely symbolic treatment of mathematical logic. And his treatment of the paradox as a faulty inference clearly stems from his basic pragmatic inferential network principles.

The contemporary revival of the Liar Paradox stems from a linguistically and formalistically oriented treatment of philosophical problems, which is quite different from that of Koyré or Peirce. The subject, "this sentence," is considered by many logicians (Tarski, Carnap, etc.) to be acceptable as an abbreviation for the whole sentence, and the paradox in ordinary language is then found to follow in the proper fashion.[9] Thus the paradox is presented as a device for showing the inadequacy of ordinary language and the need for artificially constructed and logically precise languages. No one has ever attempted to show that this paradox could be derived from Frege's logic; nevertheless, in view of his clear belief that logical analysis begins in common-sense language and proceeds by "applying a microscope to what lies before our eyes," a projection of his devices for treating this paradox, which is supposedly contained in ordinary language, seems highly desirable. Further since Frege criticised the formalists' analyses of mathematics, it seems especially pertinent to examine the bases in his thought for analyzing this philosophical problem, so close to the heart of formalistic conceptions.

My account of Frege's view of the problem is based upon a single passage from "Sinn and Bedeutung" wherein Frege rejects the possibility of treating the thought (*Gedanke*) expressed by a sentence as the subject of another sentence in such a way that the normal reference (*Bedeutung*) of a sentence, its truth-value, becomes a predicate attributed to it.[10] Frege's point in rejecting this possibility is to make clear that his two basic distinctions, sense-reference and object-concept, cannot be "collapsed" into one or identified. He argues that a sentence, e.g.,

The thought that the world is round is true,

might appear to identify these two basic distinctions; for the subject of this sentence refers to the thought as its object—the thought (*Gedanke*) is the indirect reference, the normal sense (*Sinn*) of the sentence in the dependent clause, and the predicate has one of the two normal references of sentences, the True, as its concept-reference. He states further that such a sentence says no more than the original sentence,

The world is round,

without the predicate "true." And he argues that "A truth-value cannot be a part of a thought, anymore than, say, the sun can, for it is not a sense but an object." [11] Frege's first point, that the addition of the predicate "true" adds nothing to the content of the sentence, is obviously correct and has been accepted as a material part of the prevalent "semantical" analysis of the use of this term.[12] ("Snow is white" is true, if and only if snow is white.) But Frege is not interested in a semantic definition of the concept, true; rather, he maintains that the thought of the enlarged sentence is identical with that of the original sentence and therefore that the predicate-concept, true, is empty and the sentence is not properly formed. In other words, a concept term when attributed to a subject term must specify some particular content of the object referred to by that subject term. Frege's second point is even more important than the first. Since any proper name both expresses a sense and refers to an object, and since sentences express thoughts as their senses and refer to the True (or False) as their object, one cannot put the object, the True, into the thought expressed by the sentence because "By combining the subject and predicate, one reaches only a thought, never passes from sense to reference, never from a thought to its truth value." [13]

A further point follows from Frege's usage of the term "the True." Any attempt to treat the copula "is" as meaning "is the same as" is clearly false; for the thought which is a part of the content of the True as object cannot be equated with the object itself as a whole. Frege thus argues against the "collapse" of the thought-truth-value or sense-reference distinction with the subject-predicate or object-concept distinction. His arguments apply even more obviously against any attempt to collapse the sentence-truth-value distinction with the subject-predicate distinction. This collapse is clearly present in the sentence upon which the paradox rests: "This sentence is false." If the sentence to which the predicate "is true" is attributed is not in quotation marks, then one is merely attributing the empty predicate-concept to the object-reference of the sentence as used; that is, to the True—and this is pure redundance. If the sentence is in quotation marks, then one attributes the predicate to a physical or grammatical object—neither of which properly can receive an attribution of "true" or "false." One could attribute the word "sentence" to a sentence in quotation marks, because the sentence in quotation marks refers to this grammatical object. But this grammatical object, as a linguistic entity referred to, does not express the thought or refer to the truth-value which it does when used. It cannot therefore properly be said to be true. Only when referring to the reference of a sentence in quotes can one go to the level of the object-references of all sentences.

Further, if one were to interpret the "is" to mean "is the same as," one could identify the reference-object of the sentence as used, the True, with the True as part of the predicate. But this raises new questions about the inappropriateness of the proper name, "the True," because it expresses no sense (see Chapter 5). Surely, one cannot equate the sentence in quotation marks, the grammatical or physical entity, with the True as part of the predicate. Thus Frege cannot accept the solution of the Liar Paradox as Tarski later formulated it; but neither can he accept the statement of the difficulty in ordinary language as Tarski originally presented it. Thus, "This sentence is false" offers no difficulties for Frege. The reason is not that the subject is improperly formed as the classical solution suggests, but that the reference-object of the subject of the sentence is a mere grammatical entity to which the predicate-concept cannot apply. The fault of the formalist solution lies not only in the difficulties stemming from Frege's special conception that a truth-value is an object—the reference of a sentence. The fault lies also in the supposition that the referential content of the name named by the name in quotation marks is still contained within that name even when it is in quotation marks. Thus, in " 'p' is true," the 'p' must be referring to more than the physical or grammatical entity. This appears to introduce confusion in the use of quotation marks—at least in Frege's usage of them. From Frege's point of view, the formalists appear to have committed a higher-level error of attributing a predicate to a sentence as mentioned; i.e., to the physical or grammatical entity, when only the sentence as used is true or false. For Frege, scientific and factual statements have to have an object-reference different from their thought-sense in order to distinguish them from sentences which are merely poetic; that is, those which refer to their thoughts as references. The True as this scientific and factual ground cannot (according to Frege's principle that an object must be distinguished from a concept) ever be a reference of a predicate term. We note therefore that much of this criticism of the formalistic treatment of the Liar Paradox stems from Frege's special principles and is applicable also to classical treatments of the term "true" as a predicate of sentences.

Most logicians have rejected Frege's treatment of truth-values,[14] because it has appeared strange. My Formalist Friend has raised two sets of arguments against this account of Frege's treatment of the Liar Paradox. First, he states:

> The discussions shows confusion among three quite different things: 1] the truth-value "the True," which is of course an object and therefore cannot be referred to or expressed by any predicate, and cannot itself be predicated of anything;   2] the Tarski predicate "is true" applicable to sentences;   3] the more familiar predicate "is true" (or "is a fact" etc.) applicable to propositions of *Gedanken*.

My concern here is the fact that for Frege only the object, "the True" is philosophically significant. The "is true" or "is a fact" has been reduced to the proper use of the assertion sign as has been shown in Chapter 5. And Tarski's predicate, which is supposed to be applicable to sentences, would have been unthinkable and meaningless to Frege. It would have led to a merging of an object and a concept—and thus have violated a basic principle of Frege's throught. But it is unfair to identify this criticism with Tarski's position. For Tarski argues that his conception embraces what is philosophically significant and this would certainly include the third thing, the "is true" applicable to propositions or *Gedanken*. Further, it seems to me that Tarski outlaws the treatment of true and false as proper names referring to objects when he insists that the semantical analysis of concepts he made at the highest level of metalanguages in which these concepts can never themselves become subjects for other predicates. This is one of the devices by which the formal solution achieves its aim.[15]

Second, my Formalist Friend criticizes the

> discussion of the semantical antinomies (the least integer, Grelling's antinomy, the liar) which has little relevance to Frege, as it was not these antinomies but Russell's which

led to the downfall of Frege's system. But the discussion is unsound in itself, as in fact, you adopt Koyré's device of refuting the antinomies by quoting them in what is to begin with a weakened and unsatisfactory form. The significance of these antinomies lies in the bearing they have on the way in which a logically organized treatment of semantics can be formulated; and you show no appreciation whatever of this aspect of the matter.

My critic disapproves of me 1] for bringing in irrelevancies in treating Frege's problem of inconsistency and 2] for raising the problem of inconsistency in a non-formal way, a way contrary to the formalized linguistic treatment of later semantical theory.

These two criticisms, and even the terms in which they are expressed, arise from a conception of the logical and mathematical problems quite contrary to the one Frege held. Thus, the notion of "semantical antinomies" as distinct from logical ones was not made until Ramsey distinguished the linguistic from the logical contradictions and Tarski later formulated his semantical definition of truth. It seems to me valuable to view the whole problem of inconsistency from Frege's philosophic position. This might well give us a new perspective not only on the question of the classification of inconsistencies, but also on the meaning and function of the notion of consistency in different systems. It is sufficient, however, to note here that the criticism does stem from diverse principles. The diversity of principles will be clarified once Frege's way of treating these problems has been clearly set forth. (See Chapter 8 below.) These two kinds of inconsistency deserve treatment, not because anyone claimed they existed in Frege's system, but in order to reveal more sharply why they present no problem in his system—a system which is grounded on objects as the references of proper names in an ordinary non-artificial language. But further, from the analysis of these two types of inconsistencies, the appropriate devices for examining the class-of-classes antinomy will emerge. Further, Koyré's device of refuting the antinomies is not employed here; rather, it and other devices are referred to merely to offset Frege's approach from a still different perspective. Surely, the differences between Frege's thought and that of a formalist would account in large measure for the argument of my Formalist Friend. Frege's conception of the problem of inconsistency cannot be presented in the way in which my formalist critic demands because Frege's conception is quite contrary to that of the formalists. The critic's demand would necessitate a desertion of Frege's requirement that there be content to symbols in the very formulation of any symbolic system. Consequently, if this "weakened" way appears unsatisfactory, this merely indicates the incompatibility of the two philosophical positions on the problems of logic and mathematics.

What has been shown, then, is that these types of inconsistencies do not exist in Frege's system unless we neglect one or the other aspect of the fundamental principle of content in Frege's system—the use of proper names. This point will serve as a guide in the more complicated analysis of the class-of-classes antinomy. We have noted explicitly four misuses:

1] If it is assumed that every proper name having a publicly recognizable sense also has an object-reference, this can lead to a contradiction. Some proper names may have no reference but can still be useful. Frege determined that these be considered as referring to zero—thus indicating that there is no object-reference.

2] A contradiction may be generated by playing on alternative aspects of the sense of a given proper name expression. Such an apparent contradiction depends upon ambiguity and vagueness of the sense associated with a given proper name as it may involve reference to itself as a linguistic entity as well as reference to another object. (What would be referential-opacity for Quine is sense-ambiguity in Frege.)

3] A contradiction may be generated if Frege's basic principle "never to confuse concepts and objects" is violated.

4] A contradiction may be generated if one constructs proper names having no sense at all. Such improper "proper names" cannot be admitted into a correctly constituted logic. Otherwise, endless ambiguity and nonsense may be generated in any apparently precise system.

Improper uses of proper names—this is Frege's chief point—are the source of all possible contradictions.

7

THE CLASS-OF-CLASSES ANTINOMY

Bertrand Russell's view that all the inconsistencies such as paralogisms and the Liar Paradox involve self-reference is clearly correct. In the Liar Paradox, the reflexivity appears in the subject
of the sentence which refers to the whole sentence, while the predicate refers to a property attributable to the sentence as a whole.
In the paralogisms, a given proper name or concept term is constructed into which self-reference is built; e.g., a number referred
to by the characteristics of the name which names it or a concept
whose content is its general attributability—including its possible
attributability to itself. Here Frege's sharp distinction between an
object and a concept eliminates the possibility for the paralogism.
It is important to note the differences in the sources of the self-
reference in each case, because Frege's remedy for each inconsistency will differ accordingly. In the class-of-classes antinomy, the
distinction between an object and a concept does not solve the
problem, because one object is said to be a member of another
object. For this, then, a detailed analysis must be made of the role
of the internal relation between the linguistic elements of the
sentence on which the antinomy is built.

    Ever since 1903, when Frege reported in his "Nachwort" [1]
that Russell had written him to suggest the possibility that the
logical laws of Volume I of his *Grundgesetze* might contain a contradiction, and Frege confessed that, from his laws, the class-of-classes
antinomy could be derived, it has been accepted that Frege's
system as originally stated did contain this contradiction.[2] Even

Frege's attempt to treat this antinomy as a technical oversight which could be corrected by a simple modification of one of his laws of logic has been belabored severely. For this corrected law has been itself taken as the basis for showing that the antinomy is still contained within his system.[3] Thus, despite the flexibility of Frege's philosophic method, which apparently should be adequate for developing a logical system that could be extended into an acceptable mathematical structure, virtually no logician today thinks that Frege's analyses are an adequate basis for treatment of logico-mathematical problems. It may seem foolhardy to argue against Frege's own admission and the accepted belief which by now, after many decades, has hardened into an assumed fact in the history of logical theory; nevertheless, it seems to me that if Frege had followed his own clearly stated principles, he should never have admitted the presence of the antinomy in his system. Though the unanimity about the existence of the antinomy in his system may make such an argument as mine risky, perhaps the very diversity of opinion regarding the source of the antinomy in Frege's system gives me some grounds for raising questions about the presumed inherent fact of his system.

The significance of a re-examination of this event in logical history goes beyond a mere interest in preserving Frege's logic. For this event has become a focal point for the analysis of errors in Frege's thought. If it were the case that Frege had committed a mere logico-mathematical mistake (as Quine did for example)[4] and had his system contained a simple contradiction, his error would long since have been corrected and forgotten. But philosophers (Geach, for example) have sought to explain this "mere logico-mathematical error" in terms of Frege's basically faulty conception of language. The importance of this question, then, lies in its being a sign that philosophical principles are involved in the formulation of logico-mathematical theory. I shall argue both that Frege's real error was to admit the existence of the contradiction and also that various subsequent attempts to straighten out his thought introduce expedients diverging from Frege's original principles. Though the point about Frege's error may not be highly significant by itself, it becomes so when seen in the light of, and as a point of refraction for, the diverse principles employed in the formulation of other philosophico-logical systems. Implied in my reconstitution of Frege's logico-mathematics and also in the criticisms of the diverse reconstructions of it are broader assumptions about the nature of logico-mathematics as a discipline. Perhaps the widely accepted view that mathematical logic constitutes a scientific philosophy with a linear development to which elements are added from diverse philosophical sources (despite their erroneous bases) has definite limitations—limitations which become apparent when the view is juxtaposed against other philosophical conceptions of these same problems. No criticism of mathematical logic as a scientific body of knowledge is intended here; the criticism is only of the belief that mathematical logic is merely a scientific body of knowledge and at the same time gives a definitive treatment of philosophical and logical problems.

The argument of this chapter falls into four parts, in the first of which I shall take up the Statement of the Problem as it is found in Frege's "Nachwort" to his *Grundgesetze;* in the second I shall consider the basic solution as found in the derivation of the concept *belongs to* from the simple sentence; this leads to a third step, an account of the higher-level solution, the extension of a concept, and the notion of number; at last we shall reach a final conception of *belongs to* and our conclusion.

A. *Statement of the problem*

After Frege published the first volume of his *Grundgesetze* in 1893, Russell wrote him, explaining that Frege's notion of extension was apparently subject to the class-of-classes antinomy. Russell was not sure whether Frege's "extension" was the same as his "class." [5] In acknowledging Russell's letter, Frege states the antinomy in ordinary language much like this: A given property or concept gives rise to an extension. Thus, the property man generates the extension of the concept *man*. But the extension of the concept *man* is not a man. Nor does the extension of the concept *man* belong to the extension of the concept *man*. Therefore, one can say,

> there are extensions of concepts which do not belong to the concepts,

or further,

> there are extensions of concepts which do not belong to the extensions of the concepts.

Let us therefore consider the extension of the concept *extensions of concepts which do not belong to themselves*, and ask now whether or not this extension belongs to itself (that is, to the extension of the concept *extensions of concepts which do not belong to themselves*). If it does belong to itself, then, since this extension contains only those extensions not belonging to themselves, it cannot belong to itself. And if it does not belong to itself, then by the conceptual content of this extension (*not belong to*), it must be within the extension of the concept *extensions of concepts which do not belong to themselves*—and therefore must belong to itself. Thus a contradiction results.

I. THE CONTENT OF THE "NACHWORT"

Frege 1] agrees with Russell that the criticism is applicable to his notion of the extension of a concept, 2] maintains that he has never felt very happy with this notion, even though it apparently is derivable from his more basic terms, object and concept, 3] argues that this notion of extension as an object is basic to his treatment of number and arithmetic generally, 4] shows that the antinomy is statable within his symbolism and that it is derivable from his fifth law (and laws Vb and Vc also) of arithmetic, (which he states he never found as self-evident as he found his other arithmetical laws), 5] completes his "inquiry by reaching the falsity of (law) Vb, as the final result of a deduction . . . with regard to any second-level function that takes an argument of the second type," i.e., a first-level function of one argument, 6] points out the effect of this discovery for various important theorems which follow from the fifth law, 7] suggests a modification, and 8] proceeds to show how this modification seems to take care of the problem and does not affect the derivation of the basic theorems from the fifth law. He then 9] concludes that apparently this takes care of the problem, and that if it does not, he is sure that his basic principles (object-concept distinction) are correct and all that will be required to solve this problem is at most some other minor technical adjustment. Frege, incidentally, adhered to these basic principles throughout the rest of his life despite the fact that he did waver in his be-beliefs about the importance and necessity of his notion of the extension of a concept as the basis for grounding arithmetic in logic.

The fifth law of arithmetic is merely a restatement of the basic principle originally enunciated in *Function und Begriff* that if and only if for every object (*a*), two concepts (*f*, *g*) are equivalent, then the extensions of the concepts are equivalent. Frege expresses this in his law as follows:[6]

$$\vdash [\grave{\epsilon}f(\epsilon) = \acute{\alpha}g(\alpha)] = (\neg \alpha\!\!\!\frown f(\mathfrak{a}) = g(\mathfrak{a}))$$

The modified version of this law states this same equivalence with the addition that the objects (a) for which the concepts are equivalent are not the same as either extension. This is expressed as law V′:[7]

$$\vdash [\grave{\epsilon}f(\epsilon) = \acute{\alpha}g(\alpha)] = \neg\alpha \begin{cases} f(\mathfrak{a}) = g(\mathfrak{a}) \\ \mathfrak{a} = \grave{\epsilon}f(\epsilon) \\ \mathfrak{a} = \acute{\alpha}g(\alpha) \end{cases}$$

It should be noted that for Frege there are two possible sources of trouble in his logico-mathematical structure: the extension of a concept, and the fifth law of arithmetic (in which the notion of the extension of a concept is used). Both of these notions derive directly from his basic notions of object and concept. Throughout his life he felt these latter notions were unquestionably fundamental for all language-analysis. The fact that the analysis of the "Nachwort" centers upon the derived notions raises the question about the significance of this problem as Frege views it there.

II. SIGNIFICANCE OF THE CLASS-OF-CLASSES ANTINOMY IN THE "NACHWORT"

Frege began the "Nachwort":

Hardly anything more unfortunate can befall a scientific writer than to have one of the foundations of his edifice shaken after the work is finished.

This was the position I was placed in by a letter of Mr. Bertrand Russell, just when the printing of this volume was nearing its completion. It is a matter of my Axiom (v). I have never disguised from myself its lack of the self-evidence that belongs to the other axioms and that must properly be demanded of a logical law. And so in fact I indicated this weak point in the Preface to Vol. I (p. vii). I should gladly have dispensed with this foundation if I had known of any substitute for it. And even now I do not see how arithmetic can be scientifically established; how numbers can be apprehended as logical objects, and brought under review; unless we are permitted—at least conditionally—to pass from a concept to its extension. May I always speak of the extension of a concept—speak of a class? And if not, how are the exceptional cases recognized? Can we always infer from one concept's coinciding in extension with another concept that any object that falls under the one falls under the other likewise? These are the questions raised by Mr. Russell's communication.[8]

Thus, Frege feels that he had committed a technical blunder—not an error in logical or philosophical principles. This belief apparently gives him freedom to tinker with his technical machinery without affecting his logical or philosophical principles. Even his later thoughts on this subject[9] reiterate this belief. His opinion of the extension of a concept and of the fifth law of arithmetic does waver, though, from an assumption that they are crystal clear to the belief that they are perhaps uncertain.[10] This seems to me to reveal Frege's own uncertainty about the derivation of these two notions, despite the fact that he clung to his fundamental principles. It is worth noting that Frege's concentration on the derived notions leads to neglect of his basic logical notions by subsequent constructionist logicians and tends to emphasize his technical ineptitude in seeking to correct the apparent error in his system.

After stating the antinomy as presented by Russell, Frege raises the question: "What attitude must we adopt toward this? Must we suppose that the law of excluded middle does not hold good for classes? Or must we suppose there are cases where an unexceptionable concept has no class answering to it as its extension?"[11] He rejects both of these possibilities, holding rather that if numbers are objects defined through the notion of the extension of a concept, then the sign for the extension must be a total sign functioning as a proper name of a *bona fide* object (and no merely constructed halfway entity) subject to the law of excluded middle. Frege is thus still insisting upon the natural connection between symbols and the objects they refer to even in the case involving the linguistic constructions, the extensions of concepts. This is essential in order for him to maintain that numbers are objects, appropriate references of proper names. Yet at the same time, and contrary to his previous statements about various other notions of a class as being merely a heap or disunited group, he assumes that his notion of an extension of a concept is equivalent to Russell's notion of a class.[12] That this assumption is false I shall show in section C below. Furthermore, in protecting this notion of an extension (so badly confused with the Russellian class), as necessary for his definition of number, he exposes the fifth law of arithmetic to unwarranted criticism. This law, originally designed for moving from intensional concepts to extensional objects, is modified to play also the role of an embryonic theory of types. Since this modified law functioned both as an axiomatic law of extensionality and as a type-theory principle, it is hardly surprising that it does in fact regenerate the antinomy it was designed to prevent.

Even more important, not only does Frege focus attention upon his derived notions without distinguishing their precise significance, but also he used a *method* for treating this subject-matter which is completely foreign to the principles explicitly stated in his earlier work. That is to say, he does not raise the question in terms of the content or meaning of the notions of a class or extension of a concept—nor in terms of the significance attached to the phrase "belongs to" as used in a sentence such as,

A belongs to B,

where A is an object which is being treated as a member of class object B. In all his earlier work, the question of content or meaning would have been philosophically prior to the question asked here—and such questions of content would have been especially appropriate for a problem for which Frege himself had previously issued warnings; for he had warned about the need for care in the use of such phrases as "falls under" or "belongs to." But Frege raises the question in the "Nachwort" in a form resembling the type of question found in later logical theory: "Before we go into the matter more closely, it will be useful to track down the appearance of the contradiction, by means of our symbols." [13] This is indeed a formalist way to put the problem: expressing it in symbolic form as a means for clarifying the problem. Previously, he had criticized such formulations as being possibly misleading inventions and constructions which required a prior analysis of the content of the symbols themselves. This approach makes the problem one of technical construction, not of philosophical analysis. Thus, the very method that he uses reinforces his concentration on the derived notions of his system—these notions taken as symbolically precise even though actually confused by failure to analyze a previously recognized dangerous phrase "belongs to" and confused also by failure to distinguish his notions of the extension of a concept from other notions of a class. Under these circumstances it is not surprising that the fifth law of arithmetic apparently needed technical tinkering or that the tinkering itself, done under pressures of publication, has been found faulty. (In the Appendix, we examine subsequent interpretations of Frege's corrected fifth law.)

B.   *The basic solution: derivation of* belongs to *from the content of the simple sentence*

I.   THE DERIVATION

There are three places in which we can seek the origin of the expression "belongs to" in Frege; first, the simple sentence; second, the quantified sentence, i.e., sentences in which a first-level concept is said to fall within a second-level concept; and third, a complete judgment. In this and the two subsequent sections, I shall consider the use of this expression in each of these places. Though Frege does occasionally use expressions for "belongs to" and "not belong to," he never carried forward a detailed analysis of the meaning of these terms in his system. I shall indicate where I draw directly from Frege, where I am developing the argument beyond this material, and finally, where in fact the tendency toward the errors in linguistic usage do take place in the statement of the antinomy as it is based upon the concepts, *belongs to* and *not belong to.*

For Frege, the simple sentence,

John is a man,   [i]

contains the proper and original meaning of other such sentences as,

John is a member of the class of men,   [ii]

or

John belongs to the class, men, [iii]

or

John falls under the concept *man*. [iv]

Frege stated that sentence [iv] had the same thought (*Gedanke*) as sentence [i] above, though [iv] is expressed as a relation between two objects whereas [i] asserts the attribution of a concept to an object. He noted the desirability of italicizing the concept term, "man," in such a phrase to indicate the originally incomplete nature. Further, he noted that one could not substitute any arbitrary proper name for such constructed nominative phrases ("the concept *f*") and still have a meaningful sentence. Thus, though

The concept *square root of two* is realized

is meaningful,

John is realized

is false, even though John exists and the sentence is properly formed; that is, the subject term refers to an object and the predicate refers to a concept. This indicates the difficulty Frege foresaw in the use of such special nominative phrases which admit of special predicate-concepts. This was for him merely another indication of the great difficulty he had in clarifying his basic distinction between objects and concepts. Even the attempt to talk about a concept requires a proper nominative expression, and this, according to his principles, does properly refer to an object or individual entity. He begs for his readers' co-operation in their attempts to understand what is intended by his "hints" in making this basic distinction between object and concept.

Now Frege used the expression "belongs to" early in his work as the converse relation to that expressed by the term "falls under." [14] For our purposes, this distinction is unimportant because the antinomy arises in its reflexive use where the distinction is not statable.[15] Further, Geach and Black have used "falls under" to translate Frege's symbolic expressions used to investigate this question.[16] Thus, these expressions are equivalent and they arise originally by a transformation of a simple sentence in which the unsatisfied or incomplete condition of the original concept term is shifted to a relational expression—this expression referring to a relation holding between two objects, one of which contains the content of the original concept. Yet the expression "the concept *f*" does retain some of the significance of its origin as a concept term. One could say, using Frege's terminology, that the sense of any such expression contains as part of its significance the notion of the conceptual nature from which it was derived. This is clear from the care Frege takes to point out that there are special kinds of predicates which can be attributed to it but which cannot be attributed to other objects referred to by ordinary proper names. Frege has in his "Begriff und Gegenstand" emphasized the necessity for great care and caution in the treatment of such expressions in order that our thoughts may be properly expressed in various ways without error. He has held that language usage is not a matter of following a simple mechanical procedure and that a phrase used in different places may not have the same cognitive content.

At this point, we should pause to recognize that Frege's use of "belongs (does not belong) to" in the "Nachwort" is simply a mechanical usage without inquiry into the significance of this term. We find one further remark which emphasizes the nature of an expression containing this term "falls under" or "belongs to." Frege notes that the relational term, "belongs to" or "falls under" with the following object term, forms as a whole a legitimate predicate referring to a total concept—the content of which is identical with the original concept from which the relational expression derived. Thus: "Wenn wir sagen: 'Jesus fällt unter den Begriff *Mensch*', so ist das Prädicat (von der Copula abgesehen)

'fallend unter den Begriff *Mensch*,'

und des bedeutet dasselbe wie

'ein Mensch.'

Von diesem Prädicate ist aber die Wortverbindung

'der Begriff *Mensch*'

nur ein Theil." [17]

Now we have reached the limit of Frege's original treatment of this notion "belongs to" as it applies to sentences in which a predicate is attributed to a subject or a concept is attributed to an object. From this point onward, we find only Frege's remarks in the "Nachwort" - remarks which were based upon a neglect of the very warnings he had made as he originally formulated his notions in his "Begriff und Gegenstand". We must fill in the ground between the rudimentary statements and the refined abstractions of the "Nachwort." From these original statements, it is clear that "belongs to" is not being used to refer to the relation of property possession and can only be used where the attributive relation found in language usage is being referred to. Further, since this term derives from the attribution of a concept to an object; that is, from a statement of a property-object state of affairs, it appears that no object could be said to belong to itself; that is, be a property of itself. However, this is not the case as we shall see. Finally, it should be noted that "belongs to" derives originally from Frege's use of the simple expression "the concept f" and not "the extension of the concept f." The antinomy is based upon the reflexive expression "belongs to itself" which in fact goes beyond the original derivation of the phrase "belongs to" as noted above. No ordinary proper name can be used with this expression to yield a sentence which refers to the True; thus,

The concept *man* belongs to itself,

clearly refers to the False. Further, an oft-repeated example is clearly questionable according to Frege's principles. Thus,

The concept *concept* belongs to itself,

and its equivalent by substitution

The concept *concept* belongs to the concept *concept*,

and their equivalents (by the machinery of "Begriff und Gegenstand")

The concept *concept* is a concept,

refers to the False because the subject term refers to an object and not a concept. Rather,

The concept *concept* is an object,

does refer to the True. This again indicates Frege's difficulties with the langauge. We conceive of objects by means of concepts in thoughts in which we affirm or deny that the content of the concept is a part of the public sense expressed by the proper name referring to the object.

Further, the self-referential character of "belongs to itself" has also changed a relational term into "near-concept" term; that is, a term completeable by only one proper name. The reference of the pronoun "itself" is the object referred to by the proper name subject term. There is thus linguistic referential content in the sentence containing the expression "belongs to itself." [18] Since most objects can not be said to belong to themselves, we can say that for a given object, it does not belong to itself. Thus according to "Begriff und Gegenstand"

The concept *man* is not a man,

or

The concept *man* does not belong to the concept *man*.

"Not" can remain in the relational term, for this is not obversion. Thus

The concept *man* does not belong to itself,

or

The concept *man* does belong to the concept *does not belong to itself*.

"Not" can also be a part of the created proper name. We can thus construct this special nominative term to which I shall refer subsequently as "c-r, *does not belong to itself*" in order to indicate its relational origin and its "near-concept" character.

I shall generate the antinomy by comparing Frege's use of the expression "is equal to" with his use of "belongs to." The phrase "is equal to" refers to a relation holding between two proper names whose references are a single object in a sentence whose reference is the True.[19] This relation does not relate an object to itself, nor does it hold merely between signs. Further, this relation (as noted in Chapter 2 above) has its greatest cognitive function in statements in which the senses of the proper names differ while their references are a single object. The sentence "*a* equals *a*" has minimum cognitive significance since there is no difference in the senses expressed by the two proper names (or two occasions of the same name, depending upon whether "name" refers to the physical or grammatical object). What is most probably the case here is that the sentence is saying something about the linguistic structure itself; i.e., that the same object is the reference of a proper name "a" regardless of where it occurs in the identity sentence. Further, the concept-relation *is equal to itself* (where the pronoun performs the same function as before with "belongs to") adds the same linguistic dimension to the content of the original expression. For Frege, it is axiomatic that "for every *x, x* equals *x*." Derivatively, "No object is not equal to itself" must mean "no object referred to by a given proper name is different from the object referred to by a different physical occurrence of the same proper name." The c-r *not equal to itself* is important for Frege because it is used to define the number zero; that is, the extension of the concept "equinumerous to the concept *'not equal to itself'* " is zero.[20] Thus, for Frege, the expression *"the concept not equal to itself"* parallels in construction the expression "the concept *does not belong to itself.*" If the one is admissible, as it most certainly is for Frege, then the other should be also. Now from the fact that "every object is equal to itself," we can argue that

<blockquote>The c-r, *equal to itself*, is equal to itself.   [i]</blockquote>

And from this by the technique of "Begriff und Gegenstand", one can derive

<blockquote>The c-r, *equal to itself*, belongs to the c-r, *equal to itself*,   [ii]</blockquote>

And from [ii], since the nominative phrase in the predicate is the same as the nominative subject term, we can derive

<blockquote>The c-r, equal to itself, belongs to itself.   [iii]</blockquote>

Sentences [i], [ii], and [iii] express the same thought (*Gedanke*). Thus there is an object for which it is proper to say that it belongs to itself and it is false to hold that "No object belongs to itself."

It is worth noting that the discovery of an example of an object which belongs to itself has taken us to an object which itself is a relation involving objects and the linguistic expressions for them—a relation, furthermore, which is being used with its minimum cognitive content—the cognitive content turning on the linguistic elements themselves. Moreover, the discovery of this example yields a sentence which is using an expression "belongs to" which was coined for a given purpose: to aid in showing the difference between a concept—the reference of a predicate—and an object which might be coined from the original predicative expression. And the very difference between the concept so treated and the object to which the concept was originally attributed is now at this level of abstraction completely lost. We can now quickly generate the antinomy. Given

> The c-r, *does not belong to itself*, belongs to itself. [iv]

and

> The c-r, *does not belong to itself*, does not belong to itself. [v]

as properly formed sentences, we can expeditiously derive the one from the other. If we substitute for the pronoun in the predicate of sentence [iv] the term for which it stands, we derive

> The c-r *does not belong to itself*, belongs to the c-r, *does not belong to itself*. [vi]

And sentence [vi] collapses into sentence [v] by the machinery of "Begriff und Gegenstand" given above. In exactly the reverse direction, sentence [v] could be expanded to sentence [vi] which in turn could be collapsed into sentence [iv].

II. THE MEANINGS OF THE DERIVATION

Having generated the antinomy with Frege's original principles, we now inquire about its significance for Frege's system. The problem of meaning has three aspects: First, the meanings expressed by the sentences constructed to produce the antinomy; second, the implications of this for Frege's first derivation of the antinomy in his own symbolism; and third, the implications of this for Frege's second derivation of the antinomy using his symbol "$\xi \frown \zeta$." This last problem will be treated in Section C below.

A] Sentences [i], [ii], and [iii] all express the same thought; that is, that the object referred to by the phrase "the c-r *equal to itself*" is the same object when referred to by another occurrence of the same proper name. If we ask for the thoughts expressed by sentences [iv] and [v], we must gather these from the uses discovered for "belongs to itself" and "does not belong to itself." The only appropriate use for [iv] comes from the example of the object referred to by "The concept *equal to itself*" which belongs to itself, i.e., sentence [iii]. In sentence [iv] then, we are supposing that

The concept *does not belong to itself*

might properly function as did the expression "The concept *equal to itself*." Whether or not this is the case, we have not determined here. Similarly, we found that for most (usual) objects, it is false to say that they belong to themselves. Therefore, assuming "The concept *does not belong to itself*" is like most proper names of most ordinary objects, we can coin sentence [v] which states that it does not belong to itself. Again we do not yet know whether this is the case. In fact, without such an interpretive base, there is no way of determining which of these refers to the True and which refers to the False.

Assuming, then, the thoughts expressed by these sentences are clear, we may trace the identity of each of these thoughts (for sentences [iv] and [v] given above) through the steps which produce the antinomy. Now, if we maintain the same thought through the linguistic translations for sentences [iv] to [vi] to [v]; that is, that the concept *does not belong to itself* does belong to itself and that the predicate of sentence [v], "does not belong to itself," is taken as belonging to the object referred to by the subject term, there is clearly no problem here.

But the second glance at sentence [v] removes from us this single thought by a shift in the role played by the terms "not," "belong to," and "itself." This shift occurs because the terms "belongs to itself" and "does not belong to itself" are functioning in two capacities: first, they are terms with *bona fide* content which function as concept terms and as object terms (when in the nominative form "the concept *f*"); second, they are simple expanders of a predicate term in the linguistic process of turning a simple sentence into a relational sentence (or vice versa). Through the shift in the usages of the three terms noted above, this shift in the role of the combined phrases occurs. And from this, the contradictory thought arises. There is simply a shift from the use of the term "belongs to" from its neutral, non-content bearing use to its function as a content bearing expression. There is the shift in the significance of the "itself" from its function as a part of an identical term in a repeated complex nominative expression to its becoming a pronoun referring to the whole nominative expression as this refers to a specified object. A similar shift takes place in the use of the word "not" from its being a part of a complex nominative expression to its becoming a meaningful expression having the impact of negating the original thought in which it originally functioned. Similarly for the reverse procedure from sentence [v] to sentence [iv]. This seems to show quite clearly that the reference of "c-r, *does not belong to itself*" does not function as either the c-r, *equal to itself* or any ordinary object functions. It seems fair to conclude therefore that neither of these sentences refers to the True. They are both ambiguous and meaningless expressions. And this should not surprise us, because the expression "belongs to" has been constructed to perform a certain function. So, when it is generalized (by the use of "itself"), and treated as having a special content of its own, it is not surprising that an apparent contradiction ensues.

Finally, it should be noted that this generation of the antinomy in Frege's system has occurred without using the notorious fifth law of arithmetic or the notion of the extension of a concept. Rather, it has been produced with the simpler notion of the concept f, the principle of substitution of a name for a pronoun for which it stands, and the use of the phrase "belongs to" in its original function as stated by Frege. This indicates that the antinomy presents what is essentially a philosophico-logical problem—one prior to the derived logico-mathematical problems. A prior analysis of the content of terms and language usages appears to be essential to any logico-mathematical constructions for Frege. Evidently Frege's modifications of his logico-mathematics were too hasty. This point goes beyond the distinction made by Ramsey, for it places the class-of-classes antinomy within the realm of the philosophical or semantical inconsistencies deserving analysis prior to the construction of a derived logico-mathematical system, whereas Ramsey treated this contradiction as a purely logistical one.[21] But in order to support this conclusion for Frege's system, we must review his statements in the "Nachwort."

B]   We might hesitate to treat Frege's symbolic expression of the antinomy as involving the same content for the expression "not belongs to" as does the concept *not belongs to itself* (derived above). But we quote from the point where he says that "it is useful to track down the contradiction in our signs":

Dass Δ eine Klasse ist, die sich selbst nicht angehört,

können wir so ausdrücken:

$$\text{T}\overset{g}{\underset{}{}}\left[\begin{array}{l} g(\Delta) \\ \acute{\epsilon}(-g(\epsilon)) = \Delta \end{array}\right. \tag{1}$$

Und die Klasse der sich selbst nicht angehörenden Klassen wird so zu bezeichnen sein:

$$\acute{\epsilon}\left(\text{T}\overset{g}{\underset{}{}}\left[\begin{array}{l} g(\epsilon) \\ \acute{\epsilon}(-g(\epsilon)) = \epsilon \end{array}\right.\right) \tag{2}$$

Ich will zur Abkürzung dafür in der folgenden Ableitung das Zeichen "$\forall$" gebrauchen und dabei wegen der zweifelhaften Wahrheit den Urtheilsstrich weglassen. Demnach werde ich mit

$$\text{T}\overset{g}{\underset{}{}}\left[\begin{array}{l} g(\forall) \\ \acute{\epsilon}(-g(\epsilon)) = \forall \end{array}\right. \tag{3}$$

ausdrücken, dass die Klasse $\forall$ sich selbst angehöre.
Nach (Vb) haben wir nun

$$\left[\begin{array}{l} \left[\begin{array}{l} (-f(\forall)) = \text{T}\overset{g}{\underset{}{}}\left[\begin{array}{l} g(\forall) \\ \acute{\epsilon}(-g(\epsilon)) = \forall \end{array}\right. \\ \acute{\epsilon}(-f(\epsilon)) = \acute{\epsilon}\left(\text{T}\overset{g}{\underset{}{}}\left[\begin{array}{l} g(\epsilon) \\ \acute{\epsilon}(-g(\epsilon)) = \epsilon \end{array}\right.\right) \end{array}\right. \end{array}\right. \tag{4}$$

oder, wenn wir die Abkürzung benutzen und (IIIa) anwenden

$$\left[\begin{array}{l} \left[\begin{array}{l} f(\forall) \\ \acute{\epsilon}(-f(\epsilon)) = \forall \end{array}\right. \\ \overset{g}{\underset{}{}}\left[\begin{array}{l} g(\forall) \\ \acute{\epsilon}(-g(\epsilon)) = \forall \end{array}\right. \end{array}\right. \tag{α}$$

Nun führen wir für "f" das deutsche "g" ein:

$$
\left[\begin{array}{l}
g \left[\begin{array}{l} g(\forall) \\ \acute{\epsilon}(-g(\epsilon)) = \forall \end{array}\right. \\[2ex]
\neg g \left[\begin{array}{l} g(\forall) \\ \acute{\epsilon}(-g(\epsilon)) = \forall \end{array}\right.
\end{array}\right. \qquad (\beta)
$$

d.h.: Wenn $\forall$ sich angehört, gehört es sich nicht an. Das ist die eine Seite.[22]

If we notice the obvious similarity in expression between [1] above in which the class is constructed and [3] in which the class is being said to belong to itself, we are led immediately to agree with Geach and Black that Frege made a hasty trivial slip at this point.[23] But if we notice that Frege, in applying law Vb to formulate [4], equates [3] with "f($\forall$)" which says that $\forall$ belongs to f, we must allow that Frege did mean what he said when he held that [3] states that the class $\forall$ belongs to itself; that is, that the class of all classes *not belonging to themselves* BELONGS TO the class *not belong to itself*. If this is not the case, then how could the equation hold? And similarly, when moving from step [α] to step [β] by introducing the German "g," Frege must maintain (as he does) that since "$\forall$" refers to the class of all classes *not belonging to themselves* and since the consequence in step [β] is the contradictory of the reference of the expression in [3], it must read that the class does not belong to itself; that is, that the class *does not belong to itself* DOES NOT BELONG TO the class *does not belong to itself*. And again, Geach and Black read the antecedent and consequence in step [β] by referring back to statement [1], thus reversing Frege's statements.[24] An exactly similar reversal occurs in their interpretation of the other side of the argument.[25]

Using "b" to stand for the class *belongs to itself* and "B" to stand for the incomplete concept-relation *belongs to (itself)*, the total possible equivalent expressions could be symbolized as follows (where "iv," "v," and "vi" indicate the sentences in the original derivation given above):

$$
\begin{array}{ccccc}
\text{[vii]} & \text{[iv]} & \text{[vi]} & \text{[v]} & \text{[viii]} \\
-bBb & \leftrightarrow -bB & \leftrightarrow -bB\text{-}b & \leftrightarrow -b\overline{B} & \leftrightarrow -b\overline{B}\text{-}b
\end{array}
$$

Statement [3] is taken by Frege as equivalent with [vi] while the consequence of step [β] is equivalent with [viii]. The sentence [vii] is derivable from [iv] by the machinery of "Begriff und Gegenstand," while sentence [viii] is derived from [v] by substituting the name for the pronoun for which it stood. The point here is simply that the special significance given to the class-of-classes antinomy arises from a basic ambiguity even as the problem is placed into the very symbols by means of which Frege was attempting to clarify the issue. Geach and Black's "corrections" clearly indicate that it is impossible even to state the problem unambiguously in Frege's basic symbolism. This is a direct result of the derivation of the concept *belongs to itself* from the more primitive and fundamental conception of the content of the parts of a simple sentence, object and concept. Perhaps for Frege, this would suggest that the concept is a self-eliminating "singular point," though this is not the sort of "limiting point" suggested by Gödel.[26] The source of such a self-limiting ambiguity in Frege's symbolism lies in the fact that for him there is no primitive symbol for the relation *belongs to*. Frege's symbol "$\xi \frown \zeta$" is the closest equivalent expression (in meaning) to the Peano membership symbol "ϵ." An examination of the use of this symbol takes us to the level of Frege's derived symbols and to a new meaning for the expression "belongs to."

C. *The higher level solution*

After having presented the first pair of contradictory statements derived with the use of the Vth. law of arithmetic (discussed above), Frege derives a second pair of contradictory statements by using his symbol "$\xi \frown \zeta$." Further, he derives the contradictory of law Vb "without the use of propositions or symbols whose justification is in anyway doubtful." This is accomplished by using a still less determinate and more general notion in place of his notion for the extension of a concept *not belonging to itself*. He concludes that "it is quite impossible to give the words 'the extension of the concept '$\phi(\xi)$' such a sense that from concepts' being equal in extension we could always infer that every object falling under one falls under the other likewise." [27] Finally, he shows that "Our proposition may also be reached in another way." We shall limit the discussion to Frege's second pair of contradictory statements; for this involves the appearance of the contradiction using his symbol

"⌢" in which his argument most closely resembles that found in the familiar membership logic.

I. THE SYMBOL "⌢"

Frege introduces the symbol "⌢" to express the relationship (of belonging to) as one between objects without introducing higher level expressions. He specifies that the symbol stand between the name of two objects; thus "$\xi \frown \zeta$" when the name which replaces "ξ" refers to an object which falls under the concept the extension of which is the reference of the name filling the place indicated by "ζ." Essentially, the total expression thus refers to the True when the simple sentence from which it derives refers to the True; otherwise the total expression has the same reference as the expression "the extension of the concept *not the same as itself*," "$\acute\epsilon(\top \epsilon = \epsilon)$," that is, to zero.[28] At this point, we must recall that for Frege the extension of a concept is the value-range of a function whose value for every argument is a truth-value. And since every concept and function is defined for every possible object, the extension of any concept is a complex object tying together all possible object-arguments with the appropriate object-values, in this case, the True or the False. Thus, though the object-values of a concept are vastly more limited in number, and though a concept is defined as a specific kind of function, a concept is philosophically a more fundamental notion because it is the source of the determination of the objective concept in all symbolic usage as symbols ultimately are determinative only in a sentential context. The extension of a concept is thus a complex object which divides into two fundamental parts: all objects for which the concept has the value, the True, are attached to the True as object-value, while all objects for which the concept has the value, the False, are attached to the False as object-value. Generally, most concepts divide the total universe into a pair of object-values, each of which is joined to many argument-objects; however, some divide the universe so that only one argument-object is attached to the value, the True. This indeed is the kind of concept Frege sought in his effort to define Number. And he introduced a symbol "$/\xi$" to be used with the symbol for the extension "$\acute\epsilon\phi(\epsilon)$" to give "$/\acute\epsilon\phi(\epsilon)$."[29] This total expression is defined so that it refers to the total extension as a complex object if the extension contains more than one or no object-argument attached to the True as value. In the case that there is only one object-argument for which the concept has the value, the True, the total expression refers to that specific object-argument. In an analogous manner as noted above, Frege specifies that the total expression "$\xi \frown \zeta$" refers to the True if and only if the extension of the concept which is referred to by the name replacing "ζ" does contain the object which is referred to by the name replacing "ξ"—and contains this object as an argument attached to the value-object, the True. The use of this symbol in effect limits the extension sign so that it refers only to that part for which the concept when completed refers to the True.

Now Frege introduces his second contradiction with these words:

> Wir wollen nun sehen, wie sich die Sache gestaltet, wenn wir unser Zeichen "$\frown$" benutzen. An die Stelle von "$\forall$" wird "$\acute{\epsilon}(\top \epsilon \frown \epsilon)$" treten.[30]

Using this symbol and laws (82) and (77)—also implicating law (1) from which they derive—Frege constructs the conditional

$$\top \genfrac{}{}{0pt}{}{\acute{\epsilon}(\top \epsilon \frown \epsilon) \frown \acute{\epsilon}(\top \epsilon \frown \epsilon)}{\acute{\epsilon}(\top \epsilon \frown \epsilon) \frown \acute{\epsilon}(\top \epsilon \frown \epsilon)}$$

and its converse. Symbolically, this is a simple truth-table contradiction of the form "$p \leftrightarrow -p$," as was also derived in the original derivation. Yet this time, the linguistic ambiguity does not appear. In using the symbol "$\frown$" as the relational term between the two uses in forming the name of the extension of the concept, Frege symbolically eliminated the original linguistic ambiguity. He thus achieved, contrary to his original principles, the same kind of language structure as that found in a logic in which the membership symbol is primitive or is defined in a context in which the objects of the system are determined only intensionally (not as specified by Peano) and the linguistic elements are empty symbols subsequently interpreted. For example, in Russell's case, the linguistic structure is constructed from predicate universals (known by descriptions) at such a remove from that with which we are directly acquainted that the content of the symbols includes the linguistic elements themselves.

If, however, we emphasize the derived character of "$\xi \frown \zeta$;" that is, that the sentence in which it is used is equivalent in content with the original simple sentence in terms of which it is defined, we immediately recognize the similarity of this latest contradictory biconditional to sentences [vi] and [viii]:

$$-\text{bB-b} \leftrightarrow -\text{b}\bar{\text{B}}\text{-b}$$

At this point of course, the linguistic ambiguity re-enters. Frege's definition of this symbol warrants this reductive analysis, for he specifies as noted above, that any sentence using this symbol refers to the True when the simple sentence from which it derives refers to the True. What clearly appears to be the case in keeping with Frege's principles is that in those sentences using "$\frown$" or "belongs to" in such a way that these cannot be eliminated to form a simple sentence whose truth-value can be determined, the symbolic structure is indeterminate. As we have seen, this indeterminacy is revealed by linguistic substitutions. It is further made into a determinate contradictory sentence by the special derived symbol "$\frown$." Such derived usages as these must be excluded from the system, or some arbitrary device should be adopted to aid in the determination of the truth-value of such sentences. Perhaps a simple equivalence of "$\forall$," "$\epsilon(\top\,\epsilon\frown\epsilon)$," and related expressions with "$'\epsilon(\top\,\epsilon = \epsilon)$" (which, as noted above, refers to zero) would eliminate the source of the confusion in his system and leave intact his original logistical laws. This suggestion follows Frege's principles that any improperly used proper name should arbitrarily be determined to refer to zero. This suggestion is made without a full test of its implications, and in spite of the knowledge that the antinomy can be and has been reconstituted in diverse concealed and complicated ways in an enlarged development of other logistical systems. However, in Frege's logistical system, developed as it is with specific content and direction, the antinomy did not appear until Russell suggested the reflexive linguistic application. It seems to me that one would have to show that the development of Frege's logistic required him to adopt such a reflexive application in some one of its numerous possible appearances before one could argue definitively that his system necessarily contains the antinomy. This whole problem is of course that of the effectiveness of Frege's logistic; that is, whether his laws with this additional specification that the symbol "$'\epsilon(\top\,\epsilon\frown\epsilon)$" refer to zero can still generate the desired logico-mathematical theorems without contradiction.[31] What can be said, I believe, is that Frege's construction of his definition of number does not involve this kind of ambiguous construction found in the "Nachwort." At a minimum, it would seem that the excision of particular expressions which are referentially ambiguous should increase the effective calculability of any system and that such excision is less drastic than Frege's own futile modification of the Vth. law in the "Nachwort" and his later (1910) suggestion that classes or extensions be eliminated. These latter two devices still leave the possibility of the original ambiguity based on the relation *falls under* or *belongs to*.

II. A SECOND DEPRIVATION OF *belongs to:* THE QUANTIFIED SENTENCE

"Belongs to" is the translation of the German term *"zukommen"* in Frege's *Grundlagen*, as this key term is used in formulating the definition of number. The term reappears in the *Grundgesetze* in his more exact treatment of the definition of number. This expression is used to refer to the relation holding between a second-level concept and a first-level concept. Thus

There are two square roots of nine [a]

becomes

The number, two (or Two) belongs to the concept
square root of nine [b]

Thus, "belongs to" is being used as the converse relation of "falls within" in Frege's statement that a first-level concept falls within a second-level concept. (Frege makes this statement while treating the quantified sentence parallel to (but not identical with) the simple sentence, for he states that an object falls under a concept, while a first-level concept *falls within* a second-level concept. This distinction between "falls under" and "falls within" is extremely important. As we noted in Chapter 3, one can say that a first-level concept falls *within* a second-level concept *because* one can say that objects *a, b, c, . . .* fall *under* the first-level concept. Thus, the statement involving a *falls within* relationship is in fact a general specification about the *falls under* relationship. Now instead of translating sentence [a] into sentence [b] above, it would have been proper, but hardly rewarding, to say,

> The concept *there are two* belongs to the concept
> *square root of nine.* [c]

Here a second-level concept is being said to belong to a first-level concept as both of these concepts are being referred to by nominative terms; "belongs to" is used to refer to a relation between two objects. Now the difference between sentence [b] and sentence [c] is indicative of the difference between the notion of "belongs to" in this derivation and in the previous one. In sentence [b] the attributive character of the second-level concept (expressed by "there are") has been completely taken over by the reference of the expression "belongs to" thus leaving the substantive content to be recognized as an object, a number referred to by the proper name "the number two."

In defining cardinal number in the *Grundlagen*, Frege uses the expression "belongs to" in just this manner and then proceeds to remove this expression by the more exact definitional phrase, thus:

> the Number which belongs to the concept *f* is the extension
> of the concept 'equinumerous to the concept *f*' [32]

The function of the reference of "belongs to" is in fact taken over by the expression "equinumerous to the concept *f*." This incomplete attributive expression itself requires clarification. As noted in Chapter 3, Frege uses a geometrical analogy to illuminate the concept and the notion of the one-one relation to define "equinumerous to the concept *f*." Thus, as one can abstract the definition of line direction from the concept "parallel to line a" by defining "the direction of line a" is the extension of the concept "*parallel to line a*," so one can abstract the number belonging to a concept by a similar reference to the extension of the concept "equinumerous to the concept *f*." [33] There is one important difference between the two objects being compared in this analogy. In referring to line a, we refer to a specific entity or object, the reference of a proper name. This is not the case in using the expression "the concept *f*" in the enlarged concept "equinumerous to the concept *f*." For if the expression "the concept *f*" were taken as a proper name of an object, then only one number, the number one, can be the number of that individual entity, the object so referred to by that nominative phrase (if one could meaningfully say that an object can have a number).

Now Frege seemed to realize this when he warned us that "the concept f" was not like other nominative expressions. He argued, as we noted earlier, that there were special predicates attributable only to such expressions, because this proper name retained some of its functional character. And on this occasion, Frege is definitely interested in the attributive nature of the concept f. This fact is borne out further by Frege's use of the notion of "equinumerous" as a distinct term having special significance in this special context. The concept referred to by the term "equinumerous" is defined in terms of the one-one relation of objects falling under two different concepts. Thus, the reference of this expression is clearly defined, not as holding between the references of two proper names in their expressive-referential function (as is "is equal to") but as holding between concepts in their attributive-applicability function. This attributive-applicability function is restricted to the objects for which the concept, when completed by an object, yields the value, the True. The one-one relation holding between the objects falling under the concept f and those falling under the concept g has in turn to be defined in terms of the broader notion of relation, i.e., as a function with two or more argument-places whose value is a truth-value. Frege can then conclude that when two concepts are equinumerous, the number belonging to them is the same; and that when the number belonging to them is the same, the concepts are equinumerous; that is, the identity of the number belonging to the concepts is the same as equality in number of the two concepts, though the concepts themselves may be entirely different and the objects falling under them consequently different. Thus *"moons of Jupiter* [if we forget astronomical discoveries since Frege's day] is equinumerous to *feet of normal dog."* The extension of this special concept *equinumerous* contains only one object-argument for which the concept has the value, the True. And in accord with his use of the definite article, this extension is an object referred to by a proper name. Frege thus defines a number in a propositional context with relational content. From this, it seems clear that with the increased specification of this notion of "belongs to," no contradiction is forthcoming. Only by neglecting the particular significance in which this term is used could this be stretched in such a manner as to produce a contradiction. The steps for such a procedure seem clearly given in section B above and do not require repetition. That such a procedure is clearly not possible for this use of "belongs to" is indicated by the fact that one could not say "a number belongs to itself" in the sense in which the relational term is used in the expression "a number belongs to the concept f."

III. THE NOTION OF CARDINAL NUMBER FOR FREGE AND RUSSELL

Russell's definition of number has always been considered essentially the same as Frege's; Russell himself credited Frege with discovering it before his own independent discovery. And insofar as both men are committed to a basically linguistic, or even more narrowly, a sentential formulation of the problems of philosophy, these definitions do arise from a similar background. Yet there are significant differences in the definitions—differences correlative to those in the principles of their philosophies. (An elaboration of these differences will be developed in Chapter 8.) We note that for Russell, a number is defined as a class of classes, a group of groups—whose determination as a constructed entity[34] is shown by the one-to-one relation of the members of the classes (moons of Jupiter, feet of normal dog, etc.) belonging to the given higher level class, the number. And classes, for Russell, are extensional counterparts of predicate properties. With a single exception, Russell tends to reduce objects to identifiable properties, i.e., universals, or appropriate combinations of universals. The classes remain merely constructed objects dissolvable into the appropriate congeries of universal predicates or properties. A number is a reflexively-produced entity of this kind. That there could be other reflexively-produced entities and that one of these—the class-of-classes not belonging to itself—could occasion an antinomy is clearly a part of the constructional tendency in Russell's logic and a part of his general effort to discover and eliminate paradoxes.

For Frege, on the contrary, though there is the same reflexive movement in the definition of number, and though number is defined as the extension of a concept "equinumerous to the concept f," a number is not a class-of-classes. Rather, by constructing the dual level of concepts in language usage to express the totality of objects falling under the first-level concept, Frege discovers an entity, a *bona fide* single object. The construction leads directly to a discovery; what is discovered is not a mere construct but a natural entity—the reference of many different proper names expressing different senses. The movement through two intensional levels to the single object leads to no further hierarchical construction that might be thought necessary for mathematical functions and objects. There is no general movement toward finding paradoxes or mere linguistic constructs as such. The construct therefore is quite separate from the objects (in this case, numbers) which can be reached by such a device. Frege wishes to clarify language in order to specify objects and functions (including concepts and relations) which are the content of language. Language itself is identifiable, but is not to be confused with the subject-matter of arithmetic—numbers. Whereas Russell, by the orientation of his logic and his philosophic principles was led to discover the class-of-classes antinomy—in which the linguistic constructs are entities; Frege's treatment never pointed to this development until he was misled by the brilliant young Englishman. In conclusion, number, as the substantive content of the second-level concept, is for Frege just the device for stating generally yet precisely the "belongingness" of a concept to the objects which fall under it. No further generalization of this relationship by use of the *general* phrase "belongs to" could serve any purpose in a system directed toward linguistic precision based upon identifiable objects and their properties.

D.   *A final conception of* belongs to *and conclusion*

Frege introduces a special function, the horizontal line, which yields the value, the True, when it is completed by a sentence whose reference-object is the True and which yields the value, the False, when completed by all symbols having other references. He further holds that to this completed horizontal line a vertical line should be attached in order to make a complete assertion. In Chapter 5 this function was analogized to the object-concept structure of the simple sentence. It seems possible, therefore, to say that the horizontal line refers to a relation indicating that the thought, expressed by the sentence as asserted, *belongs to* the True. (If this analogy does have any significance (though Frege does not explicitly say that the symbol is used in this way), clearly "belongs to" as an interpretation of this symbol could in no way be related to the expression upon which the antinomy is built. In fact, this function operates as a culminating sign in the ideographic structure, bringing to a focus an entire asserted thought. Any contradictions appear-

ing at the lower levels of linguistic usage must be treated as arguments in the negated horizontal line function "$\top \xi$" for they can
not belong to the True. The negated horizontal line "does not belong
to" takes as argument-expressions all those referring to the False
or any object other than the True. No reflexive usage of this function is possible. Clearly then, no antinomy could be constructed
with this functional connective.

Having now reviewed the various sources from which the
notion of *belongs to* arises or might arise in Frege's thought, and
having shown that it becomes a symbol devoid of content when it
functions to produce the antinomy (without the introduction of the
notion of the extension of a concept or the use of the fifth law of
arithmetic), we may now raise the question of the proper status of
this phrase in the system. There seem to be two ways for Frege to
treat this. He can hold either that sentences using such expressions
are not properly constructed and must be interpreted in the more
normal form of attribution of a concept to an object, or that it is
an allowable expression but that when emptied of content and put
into logistical systems as a nominative expression ("the concept
does not belong to" or "the extension of the concept *does not belong to*")
it must be determined arbitrarily to refer to zero. These methods, I
believe, may rid his logistic of the imputation of an antinomy without changing his basic laws or his fundamental notion of the extension of a concept.[35] These methods, it seems to me, do not limit or
make necessary any change in the logistical structure of his thought
as originally expressed in his *Grundgesetze*. The notions *belongs to*
and *does-not-belong-to* are not necessary concepts for deriving arithmetic from logic. The more fundamental notion of the attribution
of a concept to an object and of a second-level concept to a first-level
concept allow a full treatment of the problems dealt with there.

This whole analysis—we have said this before—is based on
philosophical principles prior to the development of a logistical
system. The only time Frege departs from his principles and attempts
to treat a problem logistically without the prior analysis (in the
"Nachwort"), he finds that he has presumably erected a system
containing a contradiction; and others have found that his attempts
to avoid the contradiction have been in vain. This concludes the
analysis of the antinomy and more generally of the whole problem
of the existence of inconsistency in Frege's thought. That there is
no ineradicable inconsistency is not a cause for astonishment; rather

it comes as a surprise that Frege ever admitted that there was such a situation in his philosophy. Nevertheless, one major problem remains, essentially a problem of philosophical principles—not merely as they operate to avoid inconsistencies in a system, but also in determining the meaning of inconsistency for any system of thought. This question is all the more pressing simply because the criticisms of Frege's logistic have stemmed from diverse systems in which the very role of logistic itself is differently conceived. Critics of such persuasions might easily feel justified in arguing that Frege's logistic is primary (because logistic for them is primary) and that the "inconsistency" in the logistic invalidates his whole contribution. For Frege as we have seen the analysis of language usages to determine the content is philosophically prior to the construction of the axioms upon which the logistic development is built. In order then to complete this argument, I must outline the significance of inconsistency in diverse systems, in order to place in perspective criticisms made from diverse positions based upon entirely different philosophical principles from those to which Frege adhered. But this inquiry itself is philosophical, not logistical.

8

MATHEMATICAL PHILOSOPHIES
AND CONSISTENCY

The Thesis of Chapter 7, presented in an earlier version of this work, was severely criticized by my Formalist Friend. Since, I believe, his position is representative of the beliefs of many mathematical philosophers today, I quote his objections:

> You fail completely to understand the nature of Frege's most important discovery, the logistic method. The idea that the formal consequences of a set of axioms can be nullified by an appeal, over the head of the axioms, to considerations of content or meaning, and that a set of axioms might thus be justified and accepted in spite of their leading formally to false consequences, would have been unthinkable to Frege. It is true that Frege often refuted his opponents by appealing from the expressions in signs to considerations of the content, but this was always done in order to show the expressions in signs to be wrong, never to justify them as right.

This statement seems to me both paradoxical and misleading. To hold that a thinker could appeal to considerations of content to refute opponents and not to protect his own formulations from misconstruction and criticism hardly seems philosophically consistent. The statement is misleading because no argument has been made to justify a set of axioms in spite of their leading formally to false consequences. In fact, in Chapter 7 above, the problem is essentially one of determining exactly what are the proper limits of significance for the axioms from which in turn the mathematical system can be seen to develop formally. Despite the paradoxical and misleading character of this statement, it does indicate the need for an enlarged view of the diverse philosophical principles and methods used in the formulation of logistical systems. This need is pressing if we are to understand the ready, though for me incorrect, acceptance of the claim that Frege's system contains an axiomatic inconsistency and not merely an apparent inconsistency due to linguistic ambiguity.

Prima facie evidence that such a conflict of philosophical principles is involved here can be found in the often expressed notion that philosophical inquiry is posterior to axiomatic linguistic construction; that is, that one requires the instruments forged by language construction to aid in the examination of philosophical problems.[1] If, however, we use the term "philosophical" to apply to the general and prior principles governing all diverse philosophic formulations, including prior linguistic constructions, a basis for exhibiting the diversity of principles in these philosophies might be found. The common goal—that of formulating a foundations of mathematics—restricts our attention to what we termed "mathematical philosophies" at the outset of this book. A "neutral" basis—neither Fregean nor formalistic—will be taken for examining the relations of these diverse mathematical philosophies (relations which were treated from Frege's viewpoint in Chapter 4). Such a "neutral" basis will be based upon an historical survey of the emergence of mathematical philosophies as one branch of philosophy today and will necessitate a recasting of the currently accepted differences in the treatments of the foundations of mathematics. The objective is that of contrasting three particular formulations within the general branch of mathematical philosophies.

A. Mathematical philosophies

The term "mathematical philosophy" is considerably narrower than the term "philosophy of mathematics." The latter applies, quite plainly, to all philosophical conceptions of mathematics, including of course the Platonic, Humean, or Kantian, while the former applies to the philosophies consciously striving for the precision found in mathematics; that is, those philosophies cast into a mathematical form. Yet this account is not precise enough, for "mathematical philosophy" has a special application as well to the contemporary developments in mathematical logic. The terms "symbolic logic" or "mathematical logic" are widely recognized as referring to a fairly well-defined body of ideas. Generally, Leibniz's notion of a "universal characteristic" is taken as the beginning for the development of symbolic logic, and Boole, too, is generally held to be an important progenitor of contemporary mathematical logic.[2] In fact, as has been noted in Chapter 4, Frege himself stated that he was following the "leibniz-boolesche" conceptions of the identity sentence. There is thus a general belief that many thinkers have contributed to a common enterprise producing a constantly developing scientific discipline. Yet there is also a general recognition that contributions to this discipline have been made in the light of many different theories of what constitutes the common enterprise. In general the commonness of the enterprise springs from a recognition that mathematical techniques and symbolism can be applied to the signs used in logic, that logical necessity (as in Aristotle's syllogism) can be treated as a form of mathematical necessity, and this necessity can be expanded to include other kinds of logical and mathematical relations and ordering principles.

On the other hand, an obvious indication of the diverse conceptions of this common enterprise can be found in the changing philosophical principles since Leibniz's day. At present, few symbolic logicians explore at any length Leibniz's notion of a simple idea, though this was itself fundamental to his universal characteristic and calculus of signs.[3] Though Boole's work is highly valued among mathematicians and logicians, few would follow his treatment of symbolic formulations as expressions of the laws of thought. Carnap, for example, attacks this side of Boole's work as a form of left-over psychologism.[4] There is also a common element in the general commitment of mathematical philosophies to language as the concrete basis for philosophy. As we argued (Chapters 1 and 5), the sentence is the principle of philosophic unity for Frege. Now there are philosophers, among them Gilbert Ryle, for whom the sentence is the principle in terms of which philosophical analyses are made, but for whom philosophy as informal logic is quite distinct from formal or mathematical logic. Many philosophers have made significant contributions to mathematical logic, but without holding that the sentence or any aspect of language is the principle of unity for philosophy; Whitehead and Husserl exemplify this tendency. Mathematical philosophies—we have already noticed this in Chapter 4—combine a technical mathematical discipline, applying mathematical devices to logical symbolism and to inference forms, with a philosophical discipline, laying the foundations for all mathematics—and for all knowledge insofar as mathematics is thought to be the official language for all scientific expression and communication. Thus, mathematical philosophy is described in terms formerly applied only to metaphysics: it is called a science of sciences.[5] Certainly, in other periods of thought, mathematics has played a similar role of epitomizing scientific thought at its best, but the novelty of the contemporary version of this role is that this feature is combined with a conception of mathematics as a purely linguistic construction.

Robert S. Brumbaugh has noted the lengthy history of the conception of mathematics as a system of constructs in contrast to the historically more prevailing Platonic conception of mathematical subject-matter.[6] Aristotle considered the subject-matter of mathematics to be a system of constructions from elements abstracted from (i.e., considered apart from whatever existence they had in) natural bodies. Kant, in his turn, emphasized the nonexistential (physical or ideational) status of mathematical subject-matter while he clearly distinguished the philosophical or conceptual method from the mathematical or constructive method. But these conceptions of mathematics dealing with constructs also required a differentiation of mathematics from other disciplines. Most contemporary mathematical philosophies conceive of the mathematical constructions as purely symbolic and in most cases, these symbolic systems are the paradigms of completed scientific structures within a total philosophy in which knowledge is presumed to be unified or anyway unifiable in principle.

Contemporary discussions of the foundations of mathematics usually center around three labels: logicism, formalism, and intuitionism. With the exception of a few details (particularly in describing intuitionism's restrictions and treatment of the law of excluded middle), the distinctions between these conceptions of the foundations are seldom made in the same way and today the classification may perhaps be losing whatever significance it had when first suggested.[7]

Of interest for my purpose here is the current concern to relate this classification to other philosophical differences. Quine analogizes these three conceptions of the foundations of mathematics to the three conceptions of the role of the universal in medieval philosophy by paralleling the formalist, logicist, and intuitionist to the medieval nominalist, realist, and conceptualist.[8] Brumbaugh, however, has analogized the intuitionist to the Aristotelian constructivist and the formalist to Plato.[9] If one goes on the usual assumption that the medieval realists were the Platonists, then Brumbaugh's treatment of the formalist directly counters Quine's. Quine treats the formalists' structures as independent of appeal to objects outside the self-contained linguistic elements themselves (non-ontological), while this very self-containedness is characteristic of Platonic mathematical objects for Brumbaugh.

My concern here is not with determining which treatment of the foundations is really platonic realism or Aristotelian conceptualism, though the roles and kinds of objects required for a given conception of a mathematical philosophy is important. Two points are of particular significance here. First, not all currently recognized conceptions of the foundations are properly mathematical philosophies in the sense just described. Some intuitionists, Weyl[10] for example, ground their symbolic constructions in a prior conception of experience as an intuitive or intentional act, thus basing their conceptions of foundations on philosophic grounds derived from Brentano and Husserl and not on a purely linguistic or sentential analysis. However, Frege would agree with the importance the intuitionist places on entities, though he does not adopt either the limitations of the intuitionist constructions nor does his method involve an intuitional act. Second, within the linguistically oriented mathematical philosophies, there are significant differences in the logical bases which the labels of logicism and formalism have tended to obscure. Differences in the logical bases clearly imply significant differences in the conception and treatment of problems in the derived portions of mathematical logic. I wish to focus attention on these prior differences in logic.

B. *Diverse logical methods*

We focus here upon the differences in the logical foundations of three mathematical philosophies.[11] The historical coincidence of Russell's criticism of Frege's logico-mathematical constructs (Chapter 7) and Frege's criticism of the formalists' conceptions of arithmetic and geometry (Chapter 4) provides the point of focus. The juxtaposition of these three mathematical philosophies exhibits a limited but important schema of diverse logical grounds, but does not exhaust the totality of diverse mathematical philosophies—much of which will have to be passed over here.[12] The points of contrast will be their treatments of the elements of logic, the logical principles, and the notion of consistency.

I. ELEMENTS OF LOGIC

Because the sentence is usually the focus of analysis for these men, we begin with their treatments of the differences between the simple sentence, the complex or compound sentence, and the more general sentence involving the quantifier.

A] For Frege, as we have noted several times before, all sentences express thoughts and refer to an object which is a truth-value. The simple sentence has as a subject term a proper name which expresses a sense and refers to an object and as a predicate term a word or other expression which refers to a concept. Frege analyzes compound sentences (e.g., those involving clauses whose references are truth-values within a sentence whose reference is also a truth-value) in order to specify their content (thoughts and truth-values) and to indicate the possible combinations of truth-values from which new statements and combinations can be derived.[13] These sentences are of quite a different kind from the quantified sentences. These latter—sometimes called general—sentences introduce a completely different structure from which emerges a new kind of content—numbers, the logico-arithmetical objects (see Chapter 4). Frege's whole logico-mathematics thus returns to numbers as objects to which the whole structure is pinned. Enlarged and complex concepts may be introduced so long as they are properly delimited or defined. Frege anticipated no difficulties with such clearly demarcated concepts and functions nor with such specificity of objects as the structure could evolve in its subsequent development.

B]   For Russell, all sentences express beliefs. The simple sentence has as its subject-term the words "this" or "I," thus referring to a particular whole, and as predicate terms words referring to universal parts which are being affirmed of that particular whole. Russell's is basically an epistemological orientation, hence one of his chief problems is just that of clearly defining what a simple sentence is and how our knowledge is extended beyond these bare simple elementary expressions of what is given at a given moment ("white, here, now"). He introduces the distinction between knowledge by acquaintance and knowledge by description and argued that most of our knowledge is of the latter kind. Only at special points of immediate experience (statable in basic propositions) is the vast structure of knowledge fixed epistemologically. For this reason most of Frege's simple sentences would not be simple in this basic epistemological sense for Russell. "Socrates is a man" involves for the most part knowledge by description, since only for the real Socrates and his immediate acquaintances would this be immediate direct knowledge.[14] Socrates, in fact, is a most complex object, a "logical construction" from sense-data.

But in addition to the epistemological problem evolving from this conception of the simple sentence, Russell considers the logical difficulties arising from diverse language usages. Logic is the essence of philosophy, being a study of the diverse *forms* of sentences: the simple, the molecular, and the general.[15] The molecular sentences (containing "and," "or," "not," "if-then") are those in terms of which logico-mathematics is generated. The general sentences (containing the quantifiers) introduce both epistemological and logical problems. The universal sentence ("All *a* is *b*" or "For any *x*, if *x* is *a*, then *x* is *b*") may refer to itself. It is this latter fact that led Russell to the logical problem, the construction of the class-of-classes antinomy. Universal self-reference can occur and an antinomy is constructible when   1] the basic distinction between the particular whole and the universal part, which are the contents of the subject and predicate terms respectively in a simple sentence, does not carry over in sentences whose content is essentially of universal parts (such as, "Red is a color"), and 2] when the actual content of the symbols is such that they can be held to be referring to linguistic objects themselves. (Note that the quantifiers do not function as second-level classes or concepts, as for Frege, hence do not contain numerical content. Rather, the use of the term "all" introduces the epistemological problem of how one knows the totality implied by the use of "all." This epistemological treatment of universal sentence is clearly consonant with the general epistemological orientation of Russell's total logic.) Thus, for Russell, the logico-mathematical system is a formal one in which the universal predicate parts and their extensional counterparts—classes—are tied together in a vast network. This constitutes a formal construct—most of which is known by description. The logistical system is not attached to a plurality of diverse individual objects, rather to the *I* or *this* (which is the only particular existential whole). The whole structure is possible only if there is at least one universal—probably similarity, which is known by acquaintance.

c]   For formalist logicians,[16] the problems of logico-mathematics center not upon the discovery of objects and the establishing of relations between objects, nor upon the determination of beliefs involving diverse formal universal parts, their constructed extensional counterparts, and the principles required to order them properly, but upon the inferential possibilities of diverse symbolic structures. The union of logic and mathematics is achieved not by defining number in terms of a second-level linguistic concept, nor by simply expanding an intensional formal structure to include the formal structure of mathematics; rather, it is accomplished by treating the problem of logical inference as essentially a mathematical problem, properly subjected to mathematical techniques because it underlies the total structure of mathematics as a deductive science. Using well-formed formulae, these thinkers abstract inference forms (whether one treats the symbols as variables or mere schematic devices is unimportant here). The simplest inference structure is that of the sentential calculus in which relations between sentences as wholes are treated in terms of the basic connectives "and," "or," etc. (These are of course Russell's molecular sentences.) Further complexities are introduced as inference structures built from variables (or schemas) for the parts of sentences are introduced. This leads to the exploration of the monadic predicate logic, the general predicate logic of first and higher orders, and to the formation of abstractions or class objects, etc. The reflexive inquiry into the property of these diverse logical systems occurs after the construction of the systems and takes place at a metalinguistic or metalogical level. At this level various possible ways of formulating logical systems with diverse inferential possibilities can be explored (such as combinatory logic or logics based on abstraction and inclusion) and a variety of mathematical techniques can be employed to aid in the inquiry about the properties of such systems and the relative strength and weaknesses of diverse logical formulations.

Corresponding to the differences in the treatment of the sentence, there are differences in the types of objects in each logic. As noted in Chapter 3, there are ordinary, logical and philosophical objects for Frege. For Russell, there are epistemological (the *this* or *I*) and constructed linguistic objects. For the formalists, there are names of constructed class-objects (though Gödel does write of real entities, he does not specify how one determines them—e.g., proper name usage).

All expand the treatment of inference beyond the limits of the syllogism. As noted in Chapter 4, the total inferential structure is built on Frege's semantics as his axioms are grounded on truth-values. In such a semantically determined system, a metalinguistic study of the properties of the system is meaningless.[17] For Russell, the inferential structure is built on the pure a priori forms of the molecular and general sentences as these express nonempirical beliefs. For the formalists, inference structures are logico-mathematical interpretations of diverse empty linguistic constructions.

In summary then, Frege's analyses of the elements of logic are semantically grounded in objects as the references of proper names; Russell's analyses turn on the epistemic function of diverse sentential forms; and the formalists, on the syntactical inferential possibilities of diverse symbolic elements in diverse formal systems.

II. THE PRINCIPLES OF LOGIC

The differences in the elements are indicative of differences in the conceptions of the subject-matter, method, and end of logic. For Frege, the subject-matter of logic is ultimately arithmetic, the method is that of inquiry, and the end is the discovery of the link between language use and arithmetic objects and their properties and relations. For Russell, the subject-matter of logic are beliefs, the method is that of analysis of beliefs with the objective of determining the appropriate degree of certitude for a belief or system of beliefs. The problems of logico-mathematics are essentially those of achieving economy and fruitfulness in analyzing and reducing a system to its simplest beliefs needed to support a given body of beliefs. For the formalists, the subject-matter is formal linguistic systems, the method is that of constructing and interpreting such systems in order to determine the properties of such systems. Thus, the formalists determine whether every sentence statable in the system can be shown to be true or false, whether the system is complete, consistent, etc. The search for the properties of whole logico-mathematical systems has led to the introduction of new conceptions of their properties (e.g., mechanical) and new devices as aids for determining whether or not such systems do in fact have these properties (e.g., the modeling technique). The truth-table determinations of truth-values of compound sentences is an instance of a device for attributing the property, *mechanical,* to the sentential calculus.[18]

Further linguistic precision and accuracy has meant a] for Frege accurate specification of the content of every symbol which enters the logico-mathematical system so that the total system clearly refers to objects, concepts, relations, and functions in such a way that the truth or falsity of each and every part of the system is clear and so that each step in the development of its theorems is seen to be a precise consequence of the content of the previous steps b] for Russell it has meant an accurate and precise account of all the epistemological, logical, and linguistic principles governing the elaboration of the total constructed linguistic system as it expresses beliefs with the appropriate degrees of certitude and is primarily composed of knowledge by description; and c] for the formalists it has meant a detailed separation and examination of the diverse kinds of inference systems and of the linguistic structure of such inferential possibilities with a determination of the properties which can be attributed to diverse linguistic inference systems.

Failure (e.g., imprecision) in any of these logico-mathematical systems can be traced back to a lack of the primary element which would constitute precision for each system. *a*] For Frege, the system would contain a symbol whose content was unclear or ambiguous—standing for two objects or two concepts, or sometimes for a concept and sometimes for an object. *b*] For Russell, the system would entail the use of a principle which had not been clearly specified as necessary for the construction and therefore the system would not have the highest degree of certitude possible for a formal commitment. *c*] For the formalists, failure would entail the attribution of a property to a whole axiomatic system which it could be shown not to possess.

III. CONSISTENCY

The background for distinguishing the meanings of "consistency" is now complete.

A] For Frege, if a system is grounded in clearly defined concepts and properly specified objects, no inconsistency can arise. If, however, it could be shown that there was an inconsistency in one's constructs, Frege would search for the origin of such an inconsistency in the improper use of symbols; that is, in the introduction of unclear, ambiguous, or empty symbols. Thus if one uses the concept *lowest rational number* to form a proper name "the lowest rational number," one could readily be led into an inconsistency. Such an inconsistency would show that there is no such object as may be presumed to be the reference of the proper name in question. Frege recognizes the usefulness of such concepts as *lowest rational number,* simply because it is a provable mathematical truth that no object could fall under such a concept. He is, therefore, not disturbed that certain combinations of simpler concepts are incompatible, as long as the simple concepts were precisely delimited. Thus, "lowest natural number" and "rational number" are predicative expressions referring to properly delimited concepts. He further recognizes the desirability of using a proper name such as "the lowest rational number" and suggests that such expressions should be taken as referring to zero—thus indicating that the concept from which they were formed can be attributed to no object. He even uses the notion of *the object, not the same as itself* to define the number zero. Thus, consistency is originally embedded in the premises of the logico-mathematical system by the very construction of the symbolism itself. Now Frege criticizes the notion that one could prove the consistency or inconsistency of a logico-mathematical system,[19] holding that any such proof involves the use of the notion of consistency and that the use of devices such as models to prove such a property attributable to a system only makes the question a more complicated one. He argues that if an inconsistency is shown to exist in a system by the use of such a device, one can never know whether it is due to the original empty symbolic system, to the model which one uses to interpret the system, or to the incompatibility of the model and the system itself. Moreover, Frege does not believe as Russell does that puzzle construction is of material significance in the discovery of the premises for a logico-mathematical system.

B]   But Russell holds that linguistic puzzle-construction is of material aid in discovering the principles or axioms of a properly grounded logico-mathematical system. Emphasizing the intricate elements which enter into the fundamentals of a logico-mathematical system as it underlies the further complexities of a more highly developed mathematics, he discounts the human ability to construct faultlessly. Thus he uses the symbolism of logico-mathematics as a further probe to reveal various further implicit beliefs underlying the scientific enterprise. In this search for linguistic principles, he is looking for what are epistemologically hidden universal parts required for the construction of a vast inferential structure. Russell is thus not grounding his logico-mathematics in objects, in this case numbers, but in principles which themselves are grounded in the human epistemological belief structure. Russell never seeks to characterize or discover properties of his logico-mathematical system as a whole or of its principal divisions. For him, it just is a linguistic expression of the simplest principles underlying the complex human belief structure, and in particular, of beliefs about the linguistic structure in terms of which beliefs themselves are expressed. Thus, Russell's conception of the role of inconsistency in a logico-mathematical system is quite different from Frege's and Hilbert's. Its uniqueness stems, of course, from Russell's epistemological basis for logical analysis and construction.

C]   For the formalists, one of the primary objectives in logico-mathematics is just that of determining whether or not a given system is consistent. Any constructed system is a formal set of linguistic relations, so built up that various kinds of inferential possibilities are contained within it. For systems with diverse degrees of complexity, the formalists determine diverse properties; for examples, that the sentential calculus can be proved to be consistent (assuming consistency of the model) and that a predicate calculus of a certain degree of richness cannot be shown to be consistent. Contemporary formalists view Frege's work as an important beginning for logistics,[20] but a beginning never elaborated much beyond the elementary stages of logico-mathematics. Further, they credit Whitehead and Russell with further developments in logico-mathematics, albeit criticizing the mixture of linguistic and epistemological elements in that system.[21] Plainly, the philosophical principles of these systems are different. And the logistical systems themselves reflect these differences. This is shown when we recall that Frege criticized Hilbert's *Foundations of Geometry* because it is not properly grounded in the objects of geometry. Clearly Frege would have criticized Hilbert's formalistic approach to logic even more strongly. In this context Bochénski's quotations from Frege's and Hilbert's unpublished letters to each other become quite intelligible. Frege writes: "From the truth of the axioms, it follows that they do not contradict one another." Hilbert writes: "I have been accustomed to say just the reverse, if the arbitrarily posited axioms are not in mutual contradiction with the totality of their consequences, then they are true—the things defined by the axioms exist."[22]

Thus, in contrast to the usual classification of Russell and Frege as logicists opposed to the formalists, we find here that Russell appears to have somewhat more in common with the formalists. What is actually true here is that Russell's system combines formal linguistic constructs on the one hand (drawn from the forms of sentences) with epistemological grounding on the other. This combination makes it possible to find significant similarities between his logico-mathematics and that of the formalists on the one hand, and between his epistemological content analysis and Frege's object-oriented content analysis on the other. In the basic notions of the objectives of logico-mathematical inquiry (discovery of logical objects, determining certitude of beliefs, interpreting linguistic constructs), of what constitutes properly formed sentences, of how the logico-mathematical structure is constituted, of the significance of inconsistency in logico-mathematics, there is a fundamental philosophical incompatibility between these approaches. This philosophical incompatibility is not of course a demonstrated logical inconsistency. Derivation of a logical inconsistency can occur only in the context of a definite formal logical structure, but philosophical incompatibility can be shown only by a confrontation of opposed philosophical principles and methods which are assumed in any formulation of a formal logical structure. And when a given logico-mathematical system is held to be inconsistent, care must be exercised to determine whether or not the source of the inconsistency is within the formal structure or is based upon appeals to principles contrary to those upon which the formal system was originally constructed.

C. *Conclusion*

Perhaps we have achieved a little of our objective of gaining a clearer understanding of what Frege accomplished and of how what he did has been subjected to interpretive distortions due to subsequent developments in logical theory. Perhaps, in addition something has been achieved in distinguishing between logical theories which begin at different points and move in diverse ways through the perennial problems of logic; that is, perhaps Frege's starting with a semantic orientation; Russell, with a pragmatic (epistemic); and the formalist, with a syntactical; and each treating the problems taken as starting points by the others may reveal some of the diversity of bases on which logics are formulated. Or again, perhaps the differences between logics grounded in objects, beliefs, or inference forms may throw light on other formulations of logic not restricted to the generally shared objectives of the mathematical philosophies. Perhaps indeed, logic as a discipline at the heart of the philosophic enterprise is clarified and in turn throws light on other areas of human knowledge as men explore the diverse possible relations symbols bear to symbol users and the objects symbolized in contexts in which logic as a subject-matter is merged with and distinguished from (in diverse ways) the subject of other disciplines. One thing is certain. Frege's work, combining as it does the analysis of ordinary language with the precision of mathematical constructions, is indeed unique and does deserve the study which it has received during the past half-century.

SUBSEQUENT TREATMENTS OF FREGE'S "NACH-WORT" SOLUTION

I review the subsequent criticism of Frege's amended fifth law of arithmetic in order to show first, the futility of Frege's attempt to treat this problem as a mere technical oversight and second, the fact that this treatment subjected Frege's work to entirely different interpretive frameworks, simply because the approach in the "Nachwort" did not have philosophical or logical grounding in any set of principles. Thus, in treating these criticisms my purpose is quite different from the objective in earlier chapters where it was argued that criticisms of and attempts to reformulate Frege's logical principles because they caused an antinomy (Geach's analysis, for example[1]) were misguided. Here, the argument is that Frege did in fact make an error when he deserted his valid principles for a carelessly formulated answer to Russell's criticism.

I present Sobocínski's[2] and Quine's[3] criticisms of Frege's corrected fifth law, though these two men together with Geach,[4] credit Lésniewski,[5] with this reconstruction. Sobocínski states that he is presenting the formal reasons never before published, though Lésniewski had presented the essential points of his analysis in his work "On the Foundations of Mathematics." I limit the discussion to the work of Sobocínski and Quine because the former gives a detailed statement of the argument not available in Lésniewski, and Geach merely presents a generalization of Quine's recasting. Both Sobocínski and Quine give a fairly full interpretive context in developing their reconstructions.

Sobocínski has chosen to criticize Frege's derived law, V'c,[6] which reads

$$\vdash f(a) = g(a)$$
$$a = \dot{\alpha}g(\alpha)$$
$$\dot{\epsilon}f(\epsilon) = \dot{\alpha}g(\alpha)$$

and which Sobocínski has translated into his symbolism[7] as:

$$[ABab] \quad : \quad A \in Kl(a) \cdot A \in Kl(b) \cdot B \in b \cdot - (B \in Kl(b)) \to B \in a \,^8$$

This can be read as follows: For every A, B, a, b, if A is the same as the class of objects with property a, and A is the same as the class of objects with property b, and B is an object with the property b, and B is not the same as the class of objects with the property b, then B is an object with the property a. This is taken to be either equivalent to or derivable from Frege's statement: If the extension of the concept f is equal to the extension of the concept g, and if a, any object, is not identical with the extension of the concept g, then the object a falling under the concept f is identical with the object a falling under the concept g.[9]

Besides the rather obvious differences (such as shifting meanings of the symbols) in Sobocínski's translation as compared with Frege's modified law, and besides the breakdown of one of Frege's identities,

$$-f(a) = g(a)$$

so that what replaces "$f(a)$" becomes a part of the antecedent and what replaces "$g(a)$" becomes the consequence (Frege's Law IIIa allows this), there is a third crucial point. It is the difference in Sobocínski's separation of the basic identity of the extensions of concepts "$\dot{\epsilon}f(\epsilon) = \alpha g(\alpha)$" into two identities involving a neutral and non-Fregean symbol "A." [10] This substitution in fact underlies the proof of a contradiction (that A equals and does not equal B);[11] for Sobocínski insists that the symbol standing for the equality of "A" with each of the extensions should also be interpreted as one of class inclusion.[12] It is this dual treatment of "ϵ" that allows the class to be treated as an object equivalent to other objects and as a property with objects under it and from this Sobocínski's Theorem E4[13] is proved.

In the concluding portion of his paper (sections VI–VIII), Sobocínski reveals the mechanism (noted above) by which he fostered the antinomy on Frege. For the antinomy turns on a class used indiscriminately as collective and distributive. One might readily maintain that in denying the equality of the class with an object falling under the concept, Frege apparently treats the class as a simple object, and in the other identification of the equality of concepts with the equality of classes (which the modified fifth law is designed to maintain), Frege apparently treats the classes as concepts under which objects fall. Thus, this imputation of the antinomy to the modified law is not wholly unwarranted, though the devices used to "discover" it in Frege again are somewhat crude. Sobocínski (and Lésniewski) has reintroduced this ambiguity by the use of the term "A" which obviously is being used indiscriminately. Though some may feel (and I would not wholly disagree) that Sobocínski's procedure will generate an antinomy in anyone's symbolism, it appears to me that Frege's symbolism in the "Nachwort" does suggest that the use of such a procedure against him is legitimate.

To clarify the differences in philosophic principles as compared with Frege's analyses, it is worth noting that Sobocínski's analysis of the antinomy turns not merely on the distinction between the collective and distributive use of the class, but also on the determination of a correctly constituted statement as it involves a particular object referred to by the subject of the statement. In order to have a correctly formed statement, the object referred to cannot be contradictory—that is, its definition cannot contain a contradiction. If this condition were neglected, "apparent antinomies" would be created. One can determine that a name does not refer to a contradictory object only by examining the structure of the language in which the name is used and determining that the language is semantically open. Appropriate distinctions in language levels are necessary to avoid nonsense or contradictions. Sobocínski's distinctions[14] are unnecessary for Frege's total system; for Frege's distinctions between object and concept are sufficient to eliminate the construction of group objects which can be treated indiscriminately as collective and distributive on the one hand, and the sense-reference distinction can eliminate all the semantic difficulties from which "apparent" antinomies might arise on the other.

Quine's "On Frege's Way Out" [15] gives another version of this problem, a version illustrating the point that different philosophical principles may well lead to different conceptions of the significance of the class-of-classes antinomy, of the cause for it in Frege's thought, and of the proper means for eliminating it from a given logical system. Quine has noted the pressure under which Frege worked as he brought the second volume of the *Grundgesetze* to press. This could account for Frege's hasty misconception of the proper way to treat the problem (as one of logistics rather than as one involving a prior analysis of the content of symbols) as easily as it could account for his hasty and incorrect alterations in the logistical system itself. Quine gently reminds us that publication pressure may have forced both Frege and Russell tentatively to accept an unexamined and ultimately wrong logistical solution. He also notes that this incident may have more biographical than scientific value. Perhaps, I should add, it has intrinsic philosophic value as well.

Quine's paper is designed to show that his own treatment of the antinomy, though it may have certain relations to Frege's solution, actually is only tangentially so related and is more closely related to the abstractive treatment of the problem deriving from Zermelo, with aids from von Neumann's conception of the element-non-element distinction which Quine used in his later work *Mathematical Logic* (as distinct from "New Foundations for Mathematical Logic"); and it is further designed to "relate Frege's 'line of solution' to the history of set theory and also to show how it leads to a contradiction." [16] Quine treats Frege's reconstruction of his logistic to meet Russell's criticism as still construing extensions (or classes) on the one hand as groups with members and on the other as individual entities. Quine uses his notion of the unit class and "w" (a class which is equal to a member which it contains and in which it is contained) to revive the contradiction in Frege's "corrected" fifth law.

Quine thus clearly distinguishes three approaches to this problem of inconsistent self-reference: his own, Frege's, and Russell's. His use of the abstractive principle, by means of which one can decide what should be "entitized" or referred to by class names without commitment to such open sentences as "not (x is a member of x) from which the antinomy is derivable is thus distinct from Frege's attempt to limit what can properly be admitted as belonging to a given concept and consequently to the extension (or class) of that concept. And both of these are distinct from Russell's type theory which simply eliminates, as incorrectly formed, certain sentences as not being sentences at all. He feels that Frege's incompletely explored method with its still apparent difficulties is more closely akin to his own (in contrast to type theory) because they both have a problem of deciding the limits of certain language-expressions. In Frege's case, the problem is the material one of clearly defining the limits of a class or extension, whereas in the set-theoretic approach, one has the easier task of choosing where to apply the abstractive principle (or, in the later von Neumann version, where to draw the line between an element and a non-element). Yet it should be noted that Frege's problem of delimitation ultimately devolves upon the precise determination of the concepts, the natural intensional units of meaning, whereas that of Quine turns on the arbitrary selection and determination of artificially constructed extensional units. Quine takes note that Frege grounds his attributes on objects and that his logistical system is essentially non-hierarchical and reduces higher levels to lower ones.[17] He notes that this approach differs markedly from the intensional orientation of *Principia Mathematica* and that the extension of a concept for Frege requires an attribute in its construction and is not a merely constructed extensional counterpart of intensional predicates as for Whitehead and Russell.

Yet in holding that extensions of concepts are "rock-bottom" objects for Frege, Quine seems to neglect their complex character and the particular role of the concept in their construction—as contrasted with the simpler objects out of which the extensions are formed. He thus does not develop the particular significance which Frege attached to the derivation of numbers as individual entities, definable as the extension of second-level concepts in which the reduction of the hierarchy of two levels of concepts to a simple object with identifiable properties is achieved. But Quine states that he is not presenting a full picture of the problem as Frege developed it. He thus does not examine the difference in his linguistic-meaning-network as contrasted with Frege's atomistic concepts or attributes. Nevertheless, in dealing with the derived notions, Quine is quite sensitive to the differences in the formulations upon which the logico-mathematical structures are based.

Sobociński's and Quine's articles are valuable, not merely because they reveal Frege's failure in the "Nachwort" but because they illustrate how a generic topic such as that labelled the class-of-classes antinomy actually contains a nest of diverse factors—some of which are only remotely related to Frege's original problem. Under each set of different conceptions of logic, this generic topic takes on a different meaning.

NOTES

The following short titles are used in the notes for references to Gottlob Frege's writings:

Begriffsschrift
  Begriffsschrift, eine der arithmetischen nachgebildete: Formelsprache des reinen Denkens (Halle AS: Louis Nebert, 1879).

Grundlagen
  Die Grundlagen der Arithmetik (Breslau: Wilhelm Koebner, 1884). Published with English translation by J. L. Austin (Oxford: Basil Blackwell, 1950).

Function und Begriff
  Function und Begriff (Jena: Hermann Pohle, 1891). Vortrag gehalten in der Sitzung vom 9 Januar 1891 der Jenaischen Gesellschaft für Medicin und Naturwissenschaft.

Grundgesetze, I
  Grundgesetze der Arithmetik, I (Jena: Hermann Pohle, 1893).

Grundgesetze, II
  Grundgesetze der Arithmetik, II (Jena: Hermann Pohle, 1903).

"Sinn und Bedeutung"
  "Über Sinn und Bedeutung," *Zeitschrift für Philosophie und Philosophische Kritik*, C (1892), 25–50.

"Begriff und Gegenstand"
  "Über Begriff und Gegenstand," *Vierteljahrsschrift für wissenschaftliche Philosophie*, XVI (1892), 192–205.

"Geometrie, XII"
  "Über die Grundlagen der Geometrie," *Jahresbericht der Deutschen Mathematiker-Vereinigung*, XII (1903), 319–24, 368–75 (Two part article).

"Geometrie, xv"

"Über die Grundlagen der Geometrie," *Jahresbericht der Deutschen Mathematiker Vereinigung,* xv (1906) 293–309, 377–403, 423–30 (Three part article).

"Der Gedanke"

"Der Gedanke. Eine Logische Untersuchung," *Beiträge zur Philosophie des Deutschen Idealismus,* ı (1918), 58–77.

1. *Introduction*

1. Kurt Gödel writes: "Mathematical logic, which is nothing but a precise and complete formulation of formal logic, has two quite different aspects. On the one hand, it is a section of Mathematics treating of classes, relations, combinations of symbols, etc., instead of numbers, functions, geometric figures, etc. On the other hand, it is a science prior to all others, which contains the ideas and principles underlying all sciences." "Russell's Mathematical Logic," *The Philosophy of Bertrand Russell,* ed. P. A. Schilpp (New York: Tudor Publishing Co., 1951), p. 125. Russell, Carnap, Quine, Tarski, et al. would subscribe to this statement.

2. Even the translation of "Bedeutung" has caused difficulty. Bertrand Russell suggested "indication" (Nos. 475–76, *The Principles of Mathematics* 2nd. ed. [London: G. Allen & Unwin Ltd., 1937). P. E. B. Jourdain and J. Stackelroth use "denotation" in their translation from Vol. ı of the *Grundgesetze* (*Monist,* xxv (1915), 481–94; xxvi (1916), 182–99; xxvii (1917), 114–27. Rudolf Carnap used "nominatum" (Nos. 28–31, *Meaning and Necessity* [Chicago: University of Chicago Press, 1947]) as does Herbert Feigl, "On Sense and Nominatum," *Readings in Philosophical Analysis,* eds. Herbert Feigl and Wilfred Sellars (New York: Appleton-Century-Crofts, Inc., 1949), pp. 85–102. Max Black first used "reference" in "Sense and Reference," *Philosophical Review,* LVII (1948), 209–30, then changed to "denotation" in further translations from the *Grundgesetze,* "Frege Against the Formalists," *Philosophical Review,* LIX (1950), 77, n. 4, 207. Also note use of "reference" and "what... stands for" in P. T. Geach and Max Black, *Translations from the Philosophical Writings of Gottlob Frege* (Oxford: Blackwell, 1952, p. ix. A. M. and Marcelle Quinton in their translation of Frege's "Der Gedanke," *Mind,* LXV (July, 1956), 293 render "Bedeutung" loosely as "meaning."

3. Max Black, *Problems of Analysis* (Ithaca: Cornell University Press, 1954), pp. 229–54; P. T. Geach, "Frege's *Grundlagen,*" *Philosophical Review,* LX (Oct. 1951), 525–44; William Marshall, "Frege's Theory

of Functions and Objects," *Philosophical Review*, LXII (July, 1953), 374–90, also his "Sense and Reference: A Reply," *Philosophical Review*, LXV (1956), 342–61.

4. Michael Dummett, "Frege on Functions: A Reply," *Philosophical Review*, LXIV (1955), 96–107; and "Note: Frege on Functions," *Philosophical Review*, LXV (1956), 229–30. See Rulon S. Wells, "Frege's Ontology," *The Review of Metaphysics*, IV (June, 1951), 544, n. 8. "It appears that Frege simply neglects to articulate his sense-denotation distinctions with his concept of function." E. D. Klemke, "Professor Bergmann and Frege's 'Hidden Nominalism'," *Philosophical Review*, LXVIII (1959), 507–14.

5. This question is developed in Chapter 3. See Charles E. Caton, "An Apparent Difficulty in Frege's Ontology," *Philosophical Review*, LXXI (1962), 462–75.

6. *Grundgesetze der Arithmetik*, I, p. x.

7. Gustav Bergmann, *Meaning and Existence* (Madison: University of Wisconsin Press, 1960), p. 210. Also William and Martha Kneale, *The Development of Logic* (Oxford: Clarendon Press, 1962), p. 484.

8. "Inbesondere glaube ich, das die Ersetzung der Begriffe *Subject* und *Prädicat* durch Argument und Function sich auf die Dauer bewähren wird." *Begriffsschrift*, pp. vii, 2–4.

9. *Grundlagen*.

10. "Begriff und Gegenstand," 198. Also P. T. Geach and Max Black, *op. cit.*, p. 1, n. A and *Begriffsschrift*, p. 1.

11. *Grundlagen*, p. 71.

12. *Grundlagen*, p. x.

13. Peter Geach writes: "The view put forward by Frege and Wittgenstein that it is only in the context of a sentence that a name stands for something, seems to me to be certainly wrong." "Subject and Predicate," *Mind*, LIX (Oct., 1950), 461–82. See also C. G. Hempel, "On the Logical Positivists' Theory of Truth," *Analysis*, II (Jan., 1935), 49–59. Michael Dummett, "Nominalism," *Philosophical Review*, LXV (1956), 491–505.

14. *Grundlagen*, p. x. Also see Paul F. Linke, "G. Frege als Philosoph," *Zeitschrift für Philosophie Forschung* I (1946–47), 75–99.

15. "Begriff und Gegenstand," 198.

16. *Ibid.*, 193, 195–201. Wells, *op. cit.*, 549. Geach, "Frege's *Grundlagen*," 537. Klemke, *op. cit.*, 510.

17. Caton, *op. cit.*, 469.

2. *Frege's Statement of His Mature Thought*

1. "Begriff und Gegenstand," 192. Benno Kerry, "Über Anschauung und ihre psychische Verarbeitung," *Vierteljahrsschrift für wis-*

senschaftliche Philosophie, IX (1885), 433-93; X (1886), 419-67; XI (1887), 53-116, 249-307; XIII (1889), 71-124, 392-419; XIV (1890), 317-53; XV (1891), 127-67.

2. "Begriff und Gegenstand," 193, 195, 198. Also, "Geometrie, XII," 371-75.

3. "Begriff und Gegenstand," 194. But *cf.* E. E. C. Jones, "Mr. Russell's Objections to Frege's Analysis of Propositions," *Mind,* XIX (1910), 379-86, and Bertrand Russell, "Appendix A," *The Principles of Mathematics,* 2nd. ed. (London: G. Allen & Unwin Ltd., 1937, pp. 500-522.

4. *Grundlagen,* p. 77, n. 2. See also *Function und Begriff,* p. 16, where Frege states: "The linguistic form of equations is a statement."

5. Begriff und Gegenstand," 194 f. Also note P. T. Geach and Max Black, *Translations from the Philosophical Writings of Gottlob Frege* (Oxford: Blackwell, 1952), p. ix, n. 4.

6. See also, *Grundlagen,* pp. 58-67, 77, n. 2. Also, *Grundgesetze,* I, ¶11.

7. *Grundlagen,* p. 65. "This relationship [of first- to second-level concepts] however, should not be confused with the subordination of species to genus." See also *Grundlagen,* pp. 69-70.

8. *Grundlagen,* p. 65.

9. *Function und Begriff,* p. 27, n. 8; "Begriff und Gegenstand," 200, n. 1.

10. "Begriff und Gegenstand," 197-201.

11. "Begriff und Gegenstand," 201 ff.

12. "Sinn und Bedeutung," 29-31. See also Alonzo Church's review of Black's translation, *The Journal of Symbolic Logic,* XIII (March, 1948), 152-53, and *Grundlagen,* pp. x, 71-72.

13. "Sinn und Bedeutung," 25-27, also, *Grundgesetze* I, foreword. Contrast this with Paul D. Wienpahl, "Frege's 'Sinn und Bedeutung'," *Mind,* LIX (Oct., 1950), 483-94. Also, P. T. Geach, "Mr. Ill-Named," *Analysis,* IX (Oct., 1948), 14-16; Richard Rudner, "On *Sinn* as a Combination of Physical Properties," *Mind,* LXI (Jan., 1952), 82-84. Also, Michael Dummett, "Nominalism," *Philosophical Review,* LXV (1956), 491-505.

14. "Sinn und Bedeutung," 31-32. Also see "Der Gedanke," 58-77. A. M. and Marcelle Quinton, "The Thought," *Mind,* LXV (July, 1956), 289-311, Bertrand Russell, "On Denoting," *Readings in Philosophical Analysis,* ed. Herbert Feigl and Wilfred Sellars (New York: Appleton-Century-Crofts, Inc., 1949), pp. 103-5.

15. "Sinn und Bedeutung," 34. Also see "Der Gedanke," 63-66.

16. "Sinn und Bedeutung," 34-35. See *Grundgesetze,* I, foreword, pp. 182-99. See Geach and Black, *op. cit.,* p. ix, n. 5.

17. See also Wells on "commonsense" in Frege, "Frege's Ontology," *The Review of Metaphysics,* IV (June, 1951), 562.

NOTES TO PAGES 24-36

18. "Sinn und Bedeutung," 36.
19. *Ibid.,* 34.
20. *Ibid.,* 27.
21. *Ibid.,* 39.
22. *Ibid.,* 42.
23. *Ibid.,* 43.
24. *Ibid.,* 43, n.
25. "Sinn und Bedeutung," 49. Contrast A. J. Baker, "Presupposition and Types of Clause," *Mind,* LXV (July, 1956), 368–78.
26. *Function und Begriff,* p. 1. Also, *Grundgesetze,* I, introduction and p. 1.; and *Begriffsschrift.* See also Jørgen Jørgensen, *A Treatise of Formal Logic* (London: Oxford University Press, 1931), I, pp. 147–75, especially 156–59.
27. Contrast Max Black, *op. cit.,* pp. 239–43, 254.
28. See Gustav Bergmann, *Meaning and Existence* (Madison: University of Wisconsin, 1960), pp. 205–24; E. D. Klemke "Professor Bergmann and Frege's 'Hidden Nominalism'," *Philosophical Review,* LXVIII (1959), 507–14; R. Grossmann, "Frege's Ontology," *Philosophical Review,* LXX (1961), 23–40.
29. *Function und Begriff,* p. 8.
30. *Function und Begriff,* p. 10; *Grundgesetze,* I, ¶9. But *cf.* Black, *op. cit.,* p. 249, n. 6.
31. *Function und Begriff,* pp. 14–15; *Grundgesetze,* I, ¶9.
32. *Function und Begriff,* pp. 16, 18–19.
33. *Function und Begriff,* p. 18. *Grundgesetze,* I, ¶2. "Objects (*Gegenstände*) stand opposed to functions. I therefore count as an object everything that is not a function; thus, examples of objects are numbers, truth-values, and the *ranges (Werthverläufe)* to be introduced farther on." Also "Extensions of concepts are likewise objects, although concepts themselves are not." Also *Grundgesetze,* I, ¶26–33.
34. *Function und Begriff,* pp. 19–20; *Grundgesetze,* I, ¶26–33; II, ¶56–58.
35. *Function und Begriff,* pp. 21, 23; *Grundgesetze,* I, ¶5, 6. "Thus the function $—\phi(\xi)$ denotes a concept and a function $—\psi(\xi, \zeta)$ denotes a relation, whether or not $\phi(\xi)$ is a concept and $\psi(\xi, \zeta)$ is a relation. Also, I regard it (the horizontal line) as a name of a function in the way that $—\Delta$ denotes the True, if Δ is the True, and the False, if Δ is not the True." Also see *Begriffsschrift,* ¶2, 5, 6.
36. *Function und Begriff,* p. 22.
37. *Grundgesetze,* I, ¶5.
38. *Beiträge zur Philosophie des deutschen Idealismus,* I (1919), 143–47.
39. *Grundgesetze,* I, p. 3. "Thus we are finally left with the result that the number datum contains an assertion about a concept. I have

traced back number to the relations of similarity and similarity to univocal correspondence.... If my opinion is correct that arithmetic is a branch of pure logic, then a purely logical expression has to be chosen for 'correspondence'. I choose the world 'relation'." Further, "*Concept* and *Relation* are the foundation stones upon which I erect my structure." Also, *Grundlagen*, pp. 81–84. See Geach's "Frege's *Grundlagen*," *Philosophical Review*, LX, (Oct., 1951), 535 on Austin's translation of "Anzahl." Also, see *Grundgesetze*, I, ¶3, 4; and Frege's notion of correlation in "Was ist eine Funktion?" *Festschrift Ludwig Boltzmann gewidmet* (Leipzig: Ambrosius Barth, 1904), pp. 656–66.

40. *Grundgesetze*, I, ¶7, 105–6. But *cf. Begriffsschrift*, ¶8.

3. *Linguistic and Logical Content in Frege's Thought*

1. Gustav Bergmann views the problem of unity in terms of a combination of an "exemplification" approach and a "mapping" approach in the use of concepts as universals. *Meaning and Existence* (Madison: University of Wisconsin Press, 1960), pp. 205–24.

2. Rulon Wells, "Frege's Ontology," *The Review of Metaphysics*, IV, 537–73. Also see Max Black, *Problems of Analysis* (Ithaca: Cornell University Press, 1954), pp. 229–54; E. D. Klemke, "Professor Bergmann and Frege's 'Hidden Nominalism'," *Philosophical Review* LXVIII (1959), 507–14; Howard Jackson, "Frege's Ontology," *Philosophical Review*, LXIX (1960), 394–95; Charles E. Caton, "An Apparent Difficulty in Frege's Ontology," *Philosophical Review*, LXXI (1962), 462–75.

3. "Sinn und Bedeutung," 28. "It may perhaps be granted that every grammatically well-formed expression representing a proper name always has a sense."

4. R. Grossmann, "Frege's Ontology," *Philosophical Review*, LXX (1961), 28. Also, Milton Fisk, "A Paradox in Frege's Semantics," *Philosophical Studies*, XIV (June, 1963), 56–63.

5. Jackson, *op. cit.*, 394–95; Caton, *op. cit.*, 462 ff; Grossmann, *op. cit.*, 32.

6. Grossmann, *op. cit.*, 27.

7. Caton, *op. cit.*, 462.

8. Wells, "Frege's Ontology," *The Review of Metaphysics*, IV (June, 1951), 549–50; Michael Dummett, "Frege on Functions; A Reply," *Philosophical Review*, LXIV (1955), 96–107 and "Note: Frege on Functions," *Philosophical Review*, LXV (1956), 229–30; Klemke, *op. cit.*, 511–12; Grossmann, *op. cit.*, 36–37.

9. See, Caton, *op. cit.*, 465–66.

10. "Geometrie, xv," 378–79.

11. Caton, *op. cit.*, 470 ff.
12. Alonzo Church, review of Black's translation of Frege's "Sinn und Bedeutung," *The Journal of Symbolic Logic*, XIII (March, 1948), 152–53. Also Wells, *op. cit.*, 563.
13. "Sinn und Bedeutung," 37.
14. Alonzo Church, "A Formulation of the Logic of Sense and Denotation," *Structure Method and Meaning*, ed. Paul Henle, *et al.* (New York: Liberal Arts Press, 1951), pp. 3–4.
15. Rudolf Carnap, *Meaning and Necessity* (Chicago: University of Chicago Press, 1947), pp. 118–36.
16. See G. E. M. Anscombe, *An Introduction to Wittgenstein's Tractatus* (London: Hutchinson University Library, 1959), pp. 111–12. The comment on Dummett's report of Frege's unpublished writings at Münster that "Frege came to think that any such statement [using an expression such as 'the concept *horse*'] was ill-formed; a concept must not occur except predicatively" indicates that Frege still maintains ɪ] that concepts occur only predicatively and ɪɪ] that problems in understanding may arise when concepts are mentioned and not used predicatively. If, as stated, he did disallow the expression "the concept *horse*," he still has the problem of determining how to mention a concept and what the reference of such a substitute expression would be: an object or a concept. Miss Anscombe's circumlocution "the animal that both the Derby winner for 1888 and the Derby winner for 1889 are" only emphasizes the difficulty; for unless one animal won in both years, this circuitous phrase merely refers to the same object as that earlier referred to by "the concept *horse*." Dr. James Bartlett's announcement at the 1963 American Philosophical Association (ED) meetings of the impending publication of Frege's unpublished manuscripts gives hope that we shall be able to acquire more information about Frege's later thoughts on this matter.
17. *Grundlagen*, p. 80, n. 1.
18. *Grundlagen*, p. 77, n. 2.
19. *Grundgesetze der Arithmetik*, ɪɪ, pp. 253–65. Also *Grundlagen*, p. 80, n. 1. Frege's notes to P. E. B. Jourdain, "The Development of the Theories of Mathematical Logic and the Principles of Mathematics," *The Quarterly Journal of Pure and Applied Mathematics*, XLIII (1912), 241, 251–52. (Henceforth, Frege in Jourdain.)
20. P. T. Geach, "Frege's *Grundlagen*," *Philosophical Review*, LX (Oct., 1951), 543.
21. *Ibid.*, 538–39.
22. Max Black, *op. cit.*, pp. 246–50.
23. W. V. O. Quine, *From a Logical Point of View*, 2nd ed. rev. (Cambridge: Harvard University Press, 1961) pp. 12 ff., 102 ff.

24. *Grundlagen,* pp. 3–4, 76, n. 1, 88.
25. *Grundlagen,* pp. 79–80.
26. Frege formalizes the informal presentation of the *Grundlagen,* pp. 79–96 in *Grundgesetze,* I, ¶34–36.
27. *Function und Begriff,* p. 31 and *Grundgesetze,* I, ¶23–25. Also *Grundlagen,* p. 72 and, *Begriffsschrift,* p. 60. See William and and Martha Kneale, *The Development of Logic* (Oxford: Clarendon Press, 1962), p. 504.
28. The German letter "α" is used consistently for what we today call bound variables; the Greek letters generally for free variables, except for epsilon in an expression for the extension of a concept such as "έφ(ε)." In this latter case the "φ" indicates a free variable and the total expression is called a "second-level function which is no concept." That is, it has a definite object as a value when completed by a specific first-level function. Generally speaking, Roman letters are constants. (*Grundgesetze,* I, p. 38).
29. *Grundlagen,* pp. 79–80.
30. See *Grundlagen,* pp. 96–99 on the infinite as a properly defined object.
31. "Begriff und Gegenstand," 199.
32. Frege's notes to Jourdain, *op. cit.,* 241, 251–52.
33. *Grundgesetze,* II, ¶86 ff.
34. Bertrand Russell, *The Principles of Mathematics,* 2nd ed. (London: G. Allen & Unwin Ltd., 1937), pp. ix, x, xiv. Willard V. Quine, *op. cit.,* p. 76. "Frege himself, incidentally, was rather a Platonist in his own philosophy."
35. See Rulon Wells, "Is Frege's Concept of Function Valid?" *The Journal of Philosophy,* LX (Nov., 1963), 720–22.

4. The Power of Frege's Logic

1. "Über den Zweck der Begriffsschrift," *Sitzungsberichte der Jenaischen Gesellschaft für Medicin und Naturwissenschaft,* Jan. 27, 1882, 1–9. See "Anwendungun der Begriffsschrift," *ibid.,* Jan. 10, 1879, 29–34.
2. P. E. B. Jourdain, "The Development of the Theories of Mathematical Logic and the Principles of Mathematics," *The Quarterly Journal of Pure and Applied Mathematics,* XLIII (1912), 241.
3. *Ibid.,* p. 255; see also "Über die Begriffsschrift des Herrn Peano und meine eigene," *Berichte über die Verhandlungen der königlich sächsischen Gesellschaft der Wissenschaften zu Leipzig,* 1896, 361–78. See also C. I. Lewis, *A Survey of Symbolic Logic* (New York: Dover Publications, Inc., 1960), p. 115. See also Bertrand Russell "The Theory of Implication," *American Journal of Mathematics.*

xxviii (1906), 160–61 and *The Principles of Mathematics*, 2nd ed. (London: G. Allen & Unwin Ltd., 1937), pp. 447–79.

4. See Black's reduction of concepts to objects, *Problems of Analysis* (Ithaca: Cornell University Press, 1954), pp. 251–53; and Quine's conceptual network, W. V. O. Quine, *From a Logical Point of View*, 2nd. ed. rev. (Cambridge: Harvard University Press, 1961), pp. 9, 21, 47.

5. See Frege's early work, *Begriffsschrift*, ¶15. Also Jourdain, *op. cit.*, 246, n. Also G. Peano, Review of Frege's *Grundgesetze der Arithmetik*, *Rivista di Matematica*, v (1895), 122–28, Frege's reply, *ibid.*, vi (1896), 53–59, and Peano's answer *ibid*, vi (1896), 60–61. Also P. T. Geach and Max Black, *Translations from the Philosophical Writings of Gottlob Frege* (Oxford: Blackwell, 1952), pp. 160–61, n.

6. *Grundgesetze*, i, pp. 5–69.

7. *Ibid.*, p. 70 through *Grundgesetze*, ii., p. 68.

8. *Grundgesetze*, ii, pp. 69–243.

9. Frege recognizes the basic difference between the cardinal numbers and the positive whole numbers, the fractions, and the irrationals. "Die Anzahlen antworten auf die Frage: 'wieviele Gegenstände einer gewissen Art giebt es?' während die reellen Zahlen als Maasszahlen betrachtet werden können, die angeben, wie gross eine Grösse verglichen mit einer Einheitgrösse ist." "The cardinal numbers answer the question: 'how many objects of a certain kind are there?' while the real numbers can be considered as measuring numbers, which state how great a quantity is compared with a unit quantity." (Throughout this exposition, I have used the word "number" as short for "cardinal number.") *Ibid.*, pp. 155–56.

10. Frege states "Der Grund dieser Misserfolge liegt in der falschen Fragestellung.... Statt zu fragen: welche Eigenschaften muss ein Gegenstand haben, um eine Grösse zu sein? muss man fragen: wie beschaffen muss ein Begriff sein, damit sein Umfang ein Grössengebiet sei?" *Ibid.*, p. 158. "The reason for these failures lies in the false putting of the question.... Instead of asking: what properties must an object have in order to be a quantity? One must ask: how must a concept be constructed in order that its extension be a quantitative region?"

11. *Grundgesetze*, i, ¶18, 20, 25, 47.

12. Frege insists upon the formality of arithmetic in the special sense in which it depends upon logical (not geometric or physical) concepts, not upon mere undefined linguistic elements. "Man kann diese Behandlung der Arithmetik vielleicht auch formal nennen, gebraucht dann aber dieses Wort nicht in dem oben dargelegten Sinne. Dann kennzeichnet es die rein logische Natur der Arithmetik,

will aber nicht besagen, dass die Zahlzeichen inhaltlose Figuren seien, die nach willkührlichen Regeln behandelt werden. Die Regeln folgen hier vielmehr nothwendig aus den Bedeutungen der Zeichen und diese Bedeutungen sind die eigentlichen Gegenstände der Arithmetik: willkührlich ist nur die Bezeichnung." ("One might perhaps also call this treatment of arithmetic formal, in that case one does not use this word in the sense set forth above. In that case it designates the purely logical nature of arithmetic, but does not mean that numerals are contentless figures which are treated according to arbitrary rules. The rules here follow rather necessarily from the references of the signs and these references are the proper objects of arithmetic: only the designations are arbitrary.") Grundgesetze, II, p. 156.

13. "Geometrie, XII," and "Geometrie, XV."

14. "Geometrie, XII," 321. "It is absolutely essential for the rigor of the mathematical inquiry not to confuse the distinction between definitions and all other sentences."

15. *Ibid.* "Axioms do not contradict one another, since they are true; this requires no proof. Definitions may not contradict one another. Such basic sentences for defining must be determined that no contradiction can occur."

16. "Geometrie, XII," 324. "If these were to contradict one another, then there would be no object, on which both of these properties could be found..."

17. *Ibid.* "If one can discover an object, which has the first property, but not the second, then the second mark is independent of the first."

18. "Geometrie, XII," 370–71.
" 'Erklärung. Wir denken uns Gegenstände, die wir Götter nennen.
Axiom 1. Jeder Gott ist allmächtig.
Axiom 2. Es gibt wenigstens einen Gott.'
Wäre dies zulässig, so wäre der ontologische Gottesbeweis glänzend gerechtfertigt. Und damit kommen wir auf den Kernpunkt. Wer den Fehler dieses Beweises ganz deutlich eingesehen hat, der kennt auch den Grundfehler der Hilbertschen Definition. Es ist die Vermengung der Begriffe erster und zweiter Stufe, wie ich sie nenne."
" 'Explanation. We think of objects which we call Gods.
Axiom 1. Every God is almighty.
Axiom 2. There is at least one God.'
If this were allowed, then the ontological proof of God would be brilliantly justified. And with this we come to the central point. Whoever comprehends quite clearly the error of this proof knows

also the basic error of the Hilbertian definition. It is the mixture of concepts of first and second level as I call them."

19. "Geometrie, XII," 374–75.

20. A. Korselt, "Über die Grundlagen der Geometrie," *Jahresbericht der Deutschen Mathematiker-Vereinigung,* XII (1903), 402–7. Korselt concluded "Aus diesen Gründen kann ich die Bedenken Herrn Freges gegen dis Hilbertsche Darstellung trotz allem Nachdenken nicht berechtigt finden."

"For these reasons and in spite of all reflections, I cannot consider justified Mr. Frege's considerations against the Hilbertian presentation."

21. "Geometrie, XV," 296–97. Frege had clearly distinguished signs which merely indicated *(andeutet)* from those which referred to *(bedeutet)* objects or concepts. *(Grundgesetze,* pars., 8, 17)

22. "Geometrie, XV," 300 f. This point can be found in Frege's *Begriffsschrift,* 55 ff, as A. T. Shearman has noted, "Definition in Symbolic Logic," *Mind,* XIX (July, 1910), 387–89.

23. "Geometrie, XV," 309. "What can be proved only by means of ambiguous signs cannot be proved."

24. "Geometrie, XV," II.

25. "Geometrie, XV," III.

26. "Geometrie, XV," III, 426. "Only true thoughts can be premises of conclusions."

27. "Geometrie, XV," 428. "No science is entirely formal."

28. "Geometrie, XV," III, 429. "However we find ourselves here in a new land."

29. A. Korselt, "Über die Logik der Geometrie," *Jahresbericht der Deutschen Mathematiker-Vereinigung,* XVII (1908) 98–124. Also see P. E. B. Jourdain, *op. cit.,* 269.

30. (Jena; Druck von F. Fromann, 1874.)

31. Published in 1884.

32. "Über formale Theorien der Arithmetik," *Sitzungsberichte der Jenaischen Gesellschaft für Medicin und Naturwissenschaft* (1885), 94–96.

33. Frege's notes to P. E. B. Jourdain, "The Development of the Theories of Mathematical Logic and the Principles of Mathematics," *The Quarterly Journal of Pure and Applied Mathematics,* XLIII (1912), 241.

34. *Grundlagen,* p. 4.

35. See Raymond L. Wilder, *op. cit.,* pp. 3–21.

36. See the Gödel numbers by which whole formulae, proofs, and even language systems can be ordered. "Über formal unentscheidbare Sätze der Principia Mathematica und verwandter Systeme I." *Monatshefte für Math. u. Physik,* XXXVIII (1931), 176–80.

37. A. J. Ayer, *Language, Truth and Logic,* 2nd ed. (London: Victor Gollanz Ltd., 1946), pp. 82–85.
38. Quine, op. cit., p. 80.
39. *Ibid.,* p. 81.
40. *Grundlagen,* pp. 48, 50, 52, 67, but especially p. 76, where he accepts Leibniz's definition of identity. Or again, *Begriffsschrift,* p. v; *Grundgesetze,* I, ¶9, his reference to the basis of the *leibniz-boolesche* logic.
41. Other logicians do treat number as a special case and arithmetic as different from geometry. For example, Carl G. Hempel, "On the Nature of Mathematical Truth," and "Geometry and Empirical Science," *Readings in Philosophical Analysis* (eds. Herbert Feigl and Wilfred Sellars (New York: Appleton-Century-Crofts, Inc., 1949), pp. 222–49. For Hempel, arithmetic is an analytic but contentful series of truths; geometry is a schematically valid, conventionally agreed-upon system of symbols which may be interpreted empirically in different ways. It seems not unlikely that the question of the priority of cardinal versus ordinal numbers rests ultimately on the kind of principles appealed to in the philosophical foundations of mathematics. Hermann Weyl, *Philosophy of Mathematics and Natural Science,* trans. Olaf Helmer (Princeton: Princeton University Press, 1949), pp. 34–35.
42. For example, Rudolf Carnap states that the "initiation of the syntactical method by Frege and Hilbert" was "a decisive step in the development of logic." *Formalization of Logic* Studies in Semantics, Vol. II (Cambridge: Harvard University Press, 1943), p. x. Again, in *Foundations of Logic and Mathematics,* (p. 18) Carnap writes: "Frege was the first to formulate explicitly and to fulfil strictly the requirement of formality, i.e., of a formulation of rules of logic without any reference to designata." Yet Carnap wavers on this point. He also writes in *Formalization of Logic* (p. 6) that Frege "recognized the importance of formal method . . . while simultaneously insisting that a logical system should not be regarded merely as a formal calculus but should, in addition, be understood as expressing thoughts." I. M. Bochénski has also indicated an ambivalence toward Frege's logic, in part by noting the opposition between Frege and Hilbert, *op. cit.,* pp. 292–93. Yet he states of Frege's Euclidean conception of proof that "Frege's program of thorough proof was later carried out in mathematics by Hilbert," p. 238. This is in spite of the fact that he also recognizes that Frege's axioms and theorems were not semantically meaningless, p. 287. He also holds that a metalogic is implicit in Frege's theory of proof, p. 284. He thus interprets Frege as a precursor of the formalist rigor while he recognizes that Frege is not a formalist and does not construct an

uninterpreted system. He thus passes over the basic philosophical differences to emphasize the formal similarities.

43. W. V. Quine, "On Frege's Way Out," *Mind*, LXIV (April, 1955), 145–59.

44. Kurt Gödel, "Russell's Mathematical Logic," *The Philosophy of Bertrand Russell*, ed. P. A. Schilpp (New York: Tudor Publishing Co., 1951), p. 125; "Frege, in consequence of his painstaking analysis of proofs, had not gotten beyond the most elementary properties of the series of integers...." Wells, "Frege's Ontology," *The Review of Metaphysics*, IV (June, 1951), 560–62. See Quine, *op. cit.*, p. 76; C. I. Lewis, *op. cit.*, pp. 114–15.

45. *Grundgesetze*, I, pp. 1 ff. Also note his "Kritische Beleuchtung einiger Punkte in E. Schröders *Vorlesungen über die Algebra der Logik*," *Archiv für systematische Philosophie*, I (1895), 433–56. Also *Grundgesetze*, II, ¶56–68, 86–137, 138–55, 146–47. Also "Über formale Theorien der Arithmetik," *Sitzungsberichte der Jenaischen Gesellschaft für Medicin und Naturwissenschaft* (1885), and "Le Nombre entire," *Revue de Metaphysique et de Morale*, III (1895), 73–78. Counter-criticisms and interchanges developed between Frege and Thomae in *Jahresbericht der Deutschen Mathematiker-Vereinigung*, XV (1906), 434–38, 586–92; XVII (1908), 52–56.

46. "Geometrie, XII," 371. Frege observes: "Diesem Unterschiede in den Zeichen entspricht natürlich ein solcher im Reiche der Bedeutungen: dem Eigennamen der Gegenstand, dem prädikativen Teile etwas, was ich Begriff nenne. Dies soll keine Definition sein; denn das Zerfallen in einen gesättigten und einen ungesättigten Teil muss als logische Urerscheinung angesehen werden, die einfach anerkannt werden muss, aber nicht auf Einfacheres züruckgeführt werden kann." "To this distinction in signs corresponds naturally one in the realm of references: to the proper name, the object; to the predicative part something which I call a concept. This is not meant to be a definition, for the breakdown into a satisfied and an unsatisfied part must be considered as a logically original phenomenon which must be simply recognized, but cannot be reduced to further simples." See Max Black, *op. cit.*, pp. 229–46. Contrast this with Frege's remark: "Ich bin mir wohl bewusst, das Ausdrücke wie 'gesättigt' und 'ungesättigt' bildlich sind und nur dazu dienen, auf das Gemeinte hinzuweisen, wobei immer auf das entgegenkommende Verständnis des Lesers gerechnet werden muss." "I am quite conscious that the expressions such as "satisfied" and "unsatisfied" are figures of speech and serve only to hint at what is meant—in connection with which one must count on the engaged understanding of the readers."

47. *Grundgesetze*, II, ¶146. Such hints are hardly implicit metalogics

except to those convinced that such a distinction is necessary. *cf.* I. M. Bochénski, *op. cit.,* p. 284; Rulon Wells, "Is Frege's Concept of Function Valid?" *The Journal of Philosophy,* LX, (Nov., 1963), 725 ff.

48. Contrast with Kurt Gödel, "Russell's Mathematical Logic," p. 147, and J. Barkley Rosser, *Logic for Mathematicians* (New York: McGraw Hill, 1953), pp. 204–7. But Bochénski writes: Frege "did not perceive the significance of this doctrine [type theory]. It [Frege's review of Schröder] is so formulated as almost to lead one to suppose that he is attacking the simple theory of types," *op. cit.,* p. 393.

49. P. E. B. Jourdain, *op. cit.,* 267. Also Peter Nidditch, "Peano and the Recognition of Frege," *Mind,* LXXII (Jan., 1963), 103–10.

5.   *The Sentence as the Principle of Philosophic Unity*

1. "Der Gedanke." 65–66. Also, William Marshall, "Frege's Theory of Functions and Objects," *Philosophical Review,* LXII (July, 1953), 374–90.

2. P. F. Strawson *Introduction to Logical Theory* (New York: John Wiley & Sons, Inc., 1952), Ch. 6, esp. p. 187. Also see his "On Referring," *Mind,* LIX (July, 1950), 320–44.

3. *Grundgesetze,* I, ¶6, 10.

4. *Function und Begriff,* pp. 21–22, esp. n. 7. R. H. Stoothoff "Note on a Doctrine of Frege," *Mind,* LXXII (Jan., 1963), 406–8.

5. *Begriffsschrift,* pp. 2–4. Also see P. E. B. Jourdain, "The Development of the Theories of Mathematical Logic and the Principles of Mathematics," *The Quarterly Journal of Pure and Applied Mathematics,* XLIII (1912), 243, which quotes *Begriffsschrift,* p. 3.

6. *Grundgesetze,* I, p. x.

7. *Grundgesetze,* I, ¶1, n. 1; also see Jourdain, *op. cit.,* 266–67.

8. Whitehead and Russell hold that the signpost indicates a complete sentence as does the period at the end of an ordinary sentence. *Principia Mathematica,* 2nd ed. (Cambridge: Cambridge University Press, 1935), I, pp. 8–9. See Bertrand Russell, *The Principles of Mathematics,* 2nd ed. (London: G. Allen & Unwin Ltd., 1937), pp. 34–35. Rudolf Carnap uses the assertion sign to indicate his L–true propositions, *Logical Foundations of Probability* (Chicago: University of Chicago Press, 1950), p. 57.
W. Quine uses the signpost "to mean that the closure of a formula is a theorem." *Mathematical Logic.* (Cambridge: Harvard University Press, 1955), pp. 88, 162.
Hans Reichenbach uses the signpost to distinguish an assertion as a logical expressive (pragmatic factor from a mere logical cognitive

(syntactical or semantical) statement. *Elements of Symbolic Logic* (New York: Macmillan Co., 1947), par. 57.

M. Polanyi interprets the signpost epistemologically as meaning "I believe. . . ." M. Polanyi, *Personal Knowledge* (Chicago: University of Chicago Press, 1958), pp. 255–56.

Max Black wonders whether the signpost is desirable in a context in which he criticizes the Tarskian concept of truth as not entirely adequate, *Language and Philosophy* (Ithaca: Cornell University Press, 1949), p. 106, n. 28.

9. See F. H. Bradley's treatment of the dual function of the Real as both the subject of all judgments and that which underlies the relation between the predicate and subject of all judgments. *The Principles of Logic*, 2nd ed. rev. (London: Oxford University Press, 1922), II, pp. 579–95; also *Appearance and Reality* (Oxford: Clarendon Press, 1946), pp. 353–54 and Chap. XXVI.

10. Frege never treats the expression "Truth is such that. . . ." in dealing with clauses in indirect discourse. "Sinn und Bedeutung," 37–39. The signpost cannot read "I believe. . . ."

6. *Problem of Inconsistency*

1. *The Principles of Mathematics*, 2nd. ed. (London: G. Allen & Unwin, Ltd., 1937), pp. xii–xiv, 101–7.
   With A. N. Whitehead *Principia Mathematica* (Cambridge: Cambridge University Press, 1935), I, pp. 63–68. See also Russell's "Mathematical Logic as based on the Theory of Types," *American Journal of Mathematics,* xxx (1908), 222–62.

2. Frank P. Ramsey, The *Foundations of Mathematics* (New York: Humanities Press, 1950), Chap. I. John Tucker challenges this classification. "The Formalisation of Set Theory," *Mind,* LXXII (Oct., 1963), 512–13.

3. Russell accepts Ramsey's modification, but does not examine the implications of it for his general conception of logic. *The Principles of Mathematics,* preface.

4. Alfred Tarski, "The Semantic Conception of Truth," *Readings in Philosophical Analysis,* eds. Herbert Feigl and Wilfred Sellars (New York: Appleton-Century-Crofts, Inc., 1949), pp. 52–84.

5. "Sinn und Bedeutung," 27–28.

6. See Nathaniel Lawrence, "Heterology and Hierarchy," *Analysis,* x (March, 1950), 77–84 and Gilbert Ryle's development of Lawrence's idea "Heterologicality," *Analysis,* xi (Jan., 1951), 61–69. Also, Joshua C. Gregory, "Heterological and Homological," *Mind,* LXI (Jan., 1952), 85–88; P. T. Geach's "Mr. Ill-Named," *Analysis,* ix (Oct., 1948), 14–16; John Tucker, *op. cit.,* 510.

7. Alexandre Koyré, "The Liar," *Philosophy and Phenomenological Research*, VI (1945/46), 344-62.

8. Manley Thompson, *The Pragmatic Philosophy of C. S. Peirce* (Chicago; University of Chicago Press, 1953), p. 55. Also see Manley Thompson, "The Logical Paradoxes and Peirce's Semiotic," *The Journal of Philosophy*, XLVI (August 18, 1949), 513-36.

9. J. Bar-Hillel's answer to Koyré, "The Revival of the Liar," *Philosophy and Phenomenological Research*, VIII (1947/48), 245-53. Also see Koyré's reply, *ibid.*, 254-55.

10. "Sinn und Bedeutung," 34-35. Also see my "A Restriction in Frege's Use of the Term 'True'," *Philosophical Studies*, VI (1955), 58-64.

11. "Sinn und Bedeutung," 35.

12. Alfred Tarski, *op. cit.*, pp. 54-55. Rudolf Carnap, *Introduction to Semantics* (Cambridge: Harvard University Press, 1942), p. 26.

13. "Sinn und Bedeutung," 35.

14. Russell denies that the True is the reference of a sentence. *The Principles of Mathematics,* p. 503. Carnap believes that this notion would be questioned by most people and is a less natural way to treat the content of sentences (*Meaning and Necessity* [Chicago: University of Chicago Press, 1947], p. 120) though he also notes that one may regard propositions as truth-values or extensions (p. 94) and refers to C. I. Lewis' notion that true sentences denote the whole world while false ones have a zero as their extensions (p. 94, n. 13). Also see C. I. Lewis, "The Modes of Meaning," *Philosophy and Phenomenological Research*, IV (1943/44), 236-50.

15. Carnap distinguishes three uses of the term "true": the absolute truth of propositions (traditional judgments), the semantical truth of sentences (traditional propositions) which is the Tarskian notion and the combination of the two in the "It is true that..." (*Introduction to Semantics*, ¶7, 17, pp. 88-93, 240-41).

Max Black writes: "More serious is the objection that this proposal [of Tarski] would make no provision for such expressions as 'The truth is hard to discover,' or others in which references to truth or falsity is made by means of substantives." *Language and Philosophy* (Ithaca: Cornell University Press, 1949), p. 106. Also Alfred Tarski, *op. cit.*, pp. 52-84.

7. The Class-of-Classes Antinomy

1. *Grundgesetze*, II, pp. 253-65; P. T. Geach and Max Black, *Translations from the Philosophical Writings of Gottob Frege* (Oxford: Blackwell, 1952), pp. 234-44.

2. Rudolf Carnap writes: "It was a decisive moment in the history of logic when, in the year 1902, a letter from Russell drew Frege's

attention to the fact that there was a contradiction in his system."
The Logical Syntax of Language (London: Kegan Paul, Trench,
Trubner & Co., Ltd., 1937), p. 137. Or again (p. 139): "For Frege
made a second mistake in not applying the type-classification of the
predicates (sentential functions), which he had constructed with such
insight and clarity, to the classes corresponding to the predicates;
instead of that, he counted the classes—and similarly the many-
termed extensions—simply as individuals (objects) quite independently of the level and kind of the sentential function which defined
the class in question. And even after the discovery of the contradiction, he still thought that he need not alter his procedure (Vol. II,
254 ff.) because he believed the names of objects and the names of
functions to be differentiated by the fact that the former have a
meaning of their own while the latter remain incomplete symbols
which only become significant after being completed by means of
other symbols."
Frank Ramsey, *The Foundations of Mathematics* (New York:
Humanities Press, 1950), pp. 1–3; J. Jørgensen, *A Treatise of Formal
Logic* (London: Oxford University Press, 1931), pp. 172–74; C. I.
Lewis, *A Survey of Symbolic Logic* (New York: Dover Publications,
Inc., 1960), pp. 114–15; William and Martha Kneale, *The Development of Logic* (Oxford: Clarendon Press, 1962), pp. 427, 652 ff; P.
T. Geach, "Frege's *Grundlagen*," Philosophical Review, LX (Oct.,
1951), 535–44; L. O. Katsoff, *A Philosophy of Mathematics* (Ames:
Iowa State College Press, 1948), pp. 24–31, 40–47; H. R. Smart,
"Frege's Logic," *The Philosophical Review,* LIV (Sept. 1945), 489–505.
3. B. Sobociński, "L'analyse de l'antinomie russellienne par Lésniewski," *Methodos.* Vol. I (1949), 94–107, 220–28, 308–16 and Vol. II
(1950), 237–57. Also, S. Lésniewski's "On the Foundation of Mathematics" (Introduction, Chaps. I, II, III, XI) *Przeglad Filosoficzny,*
XXX (1927), XXXIV (1934), Wells accepts Sobociński's proof, "Frege's
Ontology," *The Review of Metaphysics,* IV (June, 1951), 567. Also,
W. V. Quine, "On Frege's Way Out," *Mind,* LXIV (April, 1955), 145–
59. Also P. T. Geach, "On Frege's Way Out," *Mind,* LXV (July, 1956),
408–9.
4. W. V. Quine, *From a Logical Point of View,* 2nd ed. rev. (Cambridge: Harvard University Press, 1961), pp. 97–98, *Mathematical
Logic,* (Cambridge: Harvard University Press, 1951), pp. ix, 157 ff.)
and S. C. Kleene and J. B. Rosser, "The Inconsistency of Certain
Formal Logics," *Annals of Mathematics,* XXXVI (1935), 630–36.
5. "He [Frege] gives the name *Werthverlauf* to an entity which
appears to be nearly the same as what I call the class as one."
Russell, *The Principles of Mathematics,* 2nd ed. (London: G.
Allen & Unwin Ltd., 1937), p. 511.

6. *Grundgesetze*, I, ¶20, 47, 52.
7. *Grundgesetze*, II, p. 262.
8. *Grundgesetze*, II, p. 253.
9. Frege's notes to P. E. B. Jourdain, "The Development of the Theories of Mathematical Logic and the Principles of Mathematics," *The Quarterly Journal of Pure and Applied Mathematics*, XLIII (1912), 251, n. In discussing Russell's Contradiction "when classes are introduced," Frege writes:

> In my fashion of regarding concepts as functions, we can treat the principal parts of Logic without speaking of classes, as I have done in my *Begriffsschrift*, and that does not then come into consideration. Only with difficulty did I resolve to introduce classes (or extents of concepts), because the matter did not appear to me quite secure—and rightly so, as it turned out. The laws of numbers are to be developed in a purely logical manner. But numbers are objects, and in logic we have only two objects, in the first place: the two-truth-values. Our first aim, then was to obtain objects out of concepts, namely, extents of concepts or classes. By this I was constrained to overcome my resistance and to admit the passage from concepts to their extents. And, after I had made this resolution, I made a more extended use of classes than was necessary, because by that many simplifications could be reached. I confess that, by acting thus, I fell into the error of letting go too easily my initial doubts, in reliance on the fact that extents of concepts have for a long time been spoken of in Logic. The difficulties which are bound up with the use of classes vanish if only we deal with objects, concepts, and relations, and this is possible in the fundamental part of Logic. The class, namely, is something derived, whereas in the concept—as I understand the word—we have something primitive. Accordingly, also the laws of classes are less primitive than those of concepts, and it is not suitable to found Logic on the laws of classes. The primitive laws of Logic may contain nothing derived. We can, perhaps, regard Arithmetic as a further-developed Logic. But, in that, we say that in Comparison with the fundamental Logic, it is something derived. On this account I cannot think that the use of arithmetical signs ("+," "—," ":") is suitable in Logic. The sign of equality is an exception; in Arithmetic it denotes at bottom, identity, and this relation is not peculiar to Arithmetic. It would be doubtful *a priori* that it is suitable to constrain Logic in forms which originally belong to another science.

10. As for (*a*) the extension of a concept, Frege held in the "Nachwort"

that the concept was practically indispensable, *Grundgesetze*, II, pp. 254–55. "The correctness of our function of second level '*ε*f(*ε*) is brought into question thereby and yet it is so indispensable for the foundations of arithmetic." (p. 257) Also see *Grundlagen*, p. 80, n. 1, for Frege's early naïve belief that the meaning of the term was clear to everyone. *cf.*, *Grundlagen*, p. 117, See *Grundgesetze*, I, p. ix, for the necessity of the notion of the value-range in his system. And *Grundgesetze*, II, ¶146–47, 161, for Frege's belief that his notion of extension took care of the content usually designated by such terms as "class," "group," "collection," and "set." Note criticisms (given in Chapters 3–5 above) of the other notions of class, etc. Also, *Grundlagen*, pp. 39–67. But notice his later uncertainly—Frege's notes to Jourdain, *op. cit.*, 251, n. 2, 252. Regarding (*b*) the fifth law, Frege held that it was self-evident (*Function und Begriff*, p. 10). He states in *Grundgesetze*, I, p. vii of the fifth law that "I hold that it is purely logical." But also note *Grundgesetze*, II, p. 253 with its reference to *Grundgesetze*, I, p. vii.

11. *Grundgesetze*, II, pp. 254–55.

12. Though Frege had recognized earlier that Russell's use of "concept" differed from his own ("Geometrie, XII," 372, n. 2), apparently he had not seen how such a difference in a basic intensional term determined a significant difference in the derived terms "class" and "the extension of a concept..." *Vide supra* note 10 for reference to his criticism of classes.

13. "Bevor wir hierauf näher eingehen, wird es nützlich sein, dem Auftreten jenes Widerspruches mit unsern Zeichen nachzuspüren." *Grundgesetze*, II, p. 256.

14. "Begriff und Gegenstand," 196–97, n. 2. "Aehnliches kommt vor, wenn wir mit Beziehung auf den Satz 'diese Rose ist roth' sagen: das grammatische Prädicat 'ist roth' gehört zum Subjecte 'diese Rose'." It is worth quoting the remainder of this note as evidence of Frege's difficulty in explaining the notion of a concept, for this note is designed to elaborate on this special point. "Hier sind die Worte 'das grammatische Prädicat "ist roth" ' nicht grammatisches Prädicat, sondern Subject. Gerade dadurch, dass wir es ausdrücklich Prädicat nennen, rauben wir ihm diese Eigenschaft." "A similar thing happens when we say as regards the sentence 'this rose is red': Here the words 'the grammatical predicate "is red" ' are not a grammatical predicate but a subject. By the very act of explicitly calling it a predicate, we deprive it of this property."

15. *Grundgesetze*, I, p. ix. Here he uses "gehören" in the expression "an object... belongs to the group." (He also uses "angehören" in his "Geometrie, XII" where he raises the question of whether certain sciences are distinct from one another. There "belongs to" can be

read as "is part of the subject-matter of," e.g., "Does the concept *point* belong to logic?")

16. Geach and Black, *op. cit.*, pp. 237 ff.

17. "Begriff und Gegenstand," 197. "When we say 'Jesus falls under the concept *man*,' then, setting aside the copula, the predicate is:

'falling under the concept *man*'

and this refers to the same as

'a man,'

But the phrase

'the concept *man*'

is only part of this predicate."

18. See Gilbert Ryle, "Heterologicality," *Analysis*, xi, (Jan., 1951), 67: "The same inattention to grammar is the source of such paradoxes as 'The Liar,' 'the Class of Classes . . .' and 'Impredictability'."

19. My friendly formalist critic writes: "Your idea about the nature of the relation expressed by the words 'is equal to' is in my opinion about as un-Fregean as anything could be. It is true that Frege changed his view about the nature of the equality relation, but the authoritative and final version is to be found in *Grundgesetze* (Vol. I, p. 11, and elsewhere)." Frege writes: ", $\Gamma = \Delta$' bedeute das Wahre, wenn Γ dasselbe ist wie Δ; in allen andern Fällen bedeute es das Falsche." , $\Gamma = \Delta$' refers to the True, if Γ is the same as Δ; in all other cases, it refers to the False." My critic seems to hold that Frege is saying that an object is the same as itself. This perhaps can be read from Frege's statement. It seems to me more reasonable to read this statement in the light of the distinctions made in "Sinn und Bedeutung," since the *Grundgesetze* is built on the three papers expressing his matured position.

20. See *Grundgesetze*, I, p. 19 for reference to this concept. Also see *Grundlagen*, ¶74, and *Grundgesetze*, I, 57–58 for use of this concept to define the cardinal number, zero.

21. Frank P. Ramsey, *op. cit.*, Chap. I. Also John Tucker, "The Formalisation of Set Theory," *Mind*, LXXII (Oct., 1963), 512–13.

22. *Grundgesetze*, II, p. 256. This reads: "That Δ is a class which does not belong to itself, we can express thus:" And the first symbolic expression can be translated into English as: "not for every concept g, if the extension of the concept g is the same as Δ then Δ belongs to the concept g." or in other words, "there is a concept (or class) which does not belong to itself." The quotation continues: "And the class of classes not belonging to themselves can be designated

thus:" Symbolic expression [2]. "I will use the sign "∀" as short for this in the deduction that follows and moreover omit the judgment-line on account of the doubtful truth. Accordingly I shall use" —symbolic expression [3]—"to express [that the class ∀ belongs to itself]. Now we have by (Vb):" —symbolic expression [4]—"or, if we use the abbreviation and apply (IIIa)"—symbolic expression α. "Now we introduce the German 𝔤 for f" —symbolic expression β—"that is, {if ∀ belongs to itself, then it does not belong to itself.} that is one side."

23. Geach and Black have corrected Frege so that the words in brackets in note 22 above read: "that ∀ does not belong to itself.ᴱ " And their note E states: "By what is clearly a slip, Frege has 'belongs to itself.' "

24. For the words in braces in note 22, Geach and Black have "If ∀ does not belong to itself, then ∀ does belong to itself.ᴴ " And their note H states: "Frege, by a slip I have corrected here, switches 'does belong' and 'does not belong'."

25. Geach and Black's note H (given in note 24 above) is attached to Frege's reading of his symbolism in developing the other side of the argument. The derivation of the contradiction using laws Vb, IIb, and Ig is trivial.

26. Kurt Gödel, "Russell's Mathematical Logic," *The Philosophy of Bertrand Russell*, p. 150.

27. *Ibid*, pp. 260–61.

28. *Grundgesetze*, I, pp. 52–54.

29. *Grundgesetze*, I, pp. 19–20.

30. *Grundgesetze*, II, p. 257. "We will see now what occurs when we use our sign "⌢." The symbol "'ε(⊤ ε⌢ε)" replaces " ∀ .""

31. My colleague, Prof. Stanley Tennenbaum, has kindly given valuable criticism which has led to a vastly improved version of this argument. However, he has further reservations about Frege's approach to logic.

32. *Grundlagen*, ¶68.

33. *Ibid*. See also his idea that he could have illustrated this by the notion of number, *Grundlagen*, p. 76, n. 1 and *Grundgestze*, I ¶34–46. Geach also notes this "Frege's *Grundlagen*," *Philosophical Review*, LX (Oct., 1951), 537.

34. *The Principles of Mathematics*, 2nd. ed. (London: G. Allen & Unwin Ltd., 1937), pp. ix–x, chap. IX. See Carnap, *Meaning and Necessity* (Chicago: University of Chicago Press, 1947), pp. 115–17.

35. Frege's notes to Jourdain, *op. cit.*, 252. To found the 'calculus of judgments' on the 'Calculus of concepts' (which is properly a 'calculus of classes') is to reverse the correct order of things; for

classes are something derived, and can only be obtained from concepts (in my sense). But concepts are something primitive which cannot be dispensed with in Logic. We can only determine a class by giving the properties which an object must have in order to belong to the class. But these properties are the attributes (*Merkmale*) of a concept. We define a concept, and pass over from it to the class. For that reason, calculation with classes must be founded on the calculation with concepts. And the calculation with concepts is itself founded on the calculation with truth-values (which is better than saying 'calculus of judgments').

8. *Mathematical Philosophies and Consistency*

1. E.g., Bertrand Russell, *Introduction to Mathematical Philosophy* (New York: Macmillan Co., 1919), pp. ix, x; Chapters xv–xviii. Julius Weinberg, *An Examination of Logical Positivism* (London: Routledge and Kegan Paul Ltd., 1936) especially Chapter i. Or again John Tucker quotes Alonzo Church: "To give an explanation of the contradictions without having a formal guarantee of consistency is 'to abandon the notion of mathematical proof althogether'." Church's review of Finsler's "Gibt es unentscheidbare Sätze?" *Journal of Symbolic Logic*, xi (Dec., 1946), 132. John Tucker, "The Formalisation of Set Theory," *Mind*, lxxii, (Oct., 1963), 507.

2. C. I. Lewis, *A Survey of Symbolic Logic* (New York: Dover Publications, Inc., 1960), pp. 3–18, 57–71; Bertrand Russell, *Mysticism and Logic* (London: G. Allen and Unwin Ltd, 1926), p. 75 ff; Kurt Gödel, "Russell's Mathematical Logic," *The Philosophy of Bertrand Russell,* ed. P. A. Schilpp (New York: Tudor Publishing Co., 1951), p. 125. P. E. B. Jourdain, "The Development of the Theories of Mathematical Logic and the Principles of Mathematics," *The Quarterly Journal of Pure and Applied Mathematics*, xli (1910), 324–52.

3. For exceptions see Bertrand Russell's, *The Philosophy of Leibniz,* 2nd ed., (London: G. Allen and Unwin Ltd., 1937), and Gustav Bergmann, "Russell's Examination of Leibniz Examined," *Philosophy of Science,* xxiii (July, 1956), 175–203.

4. Rudolf Carnap *Logical Foundations of Probability* (Chicago: University of Chicago Press, 1950), pp. 39–40.

5. Kurt Gödel, *op. cit.*, p. 125; Bertrand Russell, *Our Knowledge of the External World* (Chicago: The Open Court Publishing Co., 1914), pp. 42–69, and the development of his logistic in *Principia Mathematica;* Rudolf Carnap, *The Logical Syntax of Language* (London: Kegan Paul, Trench, Trubner & Co., Ltd., 1937), p. xiii.

Carnap later modified this statement to include semantics, but this change does not affect this point.

6. Robert Brumbaugh, "Aristotle as a Mathematician," *The Review of Metaphysics*, VIII (March, 1955), 385–86.

7. Rudolf Carnap, "Foundations of Logic and Mathematics," *International Encyclopedia of Unified Sciences*, eds. Otto Neurath, Rudolf Carnap, Charles Morris (Chicago: University of Chicago Press, 1955) 48–51. Bertrand Russell, *The Principles of Mathematics* 2nd ed. (London: G. Allen & Unwin Ltd., 1937), pp. v–vii. Frank P. Ramsey, *The Foundations of Mathematics* (New York: Humanities Press, 1950), p. 1 ff. Kurt Gödel, *op. cit.,* pp. 125–53. Robert Wilder, *Introduction to the Foundations of Mathematics* (New York: John Wiley, 1952), p. 230.

8. *From a Logical Point of View,* 2nd ed. rev. (Cambridge: Harvard University Press, 1961), pp. 13–16.

9. Robert Brumbaugh, *op. cit.,* 387.

10. Hermann Weyl, *Space, Time, and Matter* (New York: Dover Publications, Inc., 1950), pp. 3–6. Also, his *Philosophy of Mathematics and Natural Science* (Princeton: Princeton University Press, 1949), pp. 50 ff. Brouwer also uses this same language. However, not all intuitionists are satisfied with this language; e.g., E. W. Beth, "Remarks on Intuitionist Logic," in *Constructivity in Mathematics* (Amsterdam: North-Holland Publishing Co., 1959), pp. 15–25.

11. I am especially conscious at this point of my debt to Richard McKeon whose studies on logical theory have not yet been published.

12. I omit for example all reference to the contributions of the logical positivists: Carnap, Reichenbach, Bergmann, Schlick, Hempel, etc., and to such problems as the notions of truth, the role of the different linguistic disciplines, etc.

13. "Logische Untersuchungen. Dritter Teil: Gedankengefüge," *Beitrage zur Philosophie des deutschen Idealismus*, III (1923) 36–51.

14. Whitehead and Russell, *Principia Mathematica*, 2nd. ed. (Cambridge: Cambridge University Press, 1935), p. 31 and his treatment of "Judgments of Perception," William and Martha Kneale discuss the differences between Russell's and Frege's treatment of names and descriptions. *The Development of Logic*, (Oxford: Clarendon Press, 1962), pp. 618 ff.

15. Bertrand Russell, *Our Knowledge of the External World*, pp. 42–69.

16. I refer here to D. Hilbert and W. Ackermann, *Principles of Mathematical Logic* (New York: Chelsea Publishing Co., 1950) and to the work of such men as Quine, Rosser, Church, Tarski, Gödel, and Gentzen. Note must be taken that I am concentrating on their contributions to proof theory as such and am not characterizing their

broader interests in mathematics, nor presuming a common philosophical outlook beyond that expressed by Gödel when he stated that mathematical logic was the science of sciences. Thus, Gödel entertains the hypothesis of real mathematical entities (in an intuitive arithmetic), whereas Quine identifies formalism with nominalism. Or there may be differences in emphasis on particular devices adopted for developing given portions of mathematical logic. Thus, Quine uses the tabular device of the truth-table for the sentential calculus, whereas Gentzen emphasizes the proof process. Despite these differences in intentions, there is a common view on the subject matter, the method, and the goal of logical inquiry.

Note should be made here, however, that if mathematical logic is, as some of my mathematical friends affirm, not a science of sciences, but a tiny and insignificant portion of mathematics to which a variety of mathematical devices from other mathematical disciplines are applied, then it is merely an applied science and is of little philosophical interest. If this is the case, then it does not constitute a mathematical philosophy.

17. See Rulon Wells, "Is Frege's Concept of Function Valid?" *Journal of Philosophy.* LX (Nov., 1963), 725. See also William and Martha Kneale *op. cit.,* p. 568 where they argue for the formal study of Frege's *Begriffsschrift* and Russell's *Principia.*

18. See for example, Hao Wang, "Toward Mechanical Mathematics," *The Modeling of Mind,* ed. Kenneth M. Sayre and Frederick J. Crosson (University of Notre Dame Press, 1963) pp. 91–120.

19. "Geometrie, XII," 299. Also see Chapter 4.

20. See Gödel's remarks about Frege, *op. cit.,* pp. 125–27.

21. For example, Quine criticizes *Principia Mathematica* because it neglects the use-mention distinction and is based upon intensional attributes. "Whitehead and the Rise of Modern Logic," *The Philosophy of Alfred North Whitehead,* ed. P. Arthur Schilpp (New York: Tudor Publishing Co., 1951), pp. 127–63.

22. I. M. Bochenski, A History of Formal Logic, trans. and ed. Ivo Thomas (Notre Dame: University of Notre Dame Press, 1961) pp. 292–93. William and Martha Kneale also note that Frege and Hilbert "argue at cross purposes" on the problem of consistency, *op. cit.,* pp. 686–87.

Appendix

1. "Frege's *Grundlagen,*" *Philosophical Review,* LX (Oct., 1951), 525–44.

2. B. Sobociński, "L'analyse de l'antinomie russellienne par Lésniewski," *Methodos,* I (1949), 94–107, 220–28, 308–16; II (1950), 237–57.

3. W. V. Quine, "On Frege's Way Out," *Mind*, LXIV (April, 1955), 145–59.

4. P. T. Geach, "On Frege's Way Out," *Mind*, LXV (July, 1956), 408–9.

5. "On the Foundations of Mathematics," (Introduction, Chapts. I, II, III, XI), *Przeglad Filozoficzny*, XXX (1927), XXXIV (1934). (I am greatly indebted to Daniel Kubat and to another friend who prefers to remain anonymous for assistance with Lésniewski's Polish. See also Eugene C. Luschei, *The Logical Systems of Lésniewski* (Amsterdam: North Holland Publishing Company, 1962).

6. *Grundgesetze*, II, p. 262.

7. B. Sobocínski, *op. cit.*, I, 220.

8. I am indebted to my former colleague, E. S. Robinson, for aid in making this identification, though I alone am responsible for any errors here and in the interpretation.

9. P. T. Geach and Max Black, *Translations from the Philosophical Writings of Gottlob Frege* (Oxford: Blackwell, 1952), p. 243, n. Q.

10. Sobocinski's use of "ϵ" at this point must be interpreted as "$=$" in order to translate Frege correctly, and he holds that "A ϵ Kl(a)" be interpreted as "A est l'ensemble de tour les objets 'a' ou, autrement encore 'A est un ensemble forme de tous les objets a.' " *Methodos*, I, 100.

11. *Ibid.*, 220, 228.

12. *Ibid.*, 98–99.

13. *Ibid.*, 221. Theorem E4 reads: [Ba]: B ϵ a $\rightarrow$ [$\exists$ A] · A ϵ Kl(Kl(a)).

14. *Methodos*, II, 254–57. Also see Lésniewski's "On the Foundations of Mathematics," *Przeglad Filozoficzny*, XXX, 164 ff.

15. W. V. Quine, *op. cit.*, 145–59.

16. *Ibid.*, 146.

17. *Ibid.*, 148. Quine prefers "attribute" for he fears that "concept" hints of mind and "property" suggests an essence-accident distinction.

INDEX

Abstractive principle, 166
Ackermann, Wilheim, 191
Analysis: based on common usage, 12; grounded on objects, 22; of complex sentences, 27–29; to simple concepts, 31, 43
Analytic: of arithmetic, 7, 80–81, 83–85; science, 79–81; sentence, 93
Analyticity: meaning of, 80
Andeuten. See Indicating
Anscombe, G. E. M., 175
Antinomy: Frege's admission, 4, 124–25; presumed reasons for, 5, 51; weakened statement of antinomies, 116–17; significance, 119, 122–25; stated, 120–21; derived from simple sentence, 131–33; linguistic ambiguity, 132–33, 135–36; philosophical problem, 133; inadequate solution, 163–68; other solutions, 166; import for logicians, 184–85
A priori—a posteriori, 79–81
Argument of function, 32, 34
Argument places, 36–37
Aristotle, 31, 83–84, 85, 149, 150–51
Arithmetic: different from geometry, 79–83, 180; extension of logic, 79–83, 186; analytic—a priori, 83
Assertion sign. *See* Signpost
Attitudinal clauses, 25
Austin, John L., 8
Autological, 110
Axiom: relations to definition, 72–74; proper, true, 77; independence, 77–79; systems, 85–86; of extensionality, 124
Ayer, Alfred J., 83, 180

Baker, A. J., 173
Bar-Hillel, Yehoshua, 184
Bartlett, James, 175
Bedeutung (bedeuten). See Reference
Begriffsschrift. See Ideography
Belief clauses, reference and sense, 25
Beliefs, 153–54, 156, 158
Belongs to, 125–43, 144–45, 187–88. *See also* Falls under
Bergmann, Gustav, 171, 173, 174, 190, 191
Beth, Evert W., 191
Black, Max, 1, 5, 51, 126, 135–36, 170–89 *passim*
Bochenski, I. M., 180, 182, 192
Bolzano, Bernard, 75, 79
Boole, George, 85, 86, 149
Bradley, F. H., 183
Brentano, Franz, 151
Brouwer, L. E. J., 191
Brumbaugh, Robert S., 150, 151, 191

Calculation: mechanical, 156, 191–92; of classes and judgments, 189–90
Cantor, Georg, 56, 69, 84
Carnap, Rudolf, 45–46, 80, 92, 112, 149, 170–91 *passim*
Caton, Charles E., 43, 171, 174
Church, Alonzo, 44, 45, 172, 175, 190, 191
Class. *See* Extension of concept
Classification: of inconsistencies, 107–9; of mathematical philosophies, 149–51, 159
Clauses, 25–29
Cognitive link in senses, 91–92

WARREN'S
OLDE STYLE